CASEBOOK SERIES

Marlowe: *Doctor Faustus*

Casebook Series

GENERAL EDITOR: A. E. Dyson

Jane Austen: *Emma* DAVID LODGE
T. S. Eliot: *The Waste Land* C. B. COX AND A. HINCHLIFFE
D. H. Lawrence: *Sons and Lovers* GĀMINI SALGĀDO
D. H. Lawrence: '*The Rainbow*' and '*Women in Love*' COLIN CLARKE
Marlowe: *Doctor Faustus* JOHN JUMP
John Osborne: *Look Back in Anger* J. RUSSELL TAYLOR
Pope: *The Rape of the Lock* JOHN DIXON HUNT
Shakespeare: *Antony and Cleopatra* J. RUSSELL BROWN
Shakespeare: *Hamlet* JOHN JUMP
Shakespeare: *Julius Caesar* PETER URE
Shakespeare: *Macbeth* JOHN WAIN
Shakespeare: *The Merchant of Venice* JOHN WILDERS
Shakespeare: *The Tempest* D. J. PALMER
Shakespeare: *The Winter's Tale* KENNETH MUIR
Yeats: *Last Poems* JON STALLWORTHY

IN PREPARATION

William Blake: *Songs of Innocence and Experience* MARGARET BOTTRALL
Emily Brontë: *Wuthering Heights* MIRIAM ALLOTT
Joseph Conrad: *The Secret Agent* IAN WATT
Dickens: *Bleak House* A. E. DYSON
Donne: *Songs and Sonnets* ANNE RIGHTER
George Eliot: *Middlemarch* PATRICK SWINDEN
T. S. Eliot: *Four Quartets* BERNARD BERGONZI
Henry Fielding: *Tom Jones* NEIL COMPTON
E. M. Forster: *A Passage to India* MALCOLM BRADBURY
Ben Jonson: *Volpone* JONAS BARISH
Keats: *The Odes* G. S. FRASER
Milton: '*Comus*' and '*Samson Agonistes*' STANLEY FISH
Shakespeare: *Henry IV* Parts I and II G. K. HUNTER
Shakespeare: *Henry V* MICHAEL QUINN
Shakespeare: *King Lear* FRANK KERMODE
Shakespeare: *Measure for Measure* C. K. STEAD
Shakespeare: *Othello* JOHN WAIN
Shakespeare: *Richard II* NICHOLAS BROOKE
Tennyson: *In Memoriam* JOHN DIXON HUNT
Virginia Woolf: *To The Lighthouse* MAURICE BEJA
Wordsworth: *Lyrical Ballads* ALUN JONES
Wordsworth: *The Prelude* W. J. HARVEY

Marlowe: Doctor Faustus

A CASEBOOK

EDITED BY

JOHN JUMP

Aurora Publishers Incorporated
NASHVILLE/LONDON

FIRST PUBLISHED 1969 BY
MACMILLAN AND COMPANY LIMITED
LONDON, ENGLAND

COPYRIGHT © 1970 BY
AURORA PUBLISHERS INCORPORATED
NASHVILLE, TENNESSEE 37219
LIBRARY OF CONGRESS CATALOG CARD NUMBER: 72-127572
STANDARD BOOK NUMBER: 87695-043-8
MANUFACTURED IN THE UNITED STATES OF AMERICA

CONTENTS

Acknowledgements   7

General Editor's Preface   9

Introduction   11

Part 1: *Extracts from Earlier Critics*

WALTER SCOTT, p. 25 — HENRY MAITLAND, p. 25 —
FRANCIS JEFFREY, p. 26 — WILLIAM HAZLITT, p. 27 —
CHARLES LAMB, p. 29 — J. W. VON GOETHE, p. 29 — JAMES
BROUGHTON, p. 29 — JOHN PAYNE COLLIER, p. 30 —
HENRY HALLAM, p. 30 — GEORGE HENRY LEWES, p. 31 —
H. A. TAINE, p. 32 — A. W. WARD, p. 32 — WILHELM
WAGNER, p. 33 — JOHN ADDINGTON SYMONDS, p. 35 —
A. H. BULLEN, p. 36 — HAVELOCK ELLIS, p. 37 — A. C.
SWINBURNE, p. 38 — GEORGE SANTAYANA, p. 39 —
FELIX E. SCHELLING, p. 40 — WILLIAM EMPSON, p. 41 —
LEO KIRSCHBAUM, p. 42 — UNA ELLIS-FERMOR, p. 43 —
PAUL H. KOCHER, p. 44.

Part 2: *Recent Studies*

JAMES SMITH: Marlowe's *Doctor Faustus*   49
W. W. GREG: The Damnation of Faustus   71
J. C. MAXWELL: The Sin of Faustus   89
HELEN GARDNER: The Theme of Damnation in
   Doctor Faustus   95

NICHOLAS BROOKE: The Moral Tragedy of Doctor
   Faustus   101

HARRY LEVIN: Science without Conscience   134

ROBERT ORNSTEIN: The Comic Synthesis in *Doctor
   Faustus*   165

J. P. BROCKBANK: Damned Perpetually   173

J. B. STEANE: The Instability of Faustus   177

D. J. PALMER: Magic and Poetry in *Doctor Faustus* 188

L. C. KNIGHTS: The Strange Case of *Doctor Faustus* 204

CLEANTH BROOKS: The Unity of Marlowe's *Doctor
   Faustus*   208

HAROLD HOBSON: All This and Helen, Too   222

Select Bibliography   225

Notes on Contributors   228

Index   231

ACKNOWLEDGEMENTS

Havelock Ellis, *Christopher Marlowe*, in the Mermaid series (Ernest Benn Ltd, Hill & Wang Inc.); George Santayana, *Three Philosophical Poets* (Harvard University Press); Felix E. Schelling, *English Drama* (J. M. Dent & Sons Ltd, E. P. Dutton & Co. Inc.); William Empson, *Seven Types of Ambiguity* (Chatto & Windus Ltd, New Directions Publishing Corporation; All Rights Reserved); Una Ellis-Fermor, *The Frontiers of Drama* (Methuen & Co. Ltd); Professor James Smith, 'Marlowe's *Dr Faustus*', from *Scrutiny*, VIII (1939) (Cambridge University Press); W. W. Greg, 'The Damnation of Faustus', from *Modern Language Review*, XLI (1946) (Lady Greg and Cambridge University Press); J. C. Maxwell, 'The Sin of Faustus', from *The Wind and the Rain*, IV (1947); 'Milton's "Satan" and the Theme of Damnation in Elizabethan Tragedy', from *English Studies 1948*, published for the English Association by John Murray (Publishers) Ltd and reprinted by Wm Dawson & Sons Ltd (Dame Helen Gardner, D.B.E., C.B.E.); Professor Nicholas Brooke, 'The Moral Tragedy of Doctor Faustus', from *Cambridge Journal*, V (1951–2) (Bowes & Bowes); Harry Levin, 'Science Without Conscience', from *Christopher Marlowe: The Overreacher* (Faber & Faber Ltd, Harvard University Press; © the President and Fellows of Harvard College 1952); Robert Ornstein, 'The Comic Synthesis in *Doctor Faustus*', from *Journal of English Literary History*, XXII iii (1955) (The Johns Hopkins Press); J. P. Brockbank, 'Damned Perpetually', from *Marlowe: Dr Faustus*, ed. D. Daiches, in the Studies in English Literature series (Edward Arnold (Publishers) Ltd, Barron's Educational Series Inc.); J. B. Steane, *Marlowe: A Critical Study* (Cambridge University Press); D. J. Palmer, 'Magic and Poetry in *Doctor*

Faustus', from *Critical Quarterly*, VI (1964); L. C. Knights, 'The Strange Case of Christopher Marlowe', from *Further Explorations* (Chatto & Windus Ltd, Stanford University Press; © L. C. Knights 1965); Cleanth Brooks, 'The Unity of Marlowe's *Dr Faustus*', from *To Nevill Coghill From Friends*, ed. J. Lawlor and W. H. Auden; Harold Hobson, 'All This and Helen Too', from *Sunday Times*, 20 February 1966.

GENERAL EDITOR'S PREFACE

EACH of this series of Casebooks concerns either one well-known and influential work of literature or two or three closely linked works. The main section consists of critical readings, mostly modern, brought together from journals and books. A selection of reviews and comments by the author's contemporaries is also included, and sometimes comments from the author himself. The Editor's Introduction charts the reputation of the work from its first appearance until the present time.

What is the purpose of such a collection? Chiefly, to assist reading. Our first response to literature may be, or seem to be, 'personal'. Certain qualities of vigour, profundity, beauty or 'truth to experience' strike us, and the work gains a foothold in our mind. Later, an isolated phrase or passage may return to haunt or illuminate. Where did we hear that? we wonder – it could scarcely be better put.

In these and similar ways appreciation begins, but major literature prompts to very much more. There are certain facts we need to know if we are to understand properly. Who were the author's original readers, and what assumptions did he share with them? What was his theory of literature? Was he committed to a particular historical situation, or to a set of beliefs? We need historians as well as critics to help us with this. But there are also more purely literary factors to take account of: the work's structure and rhetoric; its symbols and archetypes; its tone, genre and texture; its use of language; the words on the page. In all these matters critics can inform and enrich our individual responses by offering imaginative recreations of their own.

For the life of a book is not, after all, merely 'personal'; it is more like a tripartite dialogue, between a writer living 'then', a reader living 'now', and whatever forces of survival and honour link the two. Criticism is the public manifestation of this dialogue, a witness to the continuing power of literature to arouse and excite. It illuminates the possibilities and rewards of the dialogue, pushing 'interpretation' as far forward as it can go.

And here, indeed, is the rub: how far can it go? Where does 'interpretation' end, and nonsense begin? Why is one interpretation superior to another, and why does each age need to interpret for itself? The critic knows that his insights have value only in so far as they serve the text, and that he must take account of views differing sharply from his own. He knows that his own writing will be judged as well as the work he writes about, so that he cannot simply assert inner illumination or a differing taste.

The critical forum is a place of vigorous conflict and disagreement, but there is nothing in this to cause dismay. What is attested is the complexity of human experience and the richness of literature, not any chaos or relativity of taste. A critic is better seen, no doubt, as an explorer than as an 'authority', but explorers ought to be, and usually are, well equipped. The effect of good criticism is to convince us of what C. S. Lewis called 'the enormous extension of our being which we owe to authors'. A Casebook will be justified only if it helps to promote the same end.

A single volume can represent no more than a small selection of critical opinions. Some critics have been excluded for reasons of space, and it is hoped that readers will follow up the further suggestions in the Select Bibliography. Other contributions have been severed from their original context, to which some readers may wish to return. Indeed, if they take a hint from the critics represented here, they certainly will.

A. E. DYSON

INTRODUCTION

CHRISTOPHER MARLOWE may have written *Doctor Faustus* as early as 1588 or 1589, or he may have written it shortly before his death in May 1593. He may have written the whole of it, or he may have had a collaborator, or someone else may have finished the play after his death. Most recent critics have favoured a late date of composition, 1592–3, and have held that Marlowe had a collaborator. But the evidence is not conclusive. The reader who adopts any of the views I have listed may rest free from fear, at least for the present, that he can be proved wrong.

Extant records of performances in the Elizabethan theatres are very scanty. Nevertheless, they suffice to show that *Doctor Faustus* was one of the most successful plays of the half-century ending with the closure of the London theatres on the outbreak of the Civil War (1642). The *Diary*, or account-book, of the theatre-manager Philip Henslowe testifies to its popularity between 1594 and 1597. In 1602 Henslowe increased his investment in it by commissioning two writers to make additions to it. In 1608 a company of English players were touring Austria with it in their repertory. A year or so before the closure of the theatres, it was still being performed in the capital. This strictly theatrical evidence of its popularity is confirmed by evidence of other kinds: the large number of printed editions – at least nine between 1604 and 1631 – and the frequent references to it in the literature of the age.

No critical comments on it have survived from this early period. But it seems reasonable to guess that *Doctor Faustus* owed its popularity very largely to the awe-inspiring, even terrifying, nature of its subject and to the opportunities this gave for striking stage-effects and illusions. Support for this conjecture comes from an account, published in 1620, of how *Doctor Faustus* was produced at the Fortune theatre in Golding Lane, London. 'There indeede a man may behold shagge-hayr'd Deuills runne roaring ouer the Stage with Squibs in their mouthes, while Drummers make Thunder in the Tyring-house, and the twelue-penny Hirelings make artificiall Lightning in their Heauens' (John Melton, *Astrologaster* (1620) p. 31). Further support comes from those implacable enemies of the theatre, the Puritans, who put into circulation stories such as that of 'the *visible apparition of the Devill on the Stage at the Belsavage Play-house, in Queene* Elizabeths *dayes,* (*to the great amazement both of the Actors and Spectators*) *whiles they were there prophanely playing the History of* Faustus (the truth of which I have heard from many now alive, who well remember it,) *there being some distracted with that fearefull sight*' (W. Prynne, *Histrio-Mastix* (1633) fol. 556). Similar to this is the account, quoted in full by D. J. Palmer in his essay in the present volume, of 'Certaine Players at Exeter, acting upon the stage the tragical storie of Dr. Faustus the Conjurer', who were overcome by the horrifying conviction that 'there was one devell too many amongst them'. The performance ceased, the audience fled and the actors, 'contrarye to their custome', spent the night in scripture-reading and prayer (E. K. Chambers, *The Elizabethan Stage,* 4 vols (1923) III 424). A version of this story reached the ears of John Aubrey, the seventeenth-century antiquary.

When the theatres reopened on the restoration of the monarchy in 1660, the actors naturally hoped to see *Doctor Faustus* regain its pre-war popularity. But Samuel Pepys, taking his wife to the Red Bull theatre on 26 May 1662, found the play 'so wretchedly and poorly done, that we were sick of it'. He must have seen the slightly revised version that was printed in 1663. In this, pre-sumably out of respect for the theological bias visible in the restored dynasty, the scenes at the papal court were replaced by a scene at the court of the Soldan in Babylon. Very likely this was the version presented before royalty when, on 28 September 1675, there occurred the last recorded performance for over two hundred and twenty years.

Though Marlowe's play disappeared from the theatres for this period, Faustus himself did not. Until the close of the eighteenth century, he went on entertaining the populace in farces, pantomimes and puppet-plays. But the more cultivated members of the public had no longer any serious interest in him. Products of an age which aspired to be an age of reason, they evidently found this story of a man who sold his soul to the devil a mere barbarous survival from an age of superstition. To their polite and sceptical intelligences, such a story was, if not offensive, at all events absurd.

The Romantic challenge to eighteenth-century rationalism produced, by the early years of the nineteenth century, an intellectual atmosphere in which thoughtful persons could once more take Faustus seriously. Whether they understood the supernatural machinery literally or figuratively, they could perceive in the play a study of human aspiration and the obstacles to its fulfilment, and such a theme naturally interested a generation of readers in whom the Romantic revolt was fostering a regard for individualistic values.

We have to speak of readers rather than of theatregoers, since Marlowe's play had not yet found its way back to the stage. But it was printed in 1814, for the first time since 1663; and two more editions appeared within a dozen years. Following these publications, the formal literary criticism of *Doctor Faustus* began.

Certain of the early reactions are hostile; and even writers who are more friendly than Francis Jeffrey[1] sometimes introduce a note of apology into their remarks. Thus, C. W. Dilke, the editor of 1814, thinks *Doctor Faustus* 'by no means a favourable specimen of the plays' in his charge (*Old English Plays*, ed. C. W. Dilke, 6 vols (1814–15) I 8–9), and Henry Maitland describes it as 'exceedingly imperfect and disproportioned'. William Hazlitt echoes this; but he claims that the play is Marlowe's best, and, again echoing Maitland, he sets with him an example followed by many later critics when he picks out the rhapsody to Helen and the final soliloquy of Faustus for special

[1] Throughout this Introduction, I have refrained from giving references to passages which are included in the present volume.

praise. In his comments on Marlowe's characterization of his protagonist, he points forward to the Romantic idealization of Faustus. Admittedly, he does not argue that Marlowe was of the devil's party; he detects no 'atheism or impiety' in the play. At the same time, he reads it with a lively sympathy for the aspiring rebel who, he supposes, embodies his creator's 'lust of power' and 'hunger and thirst after unrighteousness'. Charles Lamb, similarly, finds Marlowe's Faustus more admirable than Goethe's Faust.

In Victorian criticism, the Romantic attitude gains strength. Francis Cunningham declares that 'the last scene of *Faustus* fills the soul with love and admiration as for a departed hero' (*The Works of Christopher Marlowe*, ed. F. Cunningham (1870) p. xvi); even Wilhelm Wagner, who does not regard Faustus as a hero, seems to regret that Marlowe was not liberal enough to allow him finally to escape damnation; while Havelock Ellis sees Faustus not as a sinner but as 'a hero, a Tamburlaine ... who at the thought of vaster delights has ceased to care for the finite splendours of an earthly crown'. Without completely disagreeing with such views, John Addington Symonds perceives more of the complexity of this play about a man who rejects God without denying Him. He appreciates that Marlowe's 'own audacious spirit' animates it, but he recognizes that Faustus is in revolt against nothing less than 'the eternal laws of his own nature and the world'. Symonds is perhaps the most penetrating of Marlowe's nineteenth-century critics.

During the earlier decades of the twentieth century, many commentators continued to interpret the play as on the whole inviting its readers' approval of Faustus' aspiration and rebellion. Just as Maitland protested in 1817 that Faustus does not 'seem to deserve the fearful punishment finally inflicted on him', so, according to Una M. Ellis-Fermor in 1927, 'The sin for which punishment is meted out to Faustus is more often alluded to than explained. Faustus, as far as we have been able to follow him, has been foolish and frivolous, but never criminal' (*Christopher Marlowe* (1927) p. 78). What occasion for repentance can there have been, asks F. S. Boas, in a life passed so largely in academic debate with Mephostophilis (*Christopher Marlowe* (1940) p. 211)? More positively, George Santayana presents Faustus as a martyr to the ideals of the Renaissance; and Philip Henderson, writing in 1937 as a sympathizer with the political Left, sees the play as 'simply a parable of the fight for intellectual freedom', with the Bad Angel externalizing Faustus' 'progressive and adventurous impulses' (*And Morning in his Eyes* (1937) pp. 310, 312). Having detected what he believes to be ambiguities in the final soliloquy, William Empson takes a similar line.

By this time, the play was finding its way back to the theatre. During nearly the whole of the nineteenth century, its hero had appeared on the stage only in various operatic and other more or less free adaptations of Goethe's masterpiece. Then, in 1896, there occurred the first production of Marlowe's play since 1675. Others followed at fairly long intervals until the later nineteen thirties. Since then, *Doctor Faustus* has become one of the most frequently revived of works by contemporaries of Shakespeare. There have been, among others, three productions with the Old Vic, three at Stratford-upon-Avon, a famous New York production by Orson Welles and an even more famous Oxford University Dramatic Society production in which Richard Burton and Elizabeth Taylor appeared as Faustus and Helen of Troy. The last of these has been filmed. In addition, the play has been performed repeatedly on sound radio and television.

This theatrical revival has coincided with a shift in critical attitude towards the play, though no direct connection between the two developments has yet become apparent. In general, we may say that the mid-twentieth-century critics are less ready than were their predecessors to sink everything in admiration of Faustus and more ready to believe that Marlowe presents him in such a way as to make his foolishness, and even his wickedness, unmistakable. The longer essays and extracts which compose the major part of the present volume illustrate principally this development and the continuing resistance to it.

James Smith's subtle and cogent paper is one of the authoritative early formulations of the new view. It represents the play as an allegory embodying an orthodox Christian attitude towards

Faustus' career. Writing four years later, Leo Kirschbaum is vigorous, assertive, even strident: 'there is no more obvious Christian document in all Elizabethan drama than *Doctor Faustus.*' Three years later still, W. W. Greg is lucid, patient and judicious in his promotion of very much the same interpretation of the play.

At the time of writing, Kirschbaum and Greg were engaged on their scholarly studies of the early versions of *Doctor Faustus*, studies that were in due course to lead them independently to certain revolutionary conclusions that I shall outline later. Their consequent intimacy with the text gave their critical pronouncements considerable weight. The impact of their articles, and of Smith's, shows clearly in J. C. Maxwell's note, 'The Sin of Faustus'. Helen Gardner, affected by some at least of the same influences, defines the sin in terms that differ from Maxwell's but are easily reconcilable with his. From a different angle, though on the same side in the general debate, Lily B. Campbell suggests that *Doctor Faustus* dramatizes a case of conscience such as fascinated Protestant theologians during the sixteenth century; she gives an account of one such case which instructively parallels that of Faustus, and she makes use of the play based upon it that Helen Gardner mentions in note 1 to the passage by her included in the present volume ('*Doctor Faustus*: A Case of Conscience', in *Publications of the Modern Language Association of America*, LXVII (1952) 219–39).

But the Romantic view still had, and has, its exponents. In *Christopher Marlowe: A Study of his Thought, Learning, and Character* (Chapel Hill, 1946), Paul H. Kocher argues forcibly that Marlowe was a highly subjective writer whose *Doctor Faustus* and other plays testify to 'his unremitting warfare with Christianity' (p. 330). Erich Heller's broadcast talk (printed in *The Listener*, 11 January 1962) follows a broadly similar line, though with some errors of fact. But Nicholas Brooke has provided the fullest and ablest statement in recent years of a Romantic or diabolonian interpretation. He describes *Doctor Faustus* as an inverted morality play, in which Marlowe depicts man as created desiring a greatness which his tyrannical creator has denied to him. He argues that Faustus remains admirable as long as he protests against this cruel treatment of man, and that his occasional flinchings and his movements towards repentance are his true lapses from virtue. This interpretation resembles but goes beyond that of J. A. Symonds. It encourages us to see *Doctor Faustus* as registering much the same blasphemous protest as does Byron's *Manfred* – the dramatic poem which John Wilson ('Christopher North'), reviewing it in *Blackwood's Edinburgh Magazine* (1 (1817) 289–95), thought in its catastrophe 'somewhat too much in the style' of Marlowe's play.

There is inevitably a risk that such compact summaries as I have been providing will misrepresent arguments that are often complex, and that the categorizing of individual critics as either 'Romantic' or, to borrow William Empson's term, 'neo-Christian' will force together incongruous bedfellows. But these risks must be accepted if we are to trace any kind of historical pattern in the criticism of *Doctor Faustus*. Moreover, most of the texts that I summarize and classify are reprinted at least in part in the present volume, so the reader can easily supply such amplification and qualification as he thinks necessary. He will find that Brooke, for example, fully recognizes in *Doctor Faustus* a tension between the protest he thinks dominant and other, more orthodox, tendencies. Many of the most recent commentators see the play as concerned centrally with presenting just such a tension. Harry Levin sees it as 'Marlowe's tragedy of the scientific libertine who gained control over nature while losing control of himself'. Analysing the final soliloquy, J. P. Brockbank says, 'In fear we acquiesce in the littleness and powerlessness of man, and in pity we share his sufferings and endorse his protest.' J. B. Steane describes Faustus as a professed freethinker with a deep sense of sinfulness and believes that his instability probably reflected an instability in Marlowe himself. All of these critics succeed in appraising Faustus and his career with a high degree of objectivity. Thanks initially to Smith, Kirschbaum and Greg, we have come a long way from the indulgent sentimentalism of Cunningham and the rest.

Other critics address themselves to other questions. Robert

Ornstein goes quite as far as Smith or Kirschbaum in deploring the foolishness of Faustus, but his immediate concern is with the comic spirit in the play and with the ironic light it sheds on that foolishness. D. J. Palmer discusses *Doctor Faustus* as a play about magic in which 'the magic of stage illusion' is triumphantly redeemed from the strictures of such Aristotelians as Sir Philip Sidney. L. C. Knights, agreeing with Smith regarding Marlowe's deliberate intention, tries to identify 'an unresolved emotional quality that lies behind the rational structure of the play' and that has led some critics – wrongly, in his view – into Romantic and diabolonian interpretations. Cleanth Brooks challenges the widespread view that the impressive opening scenes of *Doctor Faustus* are not adequately linked with the impressive closing scenes; his avowedly 'modern' interpretation emphasizes the relevance of the play to our own interests and preoccupations. Harold Hobson, in the last of the passages chosen for the present volume, writes with more haste than the others and seems to be on rather shaky ground when he imagines that a Protestant English audience of 1592, four years after the Armada, would have any serious misgivings about ridiculing the Pope and cardinals. But his newspaper review of the O.U.D.S. production of 1966 has the freshness of an immediate and delighted response to what was surely the most famous production of *Doctor Faustus* since Marlowe's lifetime.

We should find it easier to compare the views of the various critics if they were all talking about exactly the same play. But this is far from being the case. All modern texts of *Doctor Faustus* derive directly or indirectly from one or both of two early versions: the so-called A-version, first published in 1604, and the so-called B-version, first published in 1616. These differ widely from each other. The B-version is longer than the A-version by more than one-third. The A-version knows nothing of Bruno the antipope either at the papal or at the imperial court; it knows nothing of the plan of revenge by Benvolio and his friends or of its frustration by Faustus; it is equally ignorant of the conspiracy of the Horse-courser and his associates and of their humiliation at Vanholt; and it omits from the last three scenes a number of incidents, mainly of a supernatural or spectacular kind. In addition, all scenes occurring in both versions differ appreciably in wording, and five of them differ very widely indeed.

For a long time, editors of *Doctor Faustus* supposed that, since the longer B-version was published later than the shorter A-version, B must represent a revision and expansion of A. But in 1950 W. W. Greg demonstrated, in his great parallel-text edition of the play, that B, although not printed until twelve years after A, must already have been in existence when A was composed; and that A represents an abbreviated reconstruction of it from memory by a group of players who wished to acquire a script for performance. Leo Kirschbaum, working independently of Greg, anticipated some of his conclusions in 'The Good and Bad Quartos of *Doctor Faustus*' (*Library*, Fourth Series, XXVI (1945-1946) 272-94).

Until 1950, most editors had based their texts upon the shorter version, believing that this was the more original. Greg's demonstration that the longer version is the more original has caused editors to rely instead upon B. But they cannot rely upon it completely. When it was first printed in 1616, certain passages in the manuscript must have been illegible, for the compositor, or the scribe who prepared his copy for him, helped himself out with a printed copy of A. Clearly, in places where B is merely following A, and not succeeding in following it exactly, A itself is preferable to B. Nor are these the only circumstances in which an editor, while relying mainly upon B, may see fit to use A. But it would be inappropriate to repeat here the whole of an analysis which Greg states in detail in his parallel-text edition and which I describe fairly fully and criticize in minor respects in the Introduction to my 'Revels' edition of the play.[1]

What is relevant now is that, while most of the critics contributing 'Recent Studies' to the present volume use and quote from modern editions based mainly on the fuller B-version, a few

[1] These three paragraphs follow closely three paragraphs in section 11 of the Introduction to my Methuen's English Classics edition (1965) of *Doctor Faustus*. Elsewhere in the present Introduction I have borrowed material and formulations from my 'Revels' edition of the play.

of them use editions based on the abridged A-version. Smith does so because he was writing at a time when the A-version was still generally supposed to be the more original, Ornstein does so because even in 1955 the A-version was 'the one known to the vast majority of readers', and Steane does so nine years later still out of simple staunch conservatism. Those who prefer to discuss the more complete version use various editions of it, some adhering more and some less closely to the text as printed in 1616, some employing modern spelling and some retaining the old spelling. In this situation, an attempt by me to bring all their quotations into conformity with a single text of the play would have meant undue editorial interference. So I have recognized each contributor's right to quote from the edition of his choice and have limited myself to correcting demonstrable errors. For the reader's convenience, however, I have standardized the references given by those contributors who choose to provide them. All such references now relate to my own 'Revels' edition of the play. When referring to the A-version of any of the five scenes that differ very widely indeed in the 1604 and 1616 texts, I have prefixed the letter 'A' to the scene-number: Aiv, Avii, Ax, Axii, Axv. Appendix 1 of the 'Revels' edition contains the A-versions of these scenes.

In the 'Revels' edition, the play is divided into scenes only. For the assistance of readers who are using editions in which Act-divisions have also been imposed upon the 1616 text, I supply a table relating my scene numbers to the Act and scene numbers adopted by F. S. Boas (1932) and by Greg in his 'Conjectural Reconstruction' (1950):

> Scenes i–iv correspond to Act I, scenes i–iv.
> Scenes v–vii correspond to Act II, scenes i–iii.
> Scenes viii–x correspond to Act III, scenes i–iii.
> Scenes xi–xvii correspond to Act IV, scenes i–vii.
> Scenes xviii–xx correspond to Act V, scenes i–iii.

My decision not to standardize quotations from *Doctor Faustus* has entailed certain other decisions against standardization. For example, Faustus' companion is usually 'Mephastophilis' in 1604,

'Mephostophilis' in 1616 and 'Mephistophilis' (under Goethean influence) in the nineteenth-century editions. I have allowed each contributor to go on using the form he prefers; and my practice has been the same with regard to all other spellings that were not obviously erroneous. Nor have I denied contributors, when they quote from other works and authors, the liberty that I have left them when they quote from *Doctor Faustus*. They use the editions of their choice. Their references, too, remain keyed to those editions, and, except when a contributor has asked me to do otherwise, I have not tampered with the form of the references.

JOHN JUMP

PART ONE

Extracts from Earlier Critics, 1797-1946

WALTER SCOTT

Christopher Marlowe's *Tragicall History of Dr Faustus* – a very remarkable thing. Grand subject – end grand.

(from Scott's private notebook under the date 26 May 1797, in J. G. Lockhart, *Memoirs of the Life of Sir Walter Scott*, 7 vols (1837–8) 1 264)

HENRY MAITLAND

IT is obvious, that, as a whole, [*Doctor Faustus*] ... is exceedingly imperfect and disproportioned. The commencement and the conclusion are solemn, lofty – even magnificent – but the middle part is out of all keeping; and the ludicrous is therein not only too far prolonged, but too broadly drawn, and deeply coloured. The drama, too, comprehends a period of twenty-four years, and the actions and events are too few, and not sufficiently varied. Neither does Faustus seem to deserve the fearful punishment finally inflicted on him by Lucifer. At the same time, Marlow has shown great skill, and a deep knowledge of human nature, in not drawing Faustus as a monster of guilt and iniquity, so as to destroy all sympathy with his sufferings and fate. Though sold to Hell, he seeks rather his own enjoyment and pleasure than the misery of others, nor does he even seek them at the expense of his fellow creatures. When he delivers himself up to pleasure, his paramour is no innocent maiden whom his magic seduces, but the bright phantom of a former age, – and his licentiousness, even in its most criminal indulgencies, connects itself with the dreams of an imagination filled with all the forms of classical beauty. Goethe, on the other hand, in his powerful drama on the same subject, has driven Faustus over the edge, and down the abyss, of Sin. But we are not now going to criticise the work of the German philosopher. That we may do at another opportunity. Let us conclude with one remark – that while there is at present abroad throughout the world so mad a passion for poetry, and more especially for poetry in which the stronger passions of our nature are delineated, it is somewhat singular, that such excessive admiration is bestowed on *one* great living Poet [Byron], while (to say nothing of contemporary writers) there are so many glorious works of the mighty dead, unknown, or disregarded – works from which that illustrious person has doubtless imbibed inspiration, and which, without detracting from his well-earned fame, we must think, are far superior, in variety, depth, and energy of passion, to the best poems which his powerful genius has yet produced.

> (from 'Marlow's Tragical History of the Life and Death of Doctor Faustus', in *Blackwood's Edinburgh Magazine*, 1 (1817) 393–4)

FRANCIS JEFFREY

It is suggested, in an ingenious paper, in a late Number of the *Edinburgh Magazine*, that the general conception of this piece [Byron's *Manfred*], and much of what is excellent in the manner of its execution, have been borrowed from the *Tragical History of Dr Faustus* of Marlow; and a variety of passages are quoted, which the author considers as similar, and, in many respects, superior to others in the poem before us. . . .

But these, and many other smooth and fanciful verses in this curious old drama, prove nothing, we think, against the originality of *Manfred*; for there is nothing to be found there of the pride, the abstraction, and the heartrooted misery in which that originality consists. Faustus is a vulgar sorcerer, tempted to sell his soul to the Devil for the ordinary price of sensual pleasure, and earthly power and glory – and who shrinks and shudders in agony when the forfeit comes to be exacted. The style, too, of Marlow, though elegant and scholarlike, is weak and childish compared with the depth and force of much of what we have quoted from Lord Byron; and the disgusting buffoonery and low farce of which his piece is principally made up, place it much more in contrast, than in any terms of comparison, with that of his noble successor. In the tone and pitch of the composition, as well as in the character of the diction in the more solemn parts, the piece before us reminds us much more of the *Prometheus* of Æschylus, than of any more modern performance.

(from a review of Byron's *Manfred*, in *Edinburgh Review*, XXVIII (1817) 430–1)

WILLIAM HAZLITT

MARLOWE is a name that stands high. . . . There is a lust of power in his writings, a hunger and thirst after unrighteousness, a glow of the imagination, unhallowed by any thing but its own energies. His thoughts burn within him like a furnace with bickering flames; or throwing out black smoke and mists, that hide the dawn of genius, or like a poisonous mineral, corrode the heart. His *Life and Death of Doctor Faustus*, though an imperfect and unequal performance, is his greatest work. Faustus himself is a rude sketch, but it is a gigantic one. This character may be considered as a personification of the pride of will and eagerness of curiosity, sublimed beyond the reach of fear and remorse. He is hurried away, and, as it were, devoured by a tormenting desire to enlarge his knowledge to the utmost bounds of nature and art, and to extend his power with his knowledge. He would realise all the fictions of a lawless imagination, would solve the most subtle speculations of abstract reason; and for this purpose, sets at defiance all mortal consequences, and leagues himself with demoniacal power, with 'fate and metaphysical aid'. The idea of witchcraft and necromancy, once the dread of the vulgar and the darling of the visionary recluse, seems to have had its origin in the restless tendency of the human mind, to conceive of and aspire to more than it can achieve by natural means, and in the obscure apprehension that the gratification of this extravagant and unauthorised desire, can only be attained by the sacrifice of all our ordinary hopes, and better prospects to the infernal agents that lend themselves to its accomplishment. Such is the foundation of the present story. Faustus, in his impatience to fulfil at once and for a moment, for a few short years, all the desires and conceptions of his soul, is willing to give in exchange his soul and body to the great enemy of mankind. Whatever he fancies, becomes by this means present to his sense: whatever he commands, is done. He calls back time past, and anticipates the future: the visions of antiquity pass before him, Babylon in all its glory, Paris and Oenone: all the projects of philosophers, or creations of the poet pay tribute at his feet: all the delights of fortune, of ambition, of pleasure, and of learning are centered in his person; and from a short-lived dream of supreme felicity and drunken power, he sinks into an abyss of darkness and perdition. This is the alternative to which he submits; the bond which he signs with his blood! As the outline of the character is grand and daring, the execution is abrupt and fearful. The thoughts are vast and irregular; and the style halts and staggers under them, 'with uneasy steps'; – 'such footing found the sole of unblest feet'. There is a little fustian and incongruity of metaphor now and then, which is not very injurious to the subject. . . .

The intermediate comic parts, in which Faustus is not directly concerned, are mean and grovelling to the last degree. One of the Clowns says to another: 'Snails! what hast got there? A book? Why thou can'st not tell ne'er a word on 't.' Indeed, the ignorance and barbarism of the time, as here described, might almost justify Faustus's overstrained admiration of learning, and turn the heads of those who possessed it, from novelty and unaccustomed excitement, as the Indians are made drunk with wine! Goethe, the German poet, has written a drama on this tradition of his country, which is considered a master-piece. I cannot find, in Marlowe's play, any proofs of the atheism or impiety attributed to him, unless the belief in witchcraft and the Devil can be regarded as such; and at the time he wrote, not to have believed in both, would have been construed into the rankest atheism and irreligion. There is a delight, as Mr Lamb says, 'in dallying with interdicted subjects'; but that does not, by any means, imply either a practical or speculative disbelief of them.

(from *Lectures on the Age of Elizabeth* (1820), in *Complete Works*, ed. P. P. Howe, 20 vols (1930–4) VI 202–3, 207)

CHARLES LAMB

I throughly agree with you as to the German *Faust*, as far [as] I can do justice to it from an English translation. 'Tis a disagreeable canting tale of Seduction, which has nothing to do with the Spirit of Faustus – Curiosity. Was the dark secret to be explored to end in the seducing of a weak girl, which might have been accomplished by earthly agency? When Marlow gives *his* Faustus a mistress, he flies him at Helen, flower of Greece, to be sure, and not at Miss Betsy, or Miss Sally Thoughtless.

> Cut is the branch that bore the goodly fruit,
> And wither'd is Apollo's laurel tree:
> Faustus is dead.*

What a noble natural transition from metaphor to plain speaking! as if the figurative had flagged in description of such a Loss, and was reduced to tell the fact simply.

> (from a letter to W. Harrison Ainsworth dated 9 December 1823, in *The Works of Charles and Mary Lamb*, ed. E. V. Lucas, 7 vols (1903–5) VII 631)

J. W. VON GOETHE
(reported by H. Crabb Robinson)

I mentioned Marlowe's *Faust*. He burst out into an exclamation of praise. 'How greatly is it all planned!' He had thought of translating it. He was fully aware that Shakespeare did not stand alone.

> (from *Diary, Reminiscences, and Correspondence of Henry Crabb Robinson*, ed. T. Sadler, 3 vols (1869) II 434)

JAMES BROUGHTON

THE beauties of this play have been eloquently expatiated upon by numerous writers, and though defective as a whole, it

* Lamb evidently made his quotation from memory.

certainly merits all the praise it has received. Some exquisitely poetical passages might be selected from it, especially the apostrophe of Faustus to the shade of Helen, with his last impassioned soliloquy of agony and despair, which is surpassed by nothing in the whole circle of the English Drama, and cannot fail to excite in the reader a thrill of horror, mingled with pity for the miserable sufferer. The appearance of the devils in this scene, to bear away their victim, seems to have shocked many persons, as bordering upon profanity; and among the relaters of marvels, there was long current a story, that upon a certain occasion Satan actually made one of the party, with consequences very fearful to whose who had assumed his shape. Alleyn, the founder of Dulwich College, was the original representative of Faustus.

(from 'Life and Writings of Christopher Marlowe', in
Gentleman's Magazine, c (1830 (i)) 593)

JOHN PAYNE COLLIER

Faustus was intended to follow up the design, which may almost be said to have been accomplished in *Tamburlaine*, and to establish the use of blank-verse on the public stage. Here the poet, wishing to astonish, and to delight by astonishing, has called in the aid of magic and supernatural agency, and has wrought from his materials, a drama full of power, novelty, interest, and variety. All the serious scenes of *Faustus* eminently excite both pity and terror.

(from *The History of English Dramatic Poetry*,
3 vols (1831) III 127)

HENRY HALLAM

[*Doctor Faustus*] contains nothing, perhaps, so dramatic as the first part of the *Jew of Malta*; yet the occasional glimpses of repentance and struggles of alarmed conscience in the chief character are finely brought in. It is full of poetical beauties; but an intermixture of buffoonery weakens the effect, and leaves it on the whole rather a sketch by a great genius than a finished performance. There is an awful melancholy about Marlowe's Mephistopheles, perhaps more impressive than the malignant mirth of the fiend in the renowned work of Goethe. But the fair form of Margaret is wanting; and Marlowe has hardly earned the credit of having breathed a few casual inspirations into a greater mind than his own.

> (from *Introduction to the Literature of Europe,*
> 4 vols (1837–9) II 170–1)

GEORGE HENRY LEWES

Doctor Faustus has many magnificent passages, such as Marlowe of the 'mighty line' could not fail to write; but on the whole it is wearisome, vulgar, and ill-conceived. The lowest buffoonery, destitute of wit, fills a large portion of the scenes; and the serious parts want dramatic evolution. There is no character well drawn. The melancholy figure of Mephistopholis has a certain grandeur, but he is not the Tempter, according to the common conception, creeping to his purpose with the cunning of the serpent; nor is he the cold, ironical 'spirit that denies'; he is more like the Satan of Byron, with a touch of piety and much repentance. The language he addresses to Faustus is such as would rather frighten than seduce him.

The reader who opens *Faustus* under the impression that he is about to see a philosophical subject treated philosophically, will have mistaken both the character of Marlowe's genius and of Marlowe's epoch. *Faustus* is no more philosophical in intention than the *Jew of Malta*, or *Tamburlaine the Great*. It is simply the theatrical treatment of a popular legend, – a legend admirably characteristic of the spirit of those ages in which men, believing in the agency of the devil, would willingly have bartered their future existence for the satisfaction of present desires. . . .

The vulgar conception of this play is partly the fault of

Marlowe, and partly of his age. It might have been treated quite in conformity with the general belief; it might have been a tale of sorcery, and yet magnificently impressive. What would not Shakespeare have made of it? Nevertheless, we must in justice to Marlowe look also to the state of opinion in his time; and we shall then admit that another and higher mode of treatment would perhaps have been less acceptable to the audience. Had it been metaphysical, they would not have understood it; had the motives of Faustus been more elevated, the audience would not have believed in them. To have saved him at last, would have been to violate the legend, and to outrage their moral sense. For, why should the black arts be unpunished? why should not the sorcerer be damned? The legend was understood in its literal sense, in perfect accordance with the credulity of the audience. The symbolical significance of the legend is entirely a modern creation.

(from *The Life and Works of Goethe* (1855) pp. 469, 471)

H. A. TAINE

[MARLOWE'S Faustus is] the living, struggling, natural, personal man, not the philosophic type which Goethe has created, but a primitive and genuine man, hot-headed, fiery, the slave of his passions, the sport of his dreams, wholly engrossed in the present, molded by his lusts, contradictions, and follies, who amidst noise and starts, cries of pleasure and anguish, rolls, knowing it and willing it, down the slope and crags of his precipice.

(from *History of English Literature* (1863–4; trans. H. van Laun, 1871) bk II, ch. II iv)

A. W. WARD

[THE] moral of the tragedy . . . is simple enough, – 'unlawful things' are to be wondered at but not to be practised; yet it had its meaning for Marlowe's age, and for Marlowe's mind. His age believed that there were such possibilities of temptation as those before which Faustus succumbed; and to his mind the temptation of tampering with the inscrutable was doubtless a real seduction. No solution of the problem is proposed, or even hinted at; any such was beyond both the poet and his times; but a subjective as well as an objective significance underlies his theme, though his treatment of it is crude, and his endeavour to work it out dramatically (whatever may be the extent of interpolations by other hands in his tragedy) is imperfect.

(from *A History of English Dramatic Literature*, 3 vols (1875) I 336)

WILHELM WAGNER

MARLOWE'S Faustus is anything but a hero. He gives up heaven, and sells his soul to the Devil; but he does not derive the slightest benefit from his agreement, as he never becomes the master of the Spirit who has sworn to serve him, and employs his agency for mere frivolous uses. The thirst of supernatural knowledge is, one might say, little more than a specious pretext for Faustus to abjure God and the simple faith of his contemporaries; after a few questions about heaven, and earth, and astronomy in general, Faustus devotes himself to mere trifles and childish pastimes. If the legend meant to insinuate that the Devil and the world cannot offer us greater satisfaction than God and religion, and that by turning to the first we endanger our soul's health without gaining any corresponding advantage, simply because the Devil has nothing but trifles to offer – this is indeed sound doctrine, but does not admit of much dramatic treatment by itself. In Marlowe's play even this feature is not fully brought out in the shape of a struggle of passion and reason, but is only occasionally insinuated; and now and then we hear of Faustus' repining at his bargain, when he is regularly 'put down' by some rough words of Mephistophiles or Lucifer. When the end draws nigh, Faustus turns coward, and, though we can sympathise with his fear and lamentations, yet we cannot but feel that this end is the appropriate conclusion of his career. If Marlowe had known the legend of Theophilus, he might, perhaps, have altered this conclusion in some way or other; but still there was the didactic tendency of the legend, according to which the magician must be damned; and though Marlowe was styled an atheist by his contemporaries, his mind was not liberal enough to get over this matter of doctrine. Hence Marlowe's play is nothing but the legend dramatised, without any attempt at dramatic characterisation. The characters of the tragedy come and go like mere figures, without any internal connection with each other. They are like a phantasmagoria grouped around Faustus and Mephistophiles, who remain the same from beginning to end. Mephistophiles is, indeed, a very commonplace devil, without any distinguishing feature except a certain melancholy such as becomes a fallen angel; but this again is not a dramatic quality. The interest of the play is furnished by the first two acts, and by the fifth, i.e. Faustus' resolution to renounce divinity and adhere to the Devil, and his agreement with the latter, and then again by the payment of his self-imposed fine, when the Devil comes to fetch him. All that lies between these two extremes is merely accessory to the tale, without any intrinsic interest. Any attempt to show the doings of Faustus and the Devil within the space of four-and-twenty years was sure to prove a failure, inasmuch as all these doings were represented as so many single acts, without any internal and causal connection. Goethe, who was aware of this gap in the legend of Faustus, *invented* the tale of Gretchen and her unhappy love with Faustus. In the legend itself there was the character of Helen, whom Faustus was said to have kept as his wife; but Marlowe does not bring her before the end, and then only in order to let her disappear immediately. If Marlowe himself had not been nursed on the traditions of the Renaissance, he might have perceived that something could be made out of this appearance of Helen. Would it not have been glorious to have let Mephistophiles be cheated of his prey through the agency of one of his own spirits? Faustus' soul was full of the worship of beauty, whose power Marlowe has immortalised in many splendid passages, not the least of which are those famous lines on Helen, and Helen was an impersonation of beauty. Let her turn Faustus' mind to the sole pursuit of beauty in its widest sense, and he would thus have become averse from the Devil, who is nothing but ugliness and unsightliness!

(from Christopher Marlowe's Tragedy of Doctor Faustus,
ed. W. Wagner (1877) pp. xxxii–xxxv)

JOHN ADDINGTON SYMONDS

Doctor Faustus is more nearly allied in form to the dramatic poems of our own days, which present a psychological study of character to the reader, than any other work of our old theatre. Marlowe concentrated his energies on the delineation of the proud life and terrible death of a man in revolt against the eternal laws of his own nature and the world, defiant and desperate, plagued with remorse, alternating between the gratification of his appetites and the dread of a God whom he rejects without denying. It is this tragic figure which he drew forth from the substance of the German tale, and endowed with the breath and blood of real existence. He traced the outline with a breadth and dignity beyond the scope of the prose legend. He filled it in with the power of a great poet, with the intensity of life belonging to himself and to the age of adolescent vigour. He left us a picture of the medieval rebel, true in its minutest details to that bygone age, but animated with his own audacious spirit, no longer mythical, but vivified, a living personality. By the side of Faustus he placed the sinister and melancholy Mephistophilis, a spirit who wins souls for hell by the allurements of despair, playing with open cards and hiding no iota of the dreadfulness of damnation. He introduced good and bad angels, hovering in the air, and whispering alternately their words of warning and enticement in the ears of Faustus. The professional magicians who lend their books to the hero, the old man who entreats him to repent, the scholars who assuage his last hours with their sympathy, make up the minor persons of the drama. But each and all of these subordinate characters are dedicated to the one main purpose of expressing the psychological condition of

Faustus from various points of view: – the perplexities of his divided spirit, his waverings of anguish and remorse, the flickerings of hope extinguished in the smoke of self-abandonment to fear, the pungent pricks of conscience soothed by transient visions of delight, the prying curiosity which lulls his torment at one moment, the soul's defiance yielding to despair, and from despair recovering fresh strength to sin and suffer. To this vivisection of a ruined man, all details in the gloomy scene contribute. Even the pitiful distractions – pitiful in their leaden dulness and blunt edge of drollery – with which Faustus amuses his worse than Promethean leisure until the last hour of his contract sound, heighten the infernal effect. The stage swarms continually with devils, running at one time at their master's bidding on the sorriest errands, evoking at another the most dismal shows from hell. We are entertained with processions of the Seven Deadly Sins, and with masques of the damned 'in that vast perpetual torture-house' below. In the absence of the hero, Lucifer, Beelzebub, and Mephistophilis commune together with gross irony. The whole theatre is sulphurous with fumes of the bottomless pit.

(from *Shakspere's Predecessors in the English Drama* (1884)
pp. 631–3)

A. H. BULLEN

Dr Faustus is a work which once read can never be forgotten. It must be allowed that Marlowe did not perceive the full capabilities afforded by the legend he adopted; that crudeness of treatment is shown in making Faustus abandon the pursuit of supernatural knowledge, and turn to trivial uses the power that he had purchased at the price of his soul. This and more may be granted; but criticism is silenced when we reflect on the agony of Faustus' final soliloquy and the fervid splendour of his raptures over Helen's beauty. *Dr Faustus* is rather a series of dramatic scenes than a complete drama. Many of these scenes were the work of another hand and may be expunged with advantage.

But what remains is singularly precious. The subtler treatment of a later age can never efface from our minds the appalling realism of the catastrophe in Marlowe's play: still our sense is pierced by that last despairing cry of shrill anguish—

> Ugly Hell, gape not! Come not, Lucifer!
> I'll burn my books! Ah, Mephistophilis!

Goethe's English biographer speaks slightingly of Marlowe's play; but Goethe himself, when questioned about *Dr Faustus*, 'burst out with an exclamation of praise: How greatly was it all planned! He had thought of translating it.'

> (from *The Works of Christopher Marlowe*, ed. A. H. Bullen,
> 3 vols (1885) I xxxviii–xxxix)

HAVELOCK ELLIS

MARLOWE changed the point of view [from that which he found in the *Faustbook*]; Faust is no longer an unintelligible magician looked at from the outside, but a living man thirsting for the infinite; the sinner becomes a hero, a Tamburlaine, no longer eager to 'ride in triumph through Persepolis', who at the thought of vaster delights has ceased to care for the finite splendours of an earthly crown.

> A god is not so glorious as a king.
> I think the pleasure they enjoy in Heaven
> Cannot compare with kingly joys in earth,

once exclaimed Tamburlaine's follower, Theridamas. Faustus, in his study, realising what magic promises, thinks otherwise:

> Emperors and kings
> Are but obeyèd in their several provinces;
> Nor can they raise the wind or rend the clouds;
> But his dominion that exceeds in this
> Stretcheth as far as doth the mind of man;
> A sound magician is a demigod.

Marlowe's Faustus is not impelled like the Faustus of the legend

by the desire of 'worldly pleasure', nor, like Goethe's, by the
vanity of knowledge; it is power, power without bound, that he
desires, all that is in the world, the lust of the flesh and the lust of
the eyes and the pride of life,

> — a world of profit and delight
> Of power, of honour, and omnipotence.

This gives him a passionate energy, an emotional sensibility
which Goethe's more shifting, sceptical and complex Faust lacks.
For Marlowe, also, magic was a possible reality.

(from *Christopher Marlowe*, ed. H. Ellis (1887) pp. xxxviii–
xxxix)

A. C. SWINBURNE

THE unity of tone and purpose in *Doctor Faustus* is not unrelieved
by change of manner and variety of incident. The comic scenes,
written evidently with as little of labour as of relish, are for the
most part scarcely more than transcripts, thrown into the form
of dialogue, from a popular prose *History of Doctor Faustus*; and
therefore should be set down as little to the discredit as to the
credit of the poet. Few masterpieces of any age in any language
can stand beside this tragic poem – it has hardly the structure of a
play – for the qualities of terror and splendour, for intensity of
purpose and sublimity of note. In the vision of Helen, for example, the intense perception of loveliness gives actual sublimity to the sweetness and radiance of mere beauty in the
passionate and spontaneous selection of words the most choice
and perfect; and in like manner the sublimity of simplicity in
Marlowe's conception and expression of the agonies endured by
Faustus under the immediate imminence of his doom gives the
highest note of beauty, the quality of absolute fitness and
propriety, to the sheer straightforwardness of speech in which his
agonising horror finds vent ever more and more terrible from the
first to the last equally beautiful and fearful verse of that tremendous monologue which has no parallel in all the range of tragedy.

(from *The Age of Shakespeare* (1908) pp. 4–5)

GEORGE SANTAYANA

MARLOWE'S public would see in Doctor Faustus a man and a Christian like themselves, carried a bit too far by ambition and the love of pleasure. He is no radical unbeliever, no natural mate for the devil, conscienceless and heathen, like the typical villain of the Renaissance. On the contrary, he has become a good Protestant, and holds manfully to all those parts of the creed which express his spontaneous affections. A good angel is often overheard whispering in his ear; and if the bad angel finally prevails, it is in spite of continual remorse and hesitation on the Doctor's part. This excellent Faustus is damned by accident or by predestination; he is brow-beaten by the devil and forbidden to repent when he has really repented. The terror of the conclusion is thereby heightened; we see an essentially good man, because in a moment of infatuation he had signed away his soul, driven against his will to despair and damnation. The alternative of a happy solution lies almost at hand; and it is only a lingering taste for the lurid and the horrible, ingrained in this sort of melodrama, that sends him shrieking to hell.

What makes Marlowe's conclusion the more violent and the more unphilosophical is the fact that, to any one not dominated by convention, the good angel, in the dialogue, seems to have so much the worse of the argument. All he has to offer is sour admonition and external warnings:

> O Faustus, lay that damnèd book aside,
> And gaze not on it lest it tempt thy soul,
> And heap God's heavy wrath upon thy head.
> Read, read, the Scriptures; that is blasphemy....
> Sweet Faustus, think of heaven, and heavenly things.

To which the evil angel replies:

> No, Faustus, think of honour and of wealth.

And in another place:

> Go forward, Faustus, in that famous art,
> Wherein all nature's treasure is contained.

> Be thou on earth as Jove is in the sky,
> Lord and commander of these elements.

There can be no doubt that the devil here represents the natural ideal of Faustus, or of any child of the Renaissance; he appeals to the vague but healthy ambitions of a young soul, that would make trial of the world. In other words, this devil represents the true good, and it is no wonder if the honest Faustus cannot resist his suggestions. We like him for his love of life, for his trust in nature, for his enthusiasm for beauty. He speaks for us all when he cries:

> Was this the face that launched a thousand ships
> And burnt the topless towers of Ilium?

Even his irreverent pranks, being directed against the pope, endear him the more to an anti-clerical public; and he appeals to courtiers and cavaliers by his lofty poetical scorn for such crabbed professions as the law, medicine, or theology. In a word, Marlowe's Faustus is a martyr to everything that the Renaissance prized, – power, curious knowledge, enterprise, wealth, and beauty.

(from *Three Philosophical Poets* (1910) pp. 147–9)

FELIX E. SCHELLING

[*Doctor Faustus*] has come down to us unhappily in a fragmentary and imperfect text. *Faustus* tells the world-story of the man who, seeking for all knowledge, pledged his soul to the devil, only to find the misery of a hopeless repentance in this world and damnation in the world to come. The motive, like much of the conduct of this tragedy, is that of the old moralities, witness the alternate promptings of the good and bad angel and the dance of the seven deadly sins. More important is the typical character of Faustus who is any man and every man. But Faustus is, none the less, an individual in whose pathetic plight we are interested for himself, and the appeal of the work is primarily artistic. *Doctor Faustus* is a better play on the stage than the careless reader might suppose it; and it is worthy of note that what the old story has gained in other hands in variety of incident, by the infusion of the love story of Margaret for example, it has lost in the singleness of purpose with which Marlowe concentrates attention on his unhappy protagonist. Even the wide allegorical significance, the masterly obliteration of time and space of the second part of Goethe's *Faust* with the hero's redemption, scarcely compensate for this loss. The tragic and untimely death, too, of Marlowe, the daring character of his genius and the stories of his doubts of God have conspired to make this play one of the most interesting in our literature. Beside all this, it is unimportant what editions or translations of the *Faustbuch* Marlowe utilised in his work. His was the poetry that fired the genius of Goethe, who sophisticated with modern brilliant philosophical speculation a theme which was the product of an age of sterner and, dare we say, of sounder theology than that of his own.

(from *English Drama* (1914) p. 68)

WILLIAM EMPSON

My God, my God, look not so fierce on me;
Adders and serpents, let me breathe awhile;
Ugly Hell gape not; come not, Lucifer;
I'll burn my books. Ah Mephistophilis.

... There is *no* stress, as a matter of scansion, on the negatives, so that the main meaning is a shuddering acceptance, that informs the audience what is there. But behind this there is also a demand for the final intellectual curiosity, at whatever cost, to be satisfied:—

Let Ugly Hell gape, *show* me Lucifer;

so that perhaps, behind all his terror, it is for this reason that he is willing to abandon his learning, that he is going to a world where knowledge is immediate, and in those flames his *books* will no longer be required. Faustus is being broken; the depths of his mind are being churned to the surface; his meanings are jarring in his mouth; one cannot recite *Ugly Hell gape not* as a direct imperative like 'stop gaping there'; and it is evident that with the last two words he has abandoned the effort to organise his preferences, and is falling to the devil like a tired child.

(from *Seven Types of Ambiguity* (1930) pp. 261–2)

LEO KIRSCHBAUM

Outside the theatre, we may mightily agree or disagree with the eschatology inherent in *Doctor Faustus*. But *in* the theatre, as we watch the play, we understand and accept (if only for the nonce) that man's most precious possession is his immortal soul and that he gains Heaven or Hell by his professions and actions on earth. *In* the theatre, we accept Marlowe's premises. That these premises were inherent in his first audience is of incidental interest to us as students and appreciators of the drama. The premises are instinct in every word, line, passage, speech, action of the play. The Christian view of the world informs *Doctor Faustus* throughout – not the pagan view. If we do not accept that Faustus's selling his soul to the devil for earthly power and pleasure is a serious business, we simply are not hearing what Marlowe wrote.

Critics confound Marlowe the man and Marlowe the playwright. They consider that the man was an atheist and so interpret *Doctor Faustus*. What if the play were anonymous? What has biography to do with a play which we are presumably watching in the theatre? Whatever Marlowe was himself, there is no more obvious Christian document in all Elizabethan drama than *Doctor Faustus*. Or critics will consider the protagonist as a representative of the Renaissance superman. Whatever their feelings and thoughts on the revival of learning and the Reformation are, let them open-mindedly look at the play unfolding on the stage before them. For earthly learning, earthly power, earthly satisfaction, Faustus goes down to horrible and ever-lasting perdition. It does not matter what *you* think of Hell or what Marlowe privately thought of Hell. What does matter is that in terms of the play, Faustus is a wretched creature who for lower values gives up higher values – that the devil and Hell are omnipresent, potent, and terrifying realities. These are the values which govern the play. You must temporarily accept them while you watch the play. You need not ultimately accept them. But you should not interpret the play in the light of *your* philosophy or religion or absence of religion. You cannot do so if you hear it properly – as a play, as an entity, as a progressive action, as a quasi-morality in which is clearly set forth the hierarchy of moral values which enforces and encloses the play, which the characters in the play accept, which the playwright advances and accepts in his prologue and epilogue, which – hence – the audience must understand and accept.

(from 'Marlowe's *Faustus*: A Reconsideration', in *Review of
English Studies*, XIX (1943) 229)

UNA ELLIS-FERMOR

MARLOWE, whose tragedy appears at its height and in charac-teristic form in *Faustus*, takes up a unique position as a tragic thinker, because of the implacable paradox on which his reading of the universe rests; man's innate fallibility on the one hand, and, on the other, the infallibility demanded by inflexible law. To this paradox there is only one conclusion: 'Why then belike we must sin and so consequently die.' The precision and finality of this deduction indicate a vision terrifying alike in its assumptions and in its omissions. For implicit in Marlowe's premiss is the pre-destination of man to destruction by some determinate power capable of purpose and intention, and, as such purpose can only be sadistic, the world order it implies must derive from a Satanism more nearly absolute than that of Euripides.

But neither in this play nor elsewhere does Marlowe state this assumption in explicit terms and the implication itself rests on a few passages in *Faustus*. Even there it is rather by silence and omission that he reveals his belief that evil is not only inherent in man's destiny but both irremediable and predetermined. Only a consistent vision of a Satanic universe could beget the initial paradox; never does Marlowe raise the question: Why, if the laws of the universe be such, should man, himself a part of that universe, be so irreconcileably opposed to them? To a convinced Satanist it is, in fact, no paradox. Given a sadistic and malevolent power directing the world-order there is no inducement to postulate a further transcendent power or intelligence, relating or reconciling the contradictions of man's capacity and God's demands. And so Marlowe achieves, not a balance between two interpretations of the universe, but immobility and rigidity of protest. In his drama the spirit of man is set against the universe, but there is no equilibrium between two worlds of thought. For Marlowe, at the time of *Faustus*, did not question the nature of the world-order. He saw it steadily and saw it evil.

(from *The Frontiers of Drama* (1945) pp. 141–2)

PAUL H. KOCHER

Faustus is the only one of Marlowe's plays in which the pivotal issue is strictly religious and the whole design rests upon Protestant doctrines. This issue, stated simply, is whether Faustus shall choose God or the evil delights of witchcraft. In the first scenes we witness the temptations which lead to his fall through the witch bargain, and in subsequent scenes his agonized struggle to escape damnation by repentance. Thus the drama is not primarily one of external action but of spiritual combat within the soul of one man, waged according to the laws of the Christian world order. Now this theme allows Marlowe congenial opportunities of blaspheming without fear of being called to account. Through Faustus he can utter strictures on prayer, on Hell, on the harshness of Christian dogma, and then cover them safely with the usual orthodox replies. But withal Marlowe never lets these iconoclastic sallies overthrow the Christian emphasis of the whole. Like a crucible whose walls contain a seething liquid, the Christian structure of the play stands firm around the eruptions of blasphemy, and does not break.

(from *Christopher Marlowe: A Study of his Thought, Learning, and Character* (1946) p. 104)

PART TWO

Recent Studies

James Smith

MARLOWE'S *DOCTOR FAUSTUS*
(1939)

THE final scene in *Doctor Faustus* is more often than not treated as irrelevant to the play. In it, says one critic, 'Marlowe committed apostasy'; that is, he reversed completely the purposes and principles that had hitherto governed his writing. And as these purposes and principles are approved, one of two conclusions follows: either that the final scene is the product of a Marlowe in decline; or that he wrote it, at the best, as an exercise; at the worst as a joke, with his tongue in his cheek. There is another critic who says: 'The alternative of a happy solution lies almost at hand; and it is only a lingering taste for the lurid and the horrible, ingrained in this sort of melodrama, that sends Faustus shrieking to hell.'

To both it would seem possible to reply that no scene of such excellence – and the excellence, so far as I know, is not denied – could issue from anyone who was not both capable of and actually exerting his powers to the utmost. But this perhaps assumes as premiss a belief about life and literature which, though acknowledged outside *Scrutiny*, is not generally used as such. Therefore it is advisable to fall back on a reply that can be verified from the words of the text; and to claim that, so far from being disconnected from its predecessors, the final scene refers to them continually and is continually referred to by them.

The man who is 'sent shrieking to hell' is one who previously had vaunted:

> Thinkst thou that Faustus is so fond, to imagine,
> That after this life there is any paine?
> Tush, these are trifles and meere olde wives tales.

Whereas his ambition had been to

> ... make man to live eternally,
> Or being dead, raise them to life againe,

he is, in the last scene, reduced to lament that he cannot die:

> Or, why is this immortall that thou hast?
> Ah *Pythagoras metemsucosis*, were that true,
> This soule should flie from me, and I be changde
> Unto some brutish beast: al beasts are happy,
> For when they die,
> Their soules are soone dissolvd in elements,
> But mine must live. . . .

He finds it impossible to be rid of his soul:

> Why wert thou not a creature wanting soule?

whereas before he had thought nothing easier than to throw it away:

> Had I as many soules as there be starres,
> Ide give them al for *Mephastophilis*.

Or again:

> ... Here's the scrowle,
> Wherein thou hast given thy soule to *Lucifer*.
> — I, and body too, but what of that?

And so on: it would be possible, in illustration of this point, to transcribe whole pages of dialogue. But it is perhaps superfluous to do so, and relevant quotation will in any case be necessary later.

These references backward, once recognized, improve, I think, the last scene, however impressive in itself; and that the earlier scenes are improved by it, goes without saying. By them the play is knit into a firm if simple structure, of which it is still possible, in spite of a mutilated text, to trace the main outlines. I shall at least attempt to do so in this paper.

But first it will be necessary to discuss other and, I am afraid, more general topics. For the play makes extensive use of a system of ideas which is no longer widely familiar; and it cannot be recalled by the brief hints which, as sufficient in his time, are all that Marlowe provides.

Pared of its comic scenes, and of the not very serious ones first published in 1616, the play cannot, according to a common opinion, be interpreted wholly realistically. It is not merely a photograph, showing beings who exist side by side to influence one another. A large measure of the action takes place not so much between beings as within a single one of them, Faustus himself; of whom the Good and the Evil Angel, for example, are parts. And so, I would add, are the Old Man, Helen, Mephistophilis, even Lucifer; in a certain sense, which I shall endeavour to explain below, they are parts of Faustus. The play in other words is an allegory.

Yet obviously the Good and the Evil Angel, Helen and the rest are not merely parts of Faustus. The two angels are emissaries of powers, or representatives of orders, independent of himself; while Helen, though a shade, is more than a figment of his imagination. Hence it would appear that allegory does not altogether exclude realism; or perhaps better, that when as excellent as Marlowe's it inevitably employs realism as an instrument. For if compared with other types, its excellence will be found to be precisely this: that it is neither a puzzle, in which things are given an interest by being called other than their proper names; nor is it a scientific analysis, in which various aspects of a thing are isolated for their readier comprehension. I would say rather that it is a synthesis, rendering comprehension not so much more ready as more full.

Marlowe chooses certain characters so as to be capable of at least a double function: they are significant as symbols, in virtue of what they symbolize; but significant also as themselves, in virtue of what they are. And they are not significant now as the one thing, now as the other, by a sort of alternation; but continuously and simultaneously, as both. That they can be so, it is at least plausible to assume, is due to an affinity, or to a partial or potential identity, between what they are and what they symbolize. If the latter, establishment of the identity will be the synthesis effected. In a sense two things are distinct, and this must be acknowledged; but in a sense also they are one, and unless this is acknowledged, they cannot fully be understood, even in the sense in which they are distinct.

The Good Angel, for example, is the representative of an order of goodness, independent of Faustus in that it is not affected whether he is loyal to it or not. He can no more increase or diminish its perfection, than he can create or destroy it. But at the same time the Angel symbolizes a part of Faustus; and may do both because, though the converse is true, Faustus is by no means independent of the order. Only by loyalty can he attain his own perfection and therefore peace; if disloyal, he is tormented by regret for the perfection he has sacrificed. And so, whatever the goodness or badness of his life, the order is vindicated in him: he is evidence of it, a part of it – and to be identified with it, in this sense. But there is also a sense in which he must be kept distinct; for whereas the order's perfection is compatible with any life he may choose, only one, a good one, is compatible with his own.

All this is what the Good Angel, by multiplicity of function, is able to signify. As much Faustus as, say, reason or the power of thought, he supplies the latter, when he is loyal, with an occasion for rejoicing; if otherwise, self-reproach is as inevitable as thought. But at the same time he is none the less an angel, and as such not subject to Faustus's control: he cannot for example, as thought might, be silenced from time to time and ultimately be forgotten. So that joy and sorrow are not merely, or rather in this sense not at all, selected by Faustus for himself, according to what instinct of propriety he may possess: he suffers a sorrow which is inflicted, he receives a joy which is bestowed. Yet again, all that he receives or suffers in this way, since it comes from the Good Angel or from what the Angel represents, is in conformity with and so to speak demanded by his nature: of which the Angel continues as much as ever a part. And thus a synthesis is suggested by the allegory: that Faustus's life, though single and indivisible, is both his own and not his own. On the one hand he alone can lead it, and he cannot do other than lead it, to his profit or to his loss; on the other hand however led, it is the intimate concern of, as it is intimately concerned with, what is other than himself.

In much the same way Helen is the lust of the eyes and of the flesh, both as these are objects in an external world, other than Faustus; and as they are his own passions, leading him to seek within those objects a happiness. As both, she is able to signify that, by his nature, he is bound to the objects in one relation or another; inevitably they are part of his living. But the consequences of any relation are determined by the objects as distinct from his nature; and so there is a sense in which he and Helen must be distinct. While the Good Angel, at least as substantial as he, could ensure a lasting happiness; that proffered by Helen can be no more than momentary, for she is hardly substantial – she is a shade.

An allegorical interpretation of this kind should not perhaps be limited to space but extended also to time. I mean that, just as the spatial distinction between Faustus and the Good Angel is accepted as to some extent, though not wholly, a device (for while distinct, the two in another sense are one): so also should the temporal separation between his death and his signing of the contract. The one event follows the other after a period of twenty-four years, and the period is significant as itself; but also, I think, it is symbolical of the moment of signing. Or rather, of the moment at which Faustus determines to sign: for at that moment, and without delay, he plunges to spiritual death. He kills his soul, which does not need twenty-four years to weaken or to wither. But as death, whether spiritual or physical, does not annihilate a soul, the consequences of the determination to sign, though arriving within are not confined to a moment. Without the intervention of grace they will stretch through eternity, and can therefore be represented, if at all, only under some figure of time. And this is the purpose of the twenty-four years: which as has been said are significant as themselves – but are so only that a single moment may be the more adequately symbolized. To accomplish his purpose Marlowe might be said to write a play of which the hero is both alive and not alive. He appears to be working out as best he can his salvation, and in a sense he is doing so; but there is another sense in which he is working out neither his salvation nor his damnation. He is damned already.

Recognition of both these allegories, and that they are of complicated rather than simple type, is I think necessary to remove obstacles to the reader's enjoyment. For if it is not made, various absurdities arise which are incompatible with the reputation the play is felt to deserve. If for example the two Angels are accepted merely in their symbolical sense, as parts of Faustus, they are nothing but ideals or aspirations opposing one another within his brain. To one or other he must attach himself, but it is not yet obvious which; meanwhile he must behave impartially to both, since both are his offspring. And the two must argue for his allegiance; with the result that, as Mr Santayana says, 'the Good Angel . . . seems to have the worst of it'. But if this is so, the last scene is not only irrelevant, it is contradictory of all that precedes; and no criticism of it could be too severe. A happy ending was demanded, to justify the sound decision of an umpire; and this Marlowe, through malice or perversity, refuses to provide.

If on the other hand the Angels are accepted as at the same time angels; as representatives, that is, of orders established in a universe outside Faustus: it cannot appear doubtful even for a moment which of them should be followed. For Faustus is submitted to the universe as its creature, though a free one; and it is precisely to express this submission that he is symbolized by the Angels at all. Of these it is assumed – or rather, it would be assumed by an Elizabethan audience – that good dominates evil, so to speak absorbs it, and subordinates the ends of evil to ends of its own. Therefore there is no hope of Faustus cutting loose from what the Good Angel represents: by refusing to co-operate with it however insistently he can only prepare for himself a future punishment – and this is a form of involuntary co-operation.

On other grounds it might be said that argument is not even possible. For Faustus, no more than another man, could be argued into a choice of evil as evil. The sole problem, given the Angels as an objective evil and an objective good, is not which of them ought to be followed; but which of them will be followed in fact, and what the consequences will be.

These are to some extent displayed by behaviour on the part of the Angels which, if at first sight it might be taken for argument, is in reality very different. It will be remembered that the consequences, though they immediately supervene, are for their fuller comprehension spread over twenty-four years. Faustus is allowed to explore evil with all patience and all diligence; so that, if it does not bring happiness, the fact after such an experiment shall be more convincing; if on the other hand it brings misery, the contrast with what appeared happiness for a time shall be the sharper. During the whole of the twenty-four years each of the Angels continues in his double role: as part of Faustus, expressing his preoccupations; and as external agent, either encouraging those preoccupations or seeking to end them. As both, the Evil Angel and his associates – for he is not considered profitably, apart from the devils – are inevitably more prominent in the earlier scenes. Evil is a new toy, on which Faustus cannot cease to ponder; nor can he resist any invitations to evil that he may receive. If it is impossible the Good Angel should be silenced, he may at any rate be reduced to single lines and general warnings, such as are easily ignored.

> Sweet Faustus, thinke of heaven, and heavenly things.
> – No Faustus, thinke of honor and of wealth.
> – Of wealth,
> Why the signiory of Embden shalbe mine.

This is not an argument, by which Faustus or anyone is to be persuaded that evil is better than good; but a mere statement or illustration of the fact that, once Faustus has chosen evil, he has neither eyes nor ears save for the immediate advantages of having done so.

The gifts of the devil however neither satisfy nor last. Power and wealth, all that Faustus hitherto has obtained, are not in themselves either bad or good; and so long as they are contemplated merely, he need not be disturbed. But once the attempt is made to use them, disillusion begins. In his inexperience he thinks that, having sold himself into hell, he will be allowed to retain a portion of his integrity: to seize the opportunity, for example, of

new found wealth, to set up an orderly household. Therefore he
asks for a wife, and one is brought. But she proves stuffed with
fireworks and goes up in smoke:

> A plague on her for a hote whore,

he cries, and must henceforth content himself with the 'fairest
curtezans'.

Thus his fleshly desires are satisfied, *tant bien que mal*; but the
result is that his spiritual desires, as they are the more isolated,
become the more insistent. The devil, having already supplied a
book of spells, of planets and of herbs, is summoned to dispute
of 'divine astrologie'. The joy of learning, however, is no more
permissible to Faustus than that of domestic bliss; for if pursued
in due order and in the proper temper, it can lead to one thing
only – the knowledge, the love and ultimately the vision of God.
And all these, along with goodness, he has renounced. By a
process of reasoning which resembles, and is probably intended
to recall, the scholastic argument *a contingentia*, Faustus ascends
from a consideration of the planets to that of the moving Intelligences; and thence to the supreme Intelligence which is the origin
and mover of all.

> Tell me who made the world?

he asks, but can receive no answer. The whole economy of hell
is disturbed; Lucifer appears with his 'companion Prince',
Beelzebub, and 'looking terrible' imposes silence. But as Faustus's
mind cannot be left completely vacant there is offered him, as a
substitute for the vision of God, that of the seven deadly sins.
He watches with detachment, but not without interest; for if he
is moved to no protest against their loathsomeness, he exchanges
quips with one or two. And at the end he exclaims:

> O this feedes my soule.
> – Tut Faustus, in hel is al manner of delight.
> – O might I see hel, and returne againe, how happy were I
> then?

At this point he has fallen victim to a vice familiar to the

Fathers and to the schoolmen, but rarely mentioned as such today: that of curiosity. 'Whereas the voluptuous man', says Augustine, 'seeks after what is beautiful, melodious, sweet or smooth, the curious man seeks after the very opposites of these; not however that he may be vexed by them, but merely out of the lust to experience and to know.' This is Faustus's case: the seven sins do not move him as they would an ordinary man, and as a man should be moved. He has begun to collect sensations without judgment and without order, not as an aid to right living but merely for their own sake. And the further descent from curiosity of the senses to that of the intellect is easy. 'No longer' – to quote Augustine once again – 'is nature explored only so far as is necessary to see the eternal through the temporal', but ransacked in all its corners for the quicker compassing of 'false and earthly happiness, empty and worldly distinction'. With the magazines of science which Faustus now accumulates, he is out of the danger of knowing God; he is on the other hand the better qualified to tease Popes, oblige Duchesses and entertain Emperors.

In the passage from which the last quotation comes, and also elsewhere, Augustine connects curiosity with the conjuring and worship of devils. It is not only this which leads to the suspicion that he, or at least his doctrines, had a strong influence on *Doctor Faustus* (a direct influence I mean, and not only by way of the *Faustbook*; for as will be apparent now or later, I think Marlowe abandons the theology of the *Faustbook* for one which is more humane, as it is more traditional). That the unbounded appetite for experience or for learning was a discovery of the Renaissance is a superstition common amongst commentators: it had however been known long before, and in particular to Augustine – who was seduced into Manichaeism by the promise he would no longer need to believe, but should know; and who had, in his own magnificent image, the 'sun and moon served up to him in a dish', but found the food unsustaining. What was new in the Renaissance was the neglect of the boundaries within which, as had been taught by considered experience, this appetite must be guided if it were not to lead to disaster. And thus if any step was taken by Marlowe's contemporaries it was backward (in this matter at least) rather than forward. Marlowe also may have taken the step in *Tamburlaine*, and it seems probable that he did; but if so, he was seeking in *Doctor Faustus* to recover lost ground as speedily as possible. For evidence in support of this it is necessary to consider only the verse of the two plays, especially of the death scenes. They cannot be held – or rather they should not be held, for it seems they often are – to be mere repetitions one of another *in dispari materia*: the latter is immeasurably more mature. It is indeed fully mature, while the other, like the Renaissance in so many aspects, is no more than adolescent.

But this is a digression. The eternal, which we left Faustus neglecting, in the end cannot but avenge itself; for its only rival must sooner or later vanish, leaving an open field. By the choice of evil Faustus has forfeited not only spiritual but physical integrity, such as in the allegory is destroyed by the passage of time. An Old Man ('base and crooked age', that is *Senectus*) reminds him of this. Unable to deny it he is as never before seized with fury against an agent of good, and asks for him to be tormented. But in vain: for Mephistophilis is powerless against one who, unlike Faustus, has laid fast hold on the eternal:

> My faith, vile hel, shal triumph over thee.
> Ambitious fiends, see how the heavens smiles
> At your repulse, and laughs your state to scorne.
> Hence hel, for hence I flie unto my God.

Faustus on the contrary has nowhere to fly but to what remains of his youth; the more fleeting as youth itself is a shadow. Helen plays *Juventus*, and it is of her that he is driven to beg

> Sweete *Helen*, make me immortall with a kisse;

meaning thereby not that he himself – for to his misfortune, he is immortal already – but that what remains of youth, the present moment, shall not pass away. By the nature of things this is impossible; the twenty-four years draw to a close and before the allegory ends the last gift of the Evil Angel – for which in turn all others have been sacrificed, and all that might have come from any other source – has already crumbled in his hands.

As the attractiveness of evil gradually declines, that of good grows in inverse proportion. For it is eternal and therefore remains to draw Faustus's eyes when, the mists of evil dissolved, they are left hungry for an object. Thus the more prominent role which in the earlier scenes fell to the Evil Angel, is in the later assumed by the Good Angel and his associates: the Old Man and Faustus's own conscience. The latter, who once confined the Good Angel to the briefest of utterances, in the penultimate scene is himself forced to exclaim at length:

What wonders I have done, al *Germany* can witnes, yea all the world, for which Faustus hath lost both *Germany*, and the world, yea heaven it selfe, heaven the seate of God, the throne of the blessed, the kingdome of joy, and must remaine in hel for ever, hel, ah hel for ever, sweete friends, what shall become of Faustus, being in hel for ever? . . . Ah Gentlemen! I gave them my soule for my cunning. — God forbid. — God forbade it indeede, but Faustus hath done it: for vaine pleasure of 24. yeares hath Faustus lost eternall joy and felicitie.

The Good Angel 'gets the best of it' after all; for he or his allies speak last and, as this is not an argument but a history, he who speaks last wins.

Having forfeited the good, Faustus's knowledge of it is of course in no sense full; still, there is a degree of which he cannot be rid, sufficient to feed a regret which is his chief torment in eternity. According to Mephistophilis it is also the torment of the devils, who nevertheless do not lack diligence in or affection to evil. The two therefore – the regret and the affection – are not incompatible; and this notion may perhaps be of use in removing what appears another misunderstanding of Mr Santayana's.

'The excellent Faustus', he complains, '. . . is brow-beaten by the devil and forbidden to repent when he has actually repented.' But if so the play, as containing a contradiction, could hardly be taken seriously; or at least, no more seriously than is its source the *Faustbook*, to which Mr Santayana's words more certainly apply. Even admirers of the latter would perhaps admit this to be a mistake; and there is I think in the play, over and above what

there is in the book, something which Mr Santayana overlooks –
once again, the allegories. In so far as Marlowe's Faustus is
damned, and as he is living on earth only to exemplify in part
the sufferings of the damned, he has identified himself with the
devils as far as he possibly can. And he is kept to hell, or to
association with evil, exactly as they are: not by browbeatings
and prohibitions, but by his own free will. For they have an
affection to evil; they have so formed or deformed themselves
that they can desire only what secures them misery. Had they
for example the opportunity to escape from hell they would not
take it; though it is a place only of suffering, such as comes from
the loss of heaven. Rather than not have heaven in hell where
alone it is impossible, they would not have it at all. A state of
violent discord and disorder similar to this exists in Faustus's
soul. And this is what passages like the following, which Mr
Santayana has in mind, are intended to convey allegorically.
It is not only Lucifer who drags a reluctant Faustus from thoughts
of heaven:

> Ah Christ my Saviour,
> Seeke to save distressed Faustus soule.
> – Christ cannot save thy soule, for he is just,
> Theres none but I have intrest in the same.
> – O who art thou that lookst so terrible?
> – I am *Lucifer*. . . .
> We come to tell thee thou dost injure us.
> Thou talkst of Christ, contrary to thy promise:
> Thou shouldst not thinke of God, thinke of the devil,
> And of his dame too.

Faustus also drags himself. For Lucifer, like the Good Angel, is
here playing a double role: he is devil, but also he is part of
Faustus, who is thus agent as well as victim in his own torment.
And an interpretation of this kind should always I think be made
whenever, at first sight, it appears that Faustus's moral freedom
is being infringed. It is not, for example, only Lucifer and Beelzebub who forbid him to continue the study of 'Astrologie'; it is
his own evil will, which has already determined not to embrace
the truths to which astrology is leading. To do this he has to

exert violence on himself, not inaptly represented by a disturbance in hell; principally he has to sink deeper into hell, or to reveal a greater depth of evil in himself than has yet appeared. And as has been seen, this is what he does.

It is of course impossible to get a clear conception of his state; eternity is full of contradictions, so is evil, and little perspicuity is to be expected of a notion that combines the two. But Marlowe comes perhaps as near to a forcible expression of it as possible. Because of its complication his allegory is so to speak more than an allegory: one picture is not substituted for and therefore weakened by another; two pictures are retained, to give each other strength. Faustus suffers not merely *as though* he were struggling with an outside enemy, he has such an enemy; not merely *as though* he were torn within, he is so torn. And against Lucifer he must struggle with the persistence called for against himself: against himself with the violence for which Lucifer calls. The whole of his strength seems to lie on both sides of the struggle and therefore he is indeed, as he says, torn as by devils. But he should also add that he had an affection to the devils which tears equally.

The temporal allegory is effective in a very similar way. We can conceive of pain or sorrow persisting at its acutest only in the hope that one day it will cease: otherwise it must either blunt itself, or wear out its possessor. As he is alive Faustus has hope, and therefore pain of this intensity:

> Ah Christ my Saviour,
> Seeke to save distressed Faustus soule.

But at the same time he has no hope, for he is dead:

> I am *Lucifer*. . . .
> Thou talkst of Christ, contrary to thy promise:
> . . . thinke of the devil.

This does not of course mean that he unites contradictories in himself, as life and death; but that, since his life illustrates his death, he must be conceived as continuing after death to suffer the utmost that, in life, he has ever suffered. Yet the one condition, that of hope, has disappeared, which as far as our experience goes makes such suffering supportable.

It should perhaps be further noted that the allegories not only provide material and machinery for the body of the play, but shape it. It begins with a monologue, for example, and ends with one: as Faustus alone can commit the act for which he is to be punished, he enters alone to commit it so that responsibility shall be clear. He alone can endure the punishment, and is therefore left alone to meet it. But between these two points the stage is crowded with figures who, if they cannot commit may influence the act; or if not influence, may be influenced by it: the more fully to exhibit its nature and its workings. Only towards the end the stage thins out, and Faustus is left alone with his Scholars. They are little more than conveniences, to allow him to soliloquize in public: the solitude which he dreads nevertheless pursuing him, and so to speak commanding him to itself out of society. Similarly with the allegory of time. In the body of the play scene succeeds scene, not indeed in any order, but in one which is more of psychological than chronological significance. They are like tableaux, illustrating the possibly simultaneous aspects of a man's state of soul, rather than events in his history. But towards the end references to time begin to multiply: Faustus must back to Wittenberg, he must nurse his complacency with a 'quiet sleepe', soon sleep will not suffice and he is driven to riot and debauch. In the final monologue a clock is on the stage, faster than ordinary clocks; its second half-hour is shorter than its first; and Faustus's imagery, now seeking to halt time, now yielding to it in despair, only succeeds in making it fly the faster:

> The starres moove stil, time runs, the clocke wil strike,
> The divel wil come, and Faustus must be damnd.

The general effect is that he is rushing upon his doom. And very much the same effect, it will be suggested below, is given by the opening monologue: in which he rushes on the act from which the doom results. In both cases the intention would appear to be the same: to create the impression of asymptotic approaches to single points of time, both of supreme importance to the play.

From the one, as the consequences of an act committed in it, the whole play issues; into the other, where the consequences are resumed, the whole play is absorbed. There is however more; according to one sense of the temporal allegory both points are the same, for the consequences follow immediately upon the act. And thus the play is not only symmetrical, it has the form of a closed circle; it ends where it begins; it leaves Faustus when and as it found him. It might be compared to a spring which rushes from the ground; spreads into a pool for awhile, to allow of inspection; then withdraws as rapidly into its source.

Little space has I am afraid been left for a topic of major importance: what is the nature of the sinful act which Faustus commits? But this cannot be neglected, as it is both the strongest bond between the last scene and its predecessors, and decisive for the character of the play. I will treat it as expeditiously as possible.

The sin is pride which, according to theologians, is the form and fount of all other sin. Moreover Faustus commits it formally, that is deliberately, without the shadow of an excuse or reason save his will to do so. That is, it is not one of the sins committed in actual life, where some excuse in however small a measure is always to be found. Rather it is an abstract from them all, sin it might be said in its essence. Taking this as its theme the play is to be called not only, as hitherto, an allegory; but a morality.

Possible excuses, did Faustus possess them, would be passion or ignorance. By one or the other, as they may take a man's actions out of his power, his moral responsibility may be diminished or totally abolished. But Faustus, in his first sixty-five lines shows himself without a trace of either. He does not mention lusts of the flesh; he is free from that of gold, for he dismisses it as 'externall trash'; and from that of worldly honours, all of which, if he has desired them, he has enjoyed. And he enjoys them no longer; they are now a vanity to him, and he longs for something more.

This might of course be taken as a sign that about him ambition of some kind or other still lurks. It is however of so undetermined a nature — to the reader it is described only by negatives, as not addressed to gold, not to forensic glory, and so on — that it is hardly to be considered a passion. Rather it is an impulse to activity in general, to life itself, and without it Faustus would cease to be recognizable in any way as a human being. Even in the monologue as it stands, it must I think be confessed that he is only just recognizable: for an impulse of this kind, which though urgent is not clearly or even dimly conscious of a goal, would seem mechanical rather than human. It is machines, not men, that function without some idea of an end. And hence no doubt the mechanical qualities of the verse:

> Is to dispute well, Logickes chiefest end,
> Affoords this Art no greater myracle?
> Then reade no more, thou hast attained that end:
> A greater subject fitteth *Faustus* wit . . .

and so on. It is direct, it is economical, above all it is not inappropriate to this part of the play. But it is the price which a morality has to pay for immediate and universal relevance, that in certain aspects it appears machine-like and gaunt; for detail must as far as possible be neglected.

As for ignorance, Faustus is past master in all the arts, from logic to jurisprudence, which are useful in earthly and human affairs. He has achieved astounding success; and decides, reviewing them one by one, that none of them has anything to give him any more. Therefore it is not among them that he will find a goal to which to direct his impulse to activity. The only goal left, it seems, is that of affairs not of this earth: the supernatural rather than the natural:

> When all is done, Divinitie is best.

Opening '*Jeromes* Bible' he finds, as his first lesson in the supernatural, '*Stipendium peccati mors est.*' There is, he learns, such a possibility as that man should sin, and sin humiliates man in death. He recoils from the lesson:

> The reward of sinne is death: thats hard.

As yet however he does not reject it; and his exclamation, though irrelevant as it would be to any statement of fact, can be taken as an example of a sort of reluctance which is familiar. For a moment the acceptance of something is postponed which, it is well known, must be accepted sooner or later. But what Faustus goes on to read does more than state a possibility, it inflicts humiliation upon him: '*Si peccasse negamus, fallimur.*' As all men have sinned, Faustus has sinned, and he is already involved in death. This he rejects outright, preferring his own idea of what a fact is or should be to what, if he will open his eyes, he can see that it is (or such, at any rate, was the assumption of Marlowe and his audience). Thus he commits the sin of pride: the play has begun and, in one sense of the temporal allegory, at the same time ended.

His conscience protesting immediately, he seeks to conciliate it with the following sophism.

> If we say we have no sinne,
> We deceive our selves, and theres no truth in us.
> Why then belike
> We must sinne, and so consequently die.

If it is true that he has sinned, he says to himself he was forced into it – it was his nature to sin, he could not help himself. And conscience being thus cleared, he has no need, in spite of the Bible's assertions, to be humble. And a further conclusion follows: that if any man has sinned, he too was forced into it; if all men have done so, their nature is such as to have been designed for eternal destruction:

> I, we must die an everlasting death:
> What doctrine call you this, *Che sera, sera* . . .?

He may call it what he wishes, and it is certainly a revolting doctrine. But, rather than divinity, it is one which he has evolved for himself, by denying the basis on which all divinity rests: that sin is of its essence voluntary. But he insists on identifying the two so that, to a none too clear-sighted conscience, the rejection of divinity shall seem not only plausible but inevitable.

He no longer feels the need to review the sciences so that he may discover in what direction to employ himself. External authority denied, conscience put to sleep, there is no direction which is forbidden, none which does not, at any rate at first glance, attract. Ceasing to profess the useful arts, he will become a magician and, in

> ... a world of profit and delight,
> Of power, of honor, of omnipotence

he will be, not only King or Emperor, but a 'mighty god'. By now the verse has lost its mechanism, has begun to move with the easy enthusiasms of *Tamburlaine*: through the door of pride the passions have begun to invade Faustus, and he welcomes every one.

The rapidity of movement in this prologue, already referred to, may now perhaps be appreciated. Only nine lines are given to the crisis: four to the reading of the Bible preliminary to the act of pride, five to the apology which follows it; the act itself falling between the two groups, and being mentioned in no line. If this seems a dramatic defect, it should be reflected that, as has been said, Faustus's sin has not the shadow of an excuse. It is not the result of suasion but a pure act of the will (such as can be conceived only by abstraction) and the will turns to evil. As such the act cannot be analysed or understood: for only if it were excusable could we trace it to an origin, place ourselves at the point of view of doer, and see how – however much we deplored it – 'he came to do what he did'. In so far as anything is evil, it cannot be explained by those who recognize it as such. Marlowe therefore can do no more than observe the act of pride, mark it as it occurs, then proceed to what is his chief interest: the narration of its consequences.

These include many similar acts, which, were they not its consequences, would be equally inexplicable: Faustus's consenting to be fobbed off with 'curtezans', his acceptance of the vision of sin instead of that of God, his appeal to Helen – as though there were a chance of its success – for immortality. The tragedy of life, as presented by Marlowe in this play, is that it may be riddled with acts like these. But more striking are the occasions when Faustus – chiefly at the instance of Mephistophilis, who seems detailed for the purpose – repeats the original act in an ever grosser form.

Yet one of Mephistophilis's first speeches is no other than a rebuke to pride:

> Did not my conjuring speeches raise thee? speake.
> – That was the cause, but yet per accident,
> For when we heare one racke the name of God,
> Abjure the scriptures, and his Saviour Christ,
> Wee flye, in hope to get his glorious soule.

Faustus might learn, if he would listen, that far from receiving the omnipotence with which he flattered himself, and from freeing himself from the necessity of humiliation: there are still conditions to which he must be humbled, he is to receive nothing but at a price. And further he might reflect that, as his soul is capable of glory, it is capable of sin and damnation. But both suggestions are brushed aside; the price, he makes it clear, is to him as little as no price, for men's souls are 'vaine trifles'. These or similar words he repeats on all occasions when Mephistophilis – it almost seems of set purpose to disabuse him – bids him consider the bargain he wishes to conclude:

> But may I raise up spirits when I please? . . .
> Then theres inough for a thousand soules.

Though informed in all frankness that he receives diabolic visits only that he may be dragged down to hell, and that Lucifer shows him favour in order to make him a *socium doloris*, he protests defiantly, 'Come, I thinke hell's a fable.'

> This word damnation terrifies not him,

he says of himself:

> For he confounds hell in *Elizium*.
> His ghost be with the olde Philosophers. . . .

Such is his pride, his refusal to bow to external authority of any kind, that even on the world of spirits, of which he has no experience, he maintains his own opinion against that of one who has come direct from thence; and whom he is talking to at all, only because he believes him to have done so.

This wilful blindness, this pertinacity in self-deception, is brought out most clearly in the passage in which he enquires about the fate of Lucifer. The 'prince of devils', he is told, fell (as he himself is falling) 'by aspiring pride and insolence'. 'And what are', he goes on, 'you that live with *Lucifer*?' Mephistophilis replies:

> Unhappy spirits that fell with *Lucifer*,
> Conspir'd against our God with *Lucifer*,
> And are for ever damnd with *Lucifer*.

Almost inarticulate with rage or grief, he can do little more than repeat the name which is for him the sum of both. In reply to the next question, 'Where are you damn'd?' he can force out only two words: 'In hell'. But Faustus, insensitive to all things since he is so to his own good, continues the cross-examination

> How comes it then that thou art out of hel?

Mephistophilis bursts into lines which, in their context and by contrast with the broken utterances which have gone before, are among the most eloquent in the play:

> Why this is hel, nor am I out of it:
> Thinkst thou that I who saw the face of God,
> And tasted the eternal joyes of heaven,
> Am not tormented with ten thousand hels,
> In being depriv'd of everlasting blisse?
> O *Faustus*, leave these frivolous demaunds,
> Which strike a terror to my fainting soule.

Even Faustus it seems must be impressed. But no: with a cox-combry which may arouse either hatred or contempt he mocks:

> What, is great *Mephastophilis* so passionate? . . .
> Learne thou of *Faustus* manly fortitude,
> And scorne those joyes thou never shalt possesse.

It is as though a man, meeting another who had barely escaped from an accident with his life, informed him of a conviction that fire does not burn, stones do not crush, nor metals maim.

In this passage, as it may not seem wholly in place in a tragedy, Marlowe may be rehearsing the 'savage farce' of *The Jew of Malta*. The two plays are however closely related, and a touch of the manner of the one is perhaps not only admissible, but necessary to point the other. Both have as their theme the ghastly folly which is sin: but whereas in *The Jew*, being for the moment out of patience with mankind, Marlowe is concerned to express only the folly, what principally moves his interest in *Doctor Faustus* is still the ghastliness.

This is developed through one sin after another, following their generation as it has already been traced from the momentary, inexplicable, but undeniable beginning. It is completed and concentrated in the final scene; in which Faustus having proclaimed he is not terrified by 'the word damnation', is overwhelmed by the thing; having scorned Mephistophilis's prophecy that experience would change his mind, is compelled to cower in abjection for the prophecy to be fulfilled. The Elizabethan audience – if I may refer to it again – expected it to be fulfilled, and would have been outraged had it not been so. And so I think would any reader, however little in sympathy with the ideas in the play, if only able to see the ideas which are there.

Many readers have not been able, blinded chiefly by the prejudices of the nineteenth century. It is surprising how many even detailed opinions about Marlowe's Faustus, which are obviously incorrect once they are inquired into, are equally obviously correct of the Faust of Goethe. The one figure has been obscured, identified with the other. But he is of quite a different mettle: he does not spring from a world in which all that matters is action or enterprise, the more violent, the more inconsiderate, the better:

> Säume nicht, dich zu erdreisten,
> Wenn die Menge zaudernd schweift –

but rather from that world from which springs also Dante's Bertran de Born. The latter had not been over-considerate in action, but was humiliated by rather than proud of the fact. If he

had a scrap of Bertran's virtue – but alas! he has none – Faustus
might repeat with him:

> così s'osserva in me lo contrapasso.

SOURCE: *Scrutiny*, VIII (1939).

W. W. Greg

THE DAMNATION OF FAUSTUS
(1946)

WHEN working lately on the text of *Doctor Faustus*, I was struck by certain aspects of the story as told in Marlowe's play that I do not remember to have seen discussed in the editions with which I am familiar. I do not pretend to have read more than a little of what has been written about Marlowe as a dramatist, and it may be that there is nothing new in what I have to say; but it seemed worth while to draw attention to a few points in the picture of the hero's downfall, on the chance that they might have escaped the attention of others, as they had hitherto escaped my own.

As soon as Faustus has decided that necromancy is the only study that can give his ambition scope, he seeks the aid of his friends Valdes and Cornelius, who already are proficients in the art—

> Their conference will be a greater help to me
> Than all my labours, plod I ne'er so fast.*

Who they are we have no notion: they do not appear in the source on which Marlowe drew— 'The historie of the damnable life, and deserued death of Doctor Iohn Faustus . . . according to the true Copie printed at Franckfort, and translated into English by P. F. Gent.' — and Cornelius is certainly not the famous Cornelius Agrippa, who is mentioned in their conversation. But they must

---

* There is as yet no satisfactory critical text of *Faustus*, and I have had to do the best I could, in the light of my own study, to harmonize the rival versions as printed in the quartos of 1604 and 1616 respectively, taking from each what best illustrated the points I wished to make. In the case of such a necessarily eclectic text there seemed no object in attempting to follow the spelling of the originals, except where it possessed some significance. I have also felt free so to punctuate as best to bring out what I believe to be the sense of the original.

have been familiar figures at Wittenberg, since on learning that
Faustus is at dinner with them, his students at once conclude
that he is 'fallen into that damned art for which they two are
infamous through the world'. The pair are ready enough to
obey Faustus' invitation, for they have long sought to lead him
into forbidden ways. 'Know', says Faustus—

> Know that your words have won me at the last
> To practise magic and concealèd arts.

At the same time, though they are his 'dearest friends', he is
anxious not to appear too pliant, adding, a little clumsily (if the
1604 text is to be trusted)

> Yet not your words only, but mine own fantasy,

and he makes it plain that he is no humble seeker after instruction,
but one whose personal fame and honour are to be their main
concern—

> Then, gentle friends, aid me in this attempt,
> And I, that have with concise syllogisms
> Gravelled the pastors of the German church,
> And made the flowering pride of Wittenberg
> Swarm to my problems, as the infernal spirits
> On sweet Musaeus when he came to hell,
> Will be as cunning as Agrippa was,
> Whose shadows made all Europe honour him.

His friends are content enough to accept him on these terms.
Valdes, while hinting that common contributions deserve
common rewards—

> Faustus, these books, thy wit, and our experience
> Shall make all nations to canonize us—

paints a glowing picture of the possibilities before them, adding
however—in view of what follows a little ominously—

> If learned Faustus will be resolute.

Reassured on this score, Cornelius is ready to allow Faustus pride of place —

> Then doubt not, Faustus, but to be renowned,
> And more frequented for this mystery
> Than heretofore the Delphian oracle —

but only on condition that the profits of the enterprise are shared —

> Then tell me, Faustus, What shall we three want?

However, it soon appears that for all their sinister reputation the two are but dabblers in witchcraft. They have, indeed, called spirits from the deep, and they have come —

> The spirits tell me they can dry the sea
> And fetch the treasure of all foreign wracks,
> Yea, all the wealth that our forefathers hid
> Within the massy entrails of the earth —

but they have made no use of this knowledge, they have never become the masters — or the slaves — of the spirits. Even to raise them they must, of course, have run a mortal risk —

> Nor will we come unless he use such means
> Whereby he is in danger to be damned —

but they have been careful not to forfeit their salvation for supernatural gifts; they have never succumbed to the temptation of the spirits or made proof of their boasted powers. Nor do they mean to put their own art to the ultimate test. When Faustus eagerly demands,

> Come, show me some demonstrations magical,

Valdes proves himself a ready teacher —

> Then haste thee to some solitary grove,
> And bear wise Bacon's and Albanus' works,
> The Hebrew Psalter, and New Testament;
> And whatsoever else is requisite
> We will inform thee ere our conference cease —

and guarantees to make him proficient in the art—

> First I'll instruct thee in the rudiments,
> And then wilt thou be perfecter than I.

Knowing the depth of Faustus' learning, and satisfied of his
courage and resolution, they are anxious to form a partnership
with one whose potentialities as an adept so far exceed their own.
But Cornelius leaves us in no doubt of their intention to use
Faustus as a cat's-paw rather than run into danger themselves—

> Valdes, first let him know the words of art,
> And then, all other ceremonies learned,
> Faustus may try his cunning by himself.

The precious pair are no deeply versed magicians welcoming a
promising beginner, but merely the devil's decoys luring Faustus
along the road to destruction.* They serve their purpose in
giving a dramatic turn to the scene of his temptation, and except
for a passing mention by the students, we hear no more of them.†

Faustus goes to conjure alone, and alone he concludes his
pact with the devil. What use will he make of his hazardously
won powers? His dreams, if self-centred, are in the heroic vein:

> Oh, what a world of profit and delight,
> Of power, of honour, and omnipotence,
> Is promised to the studious artizan!
> All things that move between the quiet poles

* There is a hint that Faustus' downfall was planned by Mephostophilis from the start. Quite near the end, gloating over Faustus'
despair, he says (in the 1616 text):

> when thou took'st the book
> To view the scriptures, then I turned the leaves
> And led thine eye.

The only incident *in the play* to which this could refer is the collocation
of biblical texts that prompts Faustus to renounce divinity in the
opening scene.

† Of course, the theatrical reason for this is that Marlowe has no
further use for them, but like a good craftsman he was careful to
supply a dramatic reason in his delineation of the characters.

> Shall be at my command: emperors and kings
> Are but obeyed in their several provinces,
> But his dominion that exceeds in this
> Stretcheth as far as doth the mind of man:
> A sound magician is a demi-god!

More than mortal power and knowledge shall be his, to use in the service of his country:

> Shall I make spirits fetch me what I please?
> Resolve me of all ambiguities?
> Perform what desperate enterprise I will? ...
> I'll have them read me strange philosophy
> And tell the secrets of all foreign kings;
> I'll have them wall all Germany with brass, ...
> And chase the Prince of Parma from our land. ...

Whatever baser elements there may be in his ambition, we should, by all human standards, expect the fearless seeker after knowledge and truth, the scholar weary of the futilities of orthodox learning, to make at least no ignoble use of the power suddenly placed at his command.

Critics have complained that instead of pursuing ends worthy of his professed ideals, Faustus, once power is his, abandons these without a qualm, and shows himself content to amuse the Emperor with conjuring tricks and play childish pranks on the Pope; and they have blamed this either on a collaborator, or on the fact of Marlowe's work having been later overlaid and debased by another hand. The charge, in its crudest form, involves some disregard of the 1616 version, which is not quite as fatuous as its predecessor, but in broad outline there is no denying its justice. As to responsibility: it is of course obvious that not all the play as we have it is Marlowe's. For my own part, however, I do not believe that as originally written it differed to any material extent from what we are able to reconstruct from a comparison of the two versions in which it has come down to us. And while it is true that the middle portion, to which objection is mostly taken, shows little trace of Marlowe's hand, I see no reason to doubt that it was he who planned the whole, or that his collaborator or collaborators, whoever he or they may have been, carried out his plan substantially according to instructions. If that is so, for any fundamental fault in the design Marlowe must be held responsible.

The critics' disappointment is quite natural. Although it is difficult to see how any dramatist could have presented in language and dramatic form the revelation of a knowledge beyond the reach of human wisdom, there is no question that much more might have been done to show the wonder and uphold the dignity of the quest, and so satisfy the natural expectation of the audience. Marlowe did not do it; he deliberately turned from the attempt. Instead he showed us the betrayal of ideals, the lapse into luxury and buffoonery.

And what, in the devil's name, would the critics have? I say 'in the devil's name', because all that happens to Faustus once the pact is signed is the devil's work: 'human standards' are no longer relevant. Who but a fool, such a clever fool as Faustus, would dream that any power but evil could be won by a bargain with evil, or that truth could be wrung from the father of lies? 'All power tends to corrupt, and absolute power corrupts absolutely' is indeed an aphorism to which few Elizabethans would have subscribed; but Marlowe knew the nature of the power he put into the hands of his hero and the inevitable curse it carried with it.

Of course, Faustus' corruption is not a mechanical outcome of his pact with evil. In spite of his earnest desire to know truth, and half-hidden in the Marlowan glamour cast about him, the seeds of decay are in his character from the first – how else should he come to make his fatal bargain? Beside his passion for knowledge is a lust for riches and pleasure and power. If less single-minded, he shares Barabbas' thirst for wealth –

> I'll have them fly to India for gold,
> Ransack the ocean for orient pearl,
> And search all corners of the new-found world
> For pleasant fruits and princely delicates. . . .

Patriotism is a veil for ambition: he will

> chase the Prince of Parma from our land
> And reign sole king of all our provinces ...

> I'll join the hills that bind the Afric shore
> And make that country continent to Spain,
> And both contributary to my crown:
> The Emperor shall not live but by my leave,
> Nor any potentate in Germany.

His aspiration to be 'great emperor of the world' recalls Tamburlaine's vulgar desire for

> The sweet fruition of an earthly crown.

But Faustus' ambition is not thus limited; the promptings of his soul reveal themselves in the words of the Bad Angel:

> Be thou on earth, as Jove is in the sky,
> Lord and commander of these elements.

If there is a sensual vein in him, it is hardly seen at this stage; still his demand to 'live in all voluptuousness' anticipates later desires—

> Whilst I am here on earth let me be cloyed
> With all things that delight the heart of man;
> My four and twenty years of liberty
> I'll spend in pleasure and in dalliance—

and it may be with shrewd insight that Valdes promises 'serviceable' spirits,

> Sometimes like women or unwedded maids
> Shadowing more beauty in their airy brows
> Than in the white breasts of the Queen of Love.

But when all is said, this means no more than that Faustus is a man dazzled by the unlimited possibilities of magic, and alive enough to his own weakness to exclaim:

> The god thou serv'st is thine own appetite. ...

After Faustus has signed the bond with his blood, we can trace the stages of a gradual deterioration. His previous interview

with Mephostophilis struck the note of earnest if slightly sceptical
inquiry with which he entered on his quest:

> This word Damnation terrifies not me,
> For I confound hell in Elizium:
> My ghost be with the old philosophers!

He questions eagerly about hell, and the spirit replies:

> Why, this is hell, nor am I out of it:
> Think'st thou that I who saw the face of God
> And tasted the eternal joys of heaven,
> Am not tormented with ten thousand hells
> In being deprived of everlasting bliss? ...
> *Faustus.* What, is great Mephostophilis so passionate
> For being deprivèd of the joys of heaven?
> Learn thou of Faustus manly fortitude,
> And scorn those joys thou never shalt possess.

After the bond is signed the discussion is renewed, but while the
devil loses nothing in dignity of serious discourse, we can already
detect a change in Faustus; his sceptical levity takes on a more
truculent and jeering tone. Asked 'Where is the place that men
call hell?' Mephostophilis replies:

> Within the bowels of these elements,
> Where we are tortured and remain for ever.
> Hell hath no limits, nor is circumscribed
> In one self place, but where we are is hell,
> And where hell is, there must we ever be:
> And to conclude, when all the world dissolves
> And every creature shall be purified,
> All places shall be hell that is not heaven.
> *Faustus.* Come, I think hell's a fable.
> *Mephostophilis.* Ay, think so still, till experience change thy
> mind....
> *Faustus.* ... Think'st thou that Faustus is so fond to imagine
> That after this life there is any pain?
> Tush! these are trifles and mere old wives' tales.
> *Mephostophilis.* But I am an instance to prove the contrary;
> For I tell thee I am damned and now in hell.
> *Faustus.* Nay, and this be hell, I'll willingly be damned:
> What? sleeping, eating, walking, and disputing!

In the next scene there follows the curiously barren discussion on astronomy. It has probably been interpolated and is not altogether easy to follow, but the infernal exposition of the movements of the spheres calls forth an impatient,

> These slender questions Wagner can decide

and at the end Mephostophilis' sententious

> Per inaequalem motum respectu totius

and Faustus' half-satisfied

> Well, I am answered!

leave in the mouth the taste of dead-sea fruit. The quarrel that follows on the spirit's refusal to say who made the world leads to the intervention of Lucifer and the 'pastime' of the Seven Deadly Sins. There seems to me more savour in this than has sometimes been allowed; still it is a much shrunken Faustus who exclaims:

> Oh, this feeds my soul!

He had been no less delighted with the dance of the devils that offered him crowns and rich apparel on his signing the bond: we do not know its nature, but from his exclamation,

> Then there's enough for a thousand souls!

when told that he may conjure up such spirits at will, we may perhaps conclude that it involved a direct appeal to the senses. That would, at least, accord with his mood soon afterwards; for while it would be rash to lay much stress on his demanding 'the fairest maid in Germany, for I am wanton and lascivious' (this being perhaps an interpolation) we should allow due weight to Mephostophilis' promise:

> I'll cull thee out the fairest courtesans
> And bring them every morning to thy bed;
> She whom thine eye shall like, thy heart shall have,
> Were she as chaste as was Penelope,
> As wise as Saba, or as beautiful
> As was bright Lucifer before his fall.

So far Faustus has not left Wittenberg, and emphasis has been rather on the hollowness of his bargain in respect of any intellectual enlightenment than on the actual degradation of his character. As yet only his childish pleasure in the devil-dance and the pageant of the Sins hints at the depth of vulgar triviality into which he is doomed to descend. In company with Mephostophilis he now launches forth into the world; but his dragon-flights

> To find the secrets of astronomy
> Graven in the book of Jove's high firmament,

and

>   to prove cosmography,
> That measures coasts and kingdoms of the earth,

only land him at last in the Pope's privy-chamber to

> take some part of holy Peter's feast,

and live with dalliance in

>   the view
> Of rarest things and royal courts of kings . . .

It is true that in the fuller text of 1616 the rescue of 'holy Bruno', imperial candidate for the papal throne, lends a more serious touch to the sheer horse-play of the Roman scenes in the 1604 version, and even the 'horning' episode at the Emperor's court is at least developed into some dramatic coherence; but this only brings out more pointedly the progressive fatuity of Faustus' career, which in the clownage and conjuring tricks at Anhalt sinks to the depth of buffoonery.

If, as may be argued, the gradual deterioration of Faustus' character and the prostitution of his powers stand out less clearly than they should, this may be ascribed partly to Marlowe's negligent handling of a theme that failed to kindle his wayward inspiration, and partly to the ineptitude of his collaborator. But the logical outline is there, and I must differ from Marlowe's critics, and believe that when he sketched that outline Marlowe knew what he was about.

Another point to be borne in mind is that there is something strange and peculiar, not only in Faustus' situation, but in his nature. Once he has signed the bond, he is in the position of having of his own free will renounced salvation. So much is obvious. Less obvious is the inner change he has brought upon himself. Critics have strangely neglected the first article of the infernal compact: 'that Faustus may be a spirit in form and substance'. Presumably they have taken it to mean merely that he should be free of the bonds of flesh, so that he may be invisible at will, invulnerable, and able to change his shape, ride on dragons, and so forth. But in this play 'spirit' is used in a special sense. There is, of course, nothing very significant in the fact that, when the 'devils' dance before him, Faustus asks:

> But may I raise such spirits when I please?

that he promises to

> make my spirits pull His churches down

and bids Mephostophilis

> Ay, go, accursèd spirit to ugly hell!

or that the latter speaks of the devils as

> Unhappy spirits that fell with Lucifer —

though it is noticeable how persistently devils are called spirits in the play,* and it is worth recalling that in the *Damnable Life* Mephostophilis is regularly 'the Spirit'. What is significant is that when Faustus asks 'What is that Lucifer, thy lord?' Mephostophilis replies:

> Arch-regent and commander of all spirits

which Faustus at once interprets as 'prince of devils'; and that the Bad Angel, in reply to Faustus' cry of repentance, asserts:

> Thou art a spirit; God cannot pity thee

---

* Even in the stage directions: the first entry of the Good and Bad Angels is headed in 1616: 'Enter the Angell and Spirit.'

– a remark to which I shall return. And if there could be any doubt of the meaning of these expressions, we have the explicit statement in the *Damnable Life* that Faustus' 'request was none other than to become a devil'. Faustus then, through his bargain with hell, has himself taken on the infernal nature, although it is made clear throughout that he still retains his human soul.

This throws a new light upon the question, debated throughout the play, whether Faustus can be saved by repentance. Faustus, of course, is for ever repenting – and recanting through fear of bodily torture and death – and the Good and Bad Angels, who personate the two sides of his human nature, are for ever disputing the point:

Faustus. Contrition, prayer, repentance: what of these?
Good Angel. Oh, they are means to bring thee unto heaven.
Bad Angel. Rather illusions, fruits of lunacy

and again:

Good Angel. Never too late, if Faustus will repent.
Bad Angel. If thou repent, devils will tear thee in pieces.
Good Angel. Repent, and they shall never raze thy skin.

There are two passages that are particularly significant in this respect: and we must remember, as I have said, the double question at issue – Faustus' nature, and whether repentance can cancel a bargain. First then, the passage from which I have already quoted:

Good Angel. Faustus, repent; yet God will pity thee.
Bad Angel. Thou art a spirit; God cannot pity thee.
Faustus. Who buzzeth in mine ears, I am a spirit?
  Be I a devil, yet God may pity me;
  Yea, God will pity me if I repent.
Bad Angel. Ay, but Faustus never shall repent.

The Bad Angel evades the issue, which is left undecided.* Later

* Faustus' words are perhaps intentionally ambiguous. 'Be I a devil' may mean 'What though I am a devil', or it may mean 'Even were I a devil'. Ward insisted on the second sense, but it is not borne out by the evidence. Boas shows a correct understanding of the passage when he glosses 'spirit' as 'evil spirit, devil'.

in the same scene, when Faustus calls on Christ to save his soul, Lucifer replies with admirable logic:

> Christ cannot save thy soul, for he is just:
> There's none but I have interest in the same.*

Thus the possibility of Faustus' salvation is left nicely poised in doubt – like that of the archdeacon of scholastic speculation.

It is only when, back among his students at Wittenberg, he faces the final reckoning that Faustus regains some measure of heroic dignity. Marlowe again takes charge. But even so the years have wrought a change. His faithful Wagner is puzzled:

> I wonder what he means; if death were nigh,
> He would not banquet and carouse and swill
> Among the students, as even now he doth. . . .

This is a very different Faustus from the fearless teacher his students used to know, whose least absence from the class-room caused concern –

I wonder what's become of Faustus, that was wont to make our schools ring with *sic probo*.

One good, or at least amiable, quality – apart from a genuine tenderness towards his students – we may be tempted to claim for him throughout: a love of beauty in nature and in art:

> Have not I made blind Homer sing to me
> Of Alexander's love and Oenon's death?
> And hath not he that built the walls of Thebes
> With ravishing sound of his melodious harp
> Made music – ?

and the climax of his career is his union with the immortal beauty of Helen, to measures admittedly the most lovely that flowed from Marlowe's lyre. Is this sensitive appreciation something that has survived uncorrupted from his days of innocence? I can

---

* Compare Faustus' own lines near the end:

> Hell claims his right, and with a roaring voice
> Says, 'Faustus, come; thine hour is almost come':
> And Faustus now will come to do thee right.

find no hint of it in the austere student of the early scenes. Is it then some strange flowering of moral decay? It would seem so. What, after all, is that 'ravishing sound' but the symphony of hell? –

> Made music – with my Mephostophilis!

And Helen, what of her?

Here we come, if I mistake not, to the central theme of the damnation of Faustus. The lines in which he addresses Helen are some of the most famous in the language:

> Was this the face that launched a thousand ships
> And burnt the topless towers of Ilium?
> Sweet Helen, make me immortal with a kiss! . . .
> Here will I dwell, for heaven is in these lips,
> And all is dross that is not Helena.
> I will be Paris, and for love of thee
> Instead of Troy shall Wittenberg be sacked;
> And I will combat with weak Menelaus,
> And wear thy colours on my plumed crest:
> Yea, I will wound Achilles in the heel,
> And then return to Helen for a kiss.
> Oh, thou art fairer than the evening's air
> Clad in the beauty of a thousand stars,
> Brighter art thou than flaming Jupiter
> When he appeared to hapless Semele,
> More lovely than the monarch of the sky
> In wanton Arethusa's azured arms;
> And none but thou shalt be my paramour!

In these lines Marlowe's uncertain genius soared to its height,* but their splendour has obscured, and was perhaps meant dis-

---

* Besides a number of incidental passages of great beauty, some of which I have quoted, the play contains three that stand out above the rest and I think surpass all else that Marlowe wrote. The address to Helen is of course pure lyric; the final soliloquy is intense spiritual drama; with these, and in its different mode little below them, I would place the farewell scene with the students, which seems to prove that, had he chosen, Marlowe could have been no less an artist in prose than he was in verse.

creetly to veil, the real nature of the situation. 'Her lips suck forth my soul,' says Faustus in lines that I omitted from his speech above.* What is Helen? We are not told in so many words, but the answer is there, if we choose to look for it. When the Emperor asks him to present Alexander and his paramour before the court, Faustus (in the 1604 version) laboriously explains the nature of the figures that are to appear:

My gracious lord, I am ready to accomplish your request so far forth as by art and power of my spirit I am able to perform. . . . But, if it like your grace, it is not in my ability to present before your eyes the true substantial bodies of those two deceased princes, which long since are consumed to dust. . . . But such spirits as can lively resemble Alexander and his paramour shall appear before your grace in that manner that they best lived in, in their most flourishing estate. . . .

He adds (according to the 1616 version):

> My lord, I must forewarn your majesty
> That, when my spirits present the royal shapes
> Of Alexander and his paramour,
> Your grace demand no questions of the king,
> But in dumb silence let them come and go.

This is explicit enough; and as a reminder that the same holds for Helen, Faustus repeats the caution when he presents her to his students:

> Be silent then, for danger is in words.

Consider, too, a point critics seem to have overlooked, the circumstances in which Helen is introduced the second time. Urged by the Old Man, Faustus has attempted a last revolt; as usual he has been cowed into submission, and has renewed the blood-

---

* 'Her lips suck forth my soul: see where it flies!' Faustus of course intends the words in a merely amorous sense, confusing the physical and the spiritual in an exaggerated image that is not perhaps in the best taste. But I wonder whether Marlowe may not have had, at the back of his mind, some recollection of the *Ars Moriendi*, with its pictures of a devil dragging the naked soul out of the mouth of a dying man.

bond. He has sunk so low as to beg revenge upon his would-be saviour—

> Torment, sweet friend, that base and aged man,
> That durst dissuade me from thy Lucifer,
> With greatest torments that our hell affords.

And it is in the first place as a safeguard against relapse that he seeks possession of Helen—

> One thing, good servant, let me crave of thee
> To glut the longing of my heart's desire;
> That I may have unto my paramour
> That heavenly Helen which I saw of late,
> Whose sweet embraces may extinguish clear
> Those thoughts that may dissuade me from my vow,
> And keep mine oath I made to Lucifer.

Love and revenge are alike insurances against salvation. 'Helen' then is a 'spirit', and in this play a spirit means a devil.* In making her his paramour Faustus commits the sin of demoniality, that is, bodily intercourse with demons.†

---

* This fact has perhaps been obscured for critics by recollections of Goethe's *Faust*. Thus Ward, in a note on Faustus' address to Helen, writes: 'The outburst of Faust on beholding the real Helena (whom he had previously seen as a magical apparition) . . . should be compared.' There is, of course, no such distinction between the two appearances of Helen in Marlowe's play. It is curious, by the way, how persistently critics and editors commit the absurdity of calling the spirit in Marlowe's play 'Mephistophiles', as if this were the correct or original form and not a variant invented by Goethe a couple of centuries later.

† The *Oxford English Dictionary* defines *demoniality* as 'The nature of demons; the realm of demons, demons collectively. (Cf. *spirituality*.)' But this is not supported by the only two quotations it gives. The first, curiously enough, is the title: 'Demoniality; or Incubi and Succubi . . . by the Rev. Father Sinistrari, of Ameno . . . now first translated into English' (1879). This, even by itself, is suggestive, and anyone who has looked beyond the title of this curious and long-unprinted work by the seventeenth-century theologian Lodovico Maria Sinistrari, knows that the analogy of demoniality is not with 'spirituality' but with 'bestiality'. The worthy casuist is quite explicit. '3. Coitus igitur cum Daemone, sive Incubo, sive Succubo (qui proprie est Daemonia-

The implication of Faustus' action is made plain in the comments of the Old Man and the Angels. Immediately before the Helen episode the Old Man was still calling on Faustus to repent—

> Ah, Doctor Faustus, that I might prevail
> To guide thy steps into the way of life!

(So 1604: 1616 proceeds:)

> Though thou hast now offended like a man,
> Do not persever in it like a devil:
> Yet, yet, thou hast an amiable soul,
> If sin by custom grow not into nature. . . .

But with Faustus' union with Helen the nice balance between possible salvation and imminent damnation is upset. The Old Man, who has witnessed the meeting (according to the 1604 version), recognizes the inevitable:

> Accursèd Faustus, miserable man,
> That from thy soul exclud'st the grace of heaven
> And fliest the throne of his tribunal-seat!

The Good Angel does no less:

> O Faustus, if thou hadst given ear to me
> Innumerable joys had followed thee . . .
> Oh, thou hast lost celestial happiness. . . .

And Faustus himself, still haunted in his final agony by the idea of a salvation beyond his reach—

---

litas), specie differt a Bestialitate, nec cum ea facit unam speciem . . . 8. Ulterius in confesso est apud omnes Theologos Morales, quod longe gravior est copula cum Daemones, quam quolibet bruto. . . .' The writer also draws a distinction, repeated in his better-known work *De Delictis et Poenis* (Venice, 1700), between two varieties of demoniality, that practised by witches and warlocks with devils, and that which others commit with incubi and succubae. According to Sinistrari the first to use the term *daemonialitas*, and to distinguish it from *bestialitas*, was Johannes Caramuelis in his *Theologia Fundamentalis* (Frankfurt, 1651). The other quotation given in the dictionary is from the *Saturday Review* (1891), 'The old wives' fables . . . are those of demoniality, black masses, etc.', in which the meaning is presumably the same.

> See, see, where Christ's blood streams in the firmament!
> One drop would save my soul —

shows, in talk with his students, a terrible clarity of vision:

> A surfeit of deadly sin, that hath damned both body and soul.
> . . . Faustus' offence can ne'er be pardoned: the Serpent that
> tempted Eve may be saved, but not Faustus

and Mephostophilis echoes him:

> Ay, Faustus, now hast thou no hope of heaven!

It would be idle to speculate how far the 'atheist' Marlowe, whom gossip accused of what we call 'unnatural' vice, may have dwelt in imagination on the direst sin of which human flesh is capable. But in presenting the fall and slow moral disintegration of an ardent if erring spirit, he did not shrink from depicting, beside Faustus' spiritual sin of bartering his soul to the powers of evil, what is in effect its physical complement and counterpart, however he may have disguised it in immortal verse.

Source: *Modern Language Review*, XLI (1946).

J. C. Maxwell

THE SIN OF FAUSTUS (1947)

THERE is so little good criticism of Marlowe's *Doctor Faustus* that any addition to it is an occasion for satisfaction; and Dr Greg's recent article in the *Modern Language Review* (XLI (1946) 97–107) is particularly welcome, confirming on many points and supplementing on others the basic contribution of Mr Kirschbaum in the *Review of English Studies* (XIX (1943) 225–41). The student of those two papers has no excuse for not having a fundamentally sound conception of Marlowe's mind and art as displayed in this great play. In this note, all that I want to do is to correct what seems to me to be an error in emphasis common to the two critics. In this I have been helped by an earlier essay which, though less lucid and generally satisfactory than Kirschbaum's, is by no means entirely superseded by it, and also deserves credit for having anticipated a number of Kirschbaum's findings: that by James Smith in *Scrutiny* (VIII (1939) 36–55).

Both Kirschbaum and Greg have laid stress on the element of sensuality in Faustus as Marlowe represents him, not least in the great Helen speech (xviii 99–118), which has been made the occasion for inappropriate romanticism. The emphasis which they have given to this culminating scene* – the last before Faustus' damnation is consummated – slightly obscures some aspects of Marlowe's treatment that I take to be even more important. To Kirschbaum, for example, Faustus is a 'wretchedly irresolute hedonist' (p. 239), an 'incorrigible hedonist' (p. 238), a 'weak-willed voluptuary' (p. 239). He is all this, but this is not all that he is.

Some confusion has arisen from talk about Faustus' pro-

* Greg even refers to this scene as embodying 'the central theme of the damnation of Faustus'.

gressive degradation in the course of the action. Kirschbaum and Greg* recognize, as earlier critics often have not, that Marlowe realized very well what he was doing in depicting Faustus in such a way as to give grounds for describing him in these terms. But it is necessary to distinguish two questions: (i) what, essentially, is the nature of the sin by which Faustus brings damnation on himself? (ii) what does Marlowe represent as being the consequences of Faustus' sin in his character while he is still in the world? In Greg especially, I seem to detect a tendency to treat correct answers to the second question as if they were answers, or parts of the answer, to the first.

'In spite', he writes, 'of his earnest desire to know truth, and half-hidden in the Marlowan glamour cast about him, the seeds of decay are in his character from the first – how else should he come to make his fatal bargain? Beside his passion for knowledge is a lust for riches and pleasure and power' (p. 100). I cannot think that Greg really overlooks the fact that the spiritual ambition that leads Faustus to make 'the fatal bargain' is a sin compared with which the bodily lusts are of secondary importance, but his language is somewhat misleading.

Faustus is Everyman, and his sin is a re-enactment of the sin of Adam – pride, 'the form and fount of all other sin' (Smith, p. 49). The Chorus makes this quite plain: 'swoln with cunning, of a self-conceit' (Prol. 20); 'to practise more than heavenly power permits' (Epil. 8). This is the framework of the play, and compared with this, Faustus' final 'demoniality' (Greg, p. 106) is of secondary importance. It is only one of the fruits of the primal sin, which was a sin of the mind, not of the flesh. It is true, and important, that this sin leads to a degradation in which even the false objects of the mind give place in Faustus' eyes to more purely sensual pleasures – true also that, as Kirschbaum emphasizes, one of the things that Faustus has wanted even from the beginning is to 'live in all voluptuousness' (iii 94) – but, though possibly more contemptible to his fellow-mortals,

* Greg stresses more the degeneration, Kirschbaum the elements of sensuality present from the outset.

Faustus is not more *wicked* in respect of his indulgence in those pleasures than in his original rejection of God, any more than Milton's Satan is more wicked in the metamorphosis of *Paradise Lost*, x 503–6 than in his original rebellion. Hence to say 'with Faustus' union with Helen the nice balance between possible salvation and imminent damnation is upset' (Greg, p. 107) is true enough if it means that this act of Faustus is that in which his impenitence finally finds expression – that this union is the apparent good which he finally prefers to his salvation – but it is false if it means that this sin in its particular character is, and is bound to be, specially momentous. For the same reason I should demur to Kirschbaum's '*for the sake* of bodily pleasure, Faustus has given up the last possibility of redemption' (p. 239, my italics), as involving a measure of ambiguity that I do not think the author entirely avoids being misled by. I believe that essentially we are all in agreement – Greg justly says at the end of his paper that Marlowe 'did not shrink from depicting, beside Faustus' spiritual sin of bartering his soul to the powers of evil, what is in effect its physical complement and counterpart' (p. 107) – but I have found a tendency in students of the play, while accepting Kirschbaum's analysis, to feel that it robs Faustus of some of the dignity which they sense still to belong to him, in spite of everything. And Faustus *is* a man whom it was eminently worth Lucifer's while to gain: that he robs him of most of his dignity as well as of his soul (if the two can be so sharply distinguished) is part of the tragedy, and in pointing out what is made of Faustus it is a mistake not to pay attention also to what the Faustus is of whom that thing is made – the man whose achievements and endowments are praised in the opening and closing choruses. One way to keep a due measure of attention directed upon that side of the theme is to recognize Faustus' central act of sin for what it is.

Pride, then, is at the heart of the picture, and sensuality merely one of its fruits. What other sins go to make up the whole scheme? There is one theme of the first importance that I find mentioned only by Smith (p. 43): that of *curiosity*. Structurally, this is perhaps the most important aspect of Marlowe's treatment of sin in the play. Pride is the ultimate source of Faustus' fall, and sensuality is a pervasive element of his character after it. But it is curiosity that is most notably operative in the conduct of the action. Moreover, it is largely owing to a failure to apprehend the nature, as indeed the existence, of this sin that there have arisen the misrepresentations of Marlowe's purpose which have seen in Faustus a largely sympathetic picture of a typically Renaissance striving for 'knowledge infinite'.

Curiosity is a theme which links the intellectual and sensual aspects of Faustus' sin. It is 'the vice which has as its object the intellectual satisfaction to be derived from knowing all sensual pleasures. . . . It was, of course, considered a greater vice than the pursuit of these pleasures for their own sakes.' (See A. A. Parker, *The Allegorical Drama of Calderón* (1943) p. 196.) It is notable that it is what is really being described at certain points in the play where Kirschbaum sees only straightforward sensuality. When Mephistophilis offers the show of devils

> to delight *thy mind*,
> And let thee see what magic can perform
> (v 84–5, my italics)

it is his curiosity that he is ministering to, rather than his 'sensual satisfaction' (Kirschbaum, p. 235), though the purpose is rightly described by Kirschbaum as being 'to distract his mind from spiritual concern'. The show of the Seven Deadly Sins, again, is not just 'satisfaction of the senses' (Kirschbaum, p. 237). Smith here quotes Augustine to the effect that the curious man, as opposed to the voluptuous, seeks after the opposites of what is beautiful, etc., 'not that he may be vexed by them, but merely out of the lust to experience and to know' (p. 43). That is certainly Faustus' attitude here: 'O, how this sight doth delight my soul' (vi 170), and the fundamental unrealism of the curious man is grimly brought out in his 'O, might I see hell and return again safe, how happy were I then' (172–3). And the 'dramatic irony' noted by Kirschbaum (p. 27) in the lines, 'That sight will be as pleasing unto me / As Paradise was to Adam, the first day / Of his creation', is more forcible if we contrast Faustus' misdirected lust for knowledge with the natural and properly directed desire to know all that it concerned him to know that Adam had in the state of innocence.

If we return to follow the action chronologically, we note that Faustus' first use of his power is to ask about hell, and when he expresses doubt whether this can be hell, 'sleeping, eating, walking and *disputing*' (v 140, my italics), the 'curious' disposition is epitomized – it is none the less something that Marlowe treats on its own account because it is followed immediately by a plunge into sensuality: the two things, Marlowe indicates, go together. The 'curiously barren discussion on astronomy' (Greg, p. 101) of scene vi also falls into place from this point of view. That it is abortive is the main point of it; I think Smith (p. 42) is right in seeing, in the way it leads up to the unanswered question 'who made the world?' a reference to the argument *a contingentia*. In any case, there is a marked contrast suggested between the idle curiosity of an undisciplined mind that will not even apply itself to solving its questions for itself, and the proper use of the intellect which, even without the aid of revelation, can discover 'who made the world'.

It is not only Faustus who is obsessed by curiosity throughout the play. It is in varying degrees a characteristic vice of those who consult him, the Emperor (scene xii), the Duke of Anholt (scene xvii), even Faustus' friends the scholars (scene xviii). That the source for all these displays of Faustus' power is in the *Faust Book* does not detract from their significance in Marlowe's play; nor does the fact that 'the intellectual satisfaction to be derived from knowing all sensuous pleasures' is obviously more suitable for presentation on the stage than direct sensual enjoyment. Those facts merely show Marlowe's skill in using his material to the best effect.

The points arising out of this examination that seem to me important for the understanding of the play are: (i) No insistence on the pervading, and increasing, sensualism of Faustus ought to obscure the fact that he falls, like Man, and like Lucifer himself (iii 70), through the spiritual sin of pride. (ii) In some cases what has been taken to be straightforward sensuality has rather an intellectual quality that assimilates it to what the scholastics called 'curiosity'. (iii) That this curiosity has greater importance for the central acts than even Smith, to whom is due the credit for rediscovering this motif, has demonstrated.* (iv) In the representation of Faustus' character, the presence of this vice of curiosity mediates the transition that has sometimes seemed unduly abrupt, between the essentially spiritual pride to which he succumbs, and the direct sensuality in which his earthly career culminates. The double appearance of the succuba who impersonates Helen symbolizes this transition; she appears first to satisfy the curiosity of the Scholars, and returns to glut Faustus' sensual desire.

* But much of what I have said is implicit in his 'Faustus is out of the danger of knowing God; he is on the other hand the better qualified to tease Popes, oblige Duchesses and entertain Emperors' (p. 43).

SOURCE; *The Wind and the Rain*, IV (1947).

Helen Gardner

THE THEME OF DAMNATION
IN *DOCTOR FAUSTUS* (1948)

WE are unfortunate in possessing Marlowe's greatest play only in an obviously mutilated form; but in spite of possible distortion and some interpolation in the centre, the grandeur of the complete reversal stands out clearly. Apart from its opening and concluding choruses, which provide an archaic framework, and the short closing scene in the 1616 text, where the scholars find the mangled body of Faustus, the play begins and ends with the hero in his study. In the first scene Faustus runs through all the branches of human knowledge and finds them inadequate to his desires. Logic can only teach argument; medicine stops short where human desire is most thwarted, since it cannot defeat death; law is a mercenary pursuit; and divinity, which he comes to last, holds the greatest disappointment: it is grounded in the recognition of man's mortality and his fallibility. The two texts from Jerome's Bible insult his aspiration: *Stipendium peccati mors est*, and *Si peccasse negamus, fallimur, et nulla est in nobis veritas*.* He turns instead to magic because it is:

> a world of profit and delight,
> Of power, of honour, and omnipotence.

He decides to 'tire his brains to get a deity'. The sin of Faustus here is presumption, the aspiring above his order, or the rebellion against the law of his creation.

But when he is last seen alone in his study it is the opposite sin

---

* It is worth noting that Faustus does not complete the text, which is familiar from its use as one of the Sentences. 'If we say that we have no sin, we deceive ourselves, and the truth is not in us: but, if we confess our sins, he is faithful and just to forgive us our sins, and to cleanse us from all unrighteousness.'

which delivers him to damnation: the final sin of Faustus is despair.[1] However much he may call in his fear on God or Christ, it is the power of Lucifer and the bond with Lucifer which he really believes in. It is to Lucifer he prays: 'O, spare me, Lucifer!' and 'Ah, rend not my heart for naming of my Christ!' Donne gives presumption and despair as one of the couples which the Schoolmen have called sins against the Holy Ghost 'because naturally they shut out those meanes by which the Holy Ghost might work upon us . . . for presumption takes away the feare of God, and desperation the love of God'.[2] They are the two faces of the sin of Pride. Faustus tormented by devils is obsessed by their power; but the Old Man is safe from them, because of his faith. The great reversal from the first scene of *Doctor Faustus* to the last can be defined in different ways: from presumption to despair; from doubt of the existence of hell to belief in the reality of nothing else; from a desire to be more than man to the recognition that he has excluded himself from the promise of redemption for all mankind in Christ; from haste to sign the bond to desire for delay when the moment comes to honour it; from aspiration to deity and omnipotence to longing for extinction. At the beginning Faustus wished to rise above his humanity; at the close he would sink below it, be transformed into a beast or into 'little water-drops'. At the beginning he attempts usurpation upon God; at the close he is an usurper upon the Devil.*

As for the reward Faustus obtains, it is difficult to argue from

---

* 'The greatest sin that ever was, and that upon which even the blood of Christ Jesus hath not wrought, the sin of Angels was that *Similis ero Altissimo*, to be like God. To love our selves, to be satisfied with our selves, to finde an omnisufficiency in our selves, is an intrusion, an usurpation upon God' (*LXXX Sermons* (1640) p. 156). 'Did God ordain hell fire for us? no, but for the Devil and his Angels. And yet we that are vessels so broken, as that there is not a sheard left, to fetch water at the pit, that is, no means in our selves, to derive one drop of Christ's blood upon us, nor to wring out one tear of true repentance from us, having plung'd our selves into this everlasting, and this dark fire, which was not prepared for us: A wretched covetousness, to be intruders upon the Devil; a wretched ambition, to be usurpers upon damnation' (*XXVI Sermons* (1660) p. 273).

the play as it has come down to us, and one should not in fairness say that Faustus appears to sell his soul for the satisfaction of playing practical jokes. But there are two episodes of some significance near the beginning, in which Marlowe's hand is clearly apparent, which it is possible to argue from. Faustus takes Mephistophilis as his servant; he demands twenty-four years of 'all voluptuousness'

> Having thee ever to attend on me,
> To give me whatsoever I shall ask,
> To tell me whatsoever I demand,
> .   .   .
> And always be obedient to my will.

As the play proceeds it is clear what happens with the last clause of the agreement: the obedient servant becomes the master. It is Mephistophilis who speaks with authority as representative of 'great Lucifer', and it is Faustus who obeys. But it is the same with the other two clauses. Immediately after the bond is signed Faustus begins to ask questions, and he asks about hell. He receives what are in the context of the play true answers, but he does not believe them. He thinks hell a fable, and Mephistophilis with melancholy irony leaves the subject: 'Ay, think so, till experience change thy mind.' Then Faustus makes his first request: he asks for a wife. Here the text is plainly defective; the verse breaks down into half-lines and prose, a devil enters dressed as a woman with fireworks attached which explode. But after this horseplay, Mephistophilis resumes in dignified Marlovian verse:

> Marriage is but a ceremonial toy:
> And if thou lovest me, think no more of it.
> I'll cull thee out the fairest courtesans,
> And bring them ev'ry morning to thy bed:
> She whom thine eye shall like, thy heart shall have.

If we turn to the source, the English Faust Book, we can, I think, see the implications of the scene and conjecture why Marlowe set it here.

Doctor *Faustus* . . . bethinking himselfe of a wife called *Mephostophiles* to counsaile; which would in no wise agree: demanding of him if he would breake the couenant made with him or if hee had forgot it. Hast thou not (quoth *Mephostophiles*) sworne thy selfe an enemy to God and all creatures? To this I answere thee, thou canst not marry; thou canst not serue two masters, God, and my Prince: for wedlock is a chiefe institution ordained of God, and that hast thou promised to defie, as we doe all, and that hast thou also done: and moreouer thou hast confirmed it with thy blood: perswade thy selfe, that what thou doost in contempt of wedlock, it is all to thine owne delight.

When Faustus persists in his demand, an ugly devil appears and offers himself as a bride. On his vanishing Mephistophilis reappears to say: 'It is no iesting with us, holde thou that which thou hast vowed, and wee will perform as wee haue promised.'[3] The point of the scene is clear even in the play as we have it: Faustus's first request is met with a refusal. The source gives the full implications of that refusal, which may have been cut out to allow for more fireworks: marriage and 'the fairest courtesans' are incompatibles. Faustus has not exchanged limitations for freedom; he has merely exchanged one kind of limitation for another. Marriage belongs to the world he has left. He cannot have all he wants, for the satisfaction of some desires involves the thwarting of others.

It is the same with knowledge soon after. Faustus disputes with Mephistophilis of 'divine astrology'. The answers he gets he dismisses with contempt; he knew them already. But then he goes on to ask the great question:

Faustus. Well, I am answer'd. Now tell me who made the world.
Mephistophilis. I will not.
Faustus. Sweet Mephistophilis, tell me.
Mephistophilis. Move me not, Faustus.
Faustus. Villain, have not I bound thee to tell me any thing?
Mephistophilis. Ay, that is not against our kingdom.
     This is: thou art damn'd; think thou of hell.

Some kinds of knowledge, like some kinds of experience, Faustus has shut himself off from. He has not escaped the necessity of choice. It is a chosen path he follows to the end. Marlowe does all he can by the device of the two angels to keep before us that Faustus is still a man, and that repentance is open to him, if he will only

> Call for mercy, and avoid despair.

But he persists. His rewards are the delights of the imagination, sweet and terrible fantasies, culminating in the vision of Helen,* and the exercise of what power Mephistophilis allows him, for the practical jokes probably represent a debasing rather than an alteration of Marlowe's intention. But knowledge and felicity he has exchanged for shadows, and for power he gets slavery.

* Dr Greg has recently recovered for us the full mingling of horror and beauty in the scene in which Faustus embracing Helen cries: 'Her lips suck forth my soul: see where it flies!' He points out that Helen is a 'spirit' and that in this play a spirit is a devil. 'Faustus commits the sin of demoniality, that is bodily intercourse with demons.' See W. W. Greg, 'The Damnation of Faustus', in *Modern Language Review* (Apr 1946) pp. 97–107.

Source: 'Milton's "Satan" and the Theme of Damnation in Elizabethan Tragedy', in *English Studies*, N.S., 1 (1948). Printed here as revised for inclusion in the author's *A Reading of 'Paradise Lost'* (1965).

NOTES

1. The word *despair* or its derivative *desperate* occurs thirteen times in the play. See iii 91; v 4 and 5; vi 25 and 31; xv 23; xviii 56, 60, 64 and 71; xix 11, 88 and 97.

In *The Conflict of Conscience* by Nathaniell Woodes, Minister of Norwich, published 1581 (*A Select Collection of Old English Plays*, ed. R. Dodsley and W. C. Hazlitt, 15 vols (1874–6) VI), in which we can see the old morality play of wrongful choice, punishment, repentance and forgiveness turning into the Elizabethan tragedy of sin and retribution, the whole struggle in the final Act is between the hero's despair and the efforts of his friends to convince him that he is not beyond God's mercy. One can commend the enterprise if not the success of the Minister of Norwich in trying to put the finer points of the doctrine of justification by faith into fourteeners. Poor as his play is, it shows in a most interesting way the great debate of the sixteenth and seventeenth centuries on the freedom of the will being turned into drama. In *The Conflict of Conscience*, at the very last moment, faith conquers, and the happy ending of the old morality is preserved. [When I wrote this I was unaware that the play is found in two issues. As originally published, it ended, as in life, with the hero (Francis Spira) committing suicide. In the second issue his name was removed from the title-page and a happy ending was substituted. See the Malone Society reprint.] In *Doctor Faustus*, which retains formally much of the old morality, despair triumphs. Our understanding of some of the tragedies of Shakespeare and his contemporaries might be enriched if we thought more in terms of

> Providence, Foreknowledge, Will, and Fate,
> Fixt Fate, free will, foreknowledge absolute,

and less in terms of 'fatal flaws' and 'errors of judgement'.

2. *LXXX Sermons* (1640) p. 349.

3. *Dr Faustus*, ed. F. S. Boas (1932) App. I, pp. 181–2.

Nicholas Brooke

THE MORAL TRAGEDY OF
DOCTOR FAUSTUS (1952)

THERE has been a persistent uneasiness in recent criticism of
Elizabethan drama as to what constitutes a proper dramatic unity,
where it is that a critic may legitimately demand consistency. No
doubt the expectation of consistency is a temptation that a critic
should combat: 'the play's the thing' has been the cry since the
early years of this century, and it still is. But it is not clear that
we really know what we mean by the phrase; it has too often
been an excuse for superficial criticism, either in limiting the
quality of a play to theatrical excitement, or in contemptuous
dismissal of a serious critic's explorations into significances. The
phrase was used as a counterblast to excessive theorizing about
'characters' in the nineteenth century, just as the excellence of
Shakespeare's characterization had been asserted in the eighteenth
century as a counterblast to excessive theorizing about the unities
of time and place. Some sense of unity, some kind of consistency
has of course always been acknowledged as necessary to a good
play; and since Pope's preface at least, it has been recognized as a
quality of Shakespeare's best plays. Coleridge coined the phrase
'unity of feeling', but his exposition of the idea in *Romeo and
Juliet* is disappointing. Furthermore, Coleridge (although less
rashly than either his predecessors or successors) thought this
unity to be founded in a consistent preoccupation with character.
Detached from what now seems to be a false emphasis, the idea
remains, variously stressed in such phrases as 'unity of tone' or
'unity of impact'.

Behind such a unity there must lie some consistency of purpose,
of understanding in the author. In the complexity of a Shakes-
pearian play, any simple definition may well seem inadequate;
it does in Marlowe's plays, but not so obviously, for the range

of Marlowe's interests and abilities was far narrower. In *Tamburlaine*, we recognize a preoccupation with the faculties of man which are not all appropriate to the Scythian shepherd; it is a commonplace that the same preoccupation dominates all Marlowe's later plays, but in different forms and with an impact ever more complicated and even ambiguous. Some of the attributes of the early hero are unmistakable in the speeches of Mortimer whose zest for power is set against the sensuality of Edward II; but Mortimer is treated as a secondary character, and marks his own downfall as an orthodox operation of the wheel of fortune; finally the new king rounds off the play of ideas with the establishment of a political peace, the benevolent despotism of the Tudors. Something of the same kind would seem to be true of *The Massacre at Paris*, and even (though less clearly) of *The Jew of Malta*. In *Doctor Faustus* the implied conclusion is far less certain, but that Marlowe's main preoccupation here is still the moral one, of Man's faculties and his voluntary subjection of them to an accepted order, is beyond question.[1]

It is in the presentation of that theme, then, that we must look, if anywhere, for the consistency of attitude (it will not be more) on which the play's unity should depend. The Play is the thing, but the play is not just 'putting the *Faust Book* on the stage', nor 'exploiting a popular interest in devils and witchcraft'. Marlowe is doing both these things, and both produce their own deviations from a consistent course: but they are not what the Elizabethans would have called the 'cause' of his play. There is a principle of selection in his treatment of the *Faust Book*; and there is an interpretative interest in his handling of witchcraft evident in the (typically Elizabethan) duality of his attitude to the supernatural. On the one hand, supernatural manifestations are external to man; on the other they are partly suggested as objective realizations of psychological conflict: it is not accurate to speak of Mephostophilis solely as the former, any more than it is to speak of the Good and Bad Angels solely as the latter. Whichever they are, psychological or supernatural, their effects and activities must necessarily be the same; but the consistent co-existence of both forms is not necessary and does not take place. That this modifies the idea of individual responsibility which Marlowe develops in the play seems obvious; Faustus is, and is not, in control of the events that destroy him; but Marlowe does not clarify his thought on this matter, and if at one moment he seems clearly to imply one attitude, at another he equally clearly implies the opposite. Mr J. Smith, in an interesting essay² which fails to take sufficient account of historical context, avoids this ambiguity by finding allegory at one level only (the psychological) wherever Faustus' moral freedom is tampered with. But this does not seem to be Marlowe's meaning. Faustus attempts to assert his will in opposition to both God and devil, and he fails, as it is obvious he must. What is not so obvious is the interpretation Marlowe places on that failure; what significant change of thought caused him to turn from the story of Tamburlaine who even in death can be suggested as triumphant, to Faustus who cannot. The issue has been grossly over-simplified as between atheism and orthodox Christianity; this is particularly dangerous because these terms have changed their common meanings very considerably since the sixteenth century.

The problem, then, is to understand the terms in which Marlowe conceived his drama: to discover whether there does exist a consistency in his attitude to his theme throughout the play to form a sufficient foundation for the patent magnificence of the end. For by the end only is the play widely known, the apostrophe to Helen and Faustus's last speech: but they are sufficient to make it the only Elizabethan play outside Shakespeare that enjoys regular revival at Stratford. For the rest, the play is known to be a wandering, ill-constructed and for the most part ill-written affair. Worse than that, it is erratic in taste and seriousness: it wanders from high philosophical speculation to cheap spectacle and vulgar farce, and offers no clear continuity, no thread of development to which we can relate its flashes of greatness, its hints of profound meaning. The problem is made more difficult by the condition of the text as we have it. Dr Walter Greg³ has thoroughly worked out the relations of the two early printed texts to Marlowe's own manuscript; the details are controversial, but the main issues are no longer in doubt.

Doctor Faustus was written at the end, not at the beginning, of Marlowe's career; thus any relation of the thought of this play to Marlowe's others must be made on the asumption that it is his last, not his first important statement of his ideas. The 1616 text is the nearer to what Marlowe wrote, and it retains more fully the Morality play features which distinguish *Faustus*. It is precisely this characteristic which seems to have dictated the critical (as opposed to scholarly) preference for the 1604 text which persisted until very recently; for the less the 'machinery' was allowed to obtrude, the more easily could the play be represented as a personal tragedy, depending on the character of Faustus himself. Yet Marlowe's drama was never concerned primarily with character – his heroes are not in that sense clearly defined at all: his plays take their source from ideas, and the excitement of their presentation; and his human drama, when it can properly be said to exist, lies again more in predicament than character. It is not the stupidity of Faustus of which we are most aware at the end of the play, but his appalling situation, a man (*any* man) cut off from all contact with humanity, dragged to Hell for eternity and seeing visions of Heaven as he goes. The situation depends on the Morality of the play, and to cut that out is to cut out the foundations of the tragedy. The deficiencies of the 1604 text seem to be, as Greg suggests, caused by a need for easy theatrical effect and simple staging in the provinces; it therefore reduces not only the Morality framework (which might not be 'good theatre') but also such spectacular (and surely Marlowan) effects as the presence of the Princes of Hell overlooking the last scene; as well as making the most of opportunities for farce even at the expense of serious intent.

The deficiencies which Greg notices in the 1616 text may also, I suspect, have an important bearing on critical interpretation. Where his manuscript was damaged, the editor was forced to rely on the printed version, and further (the last infernal bar to the present inquiry) he found it necessary to tone the play down to conform with the more rigorous censorship of blasphemy. In such obvious cases as the substitution of 'Oh mercy Heaven' for 'My God, my God', the earlier text supplies the stronger line:

but I shall try to show that Marlowe's fundamental ideas in this play were blasphemous – circumspectly so, no doubt, in the first place (blasphemy was always a serious offence; Marlowe was awaiting trial for it when he was murdered) – but where they showed a little too plain, the lines may have been re-written by the editor in just those contexts of moral argument which were omitted from the 1604 text. Such a possibility (as it is based on mere conjecture) need not be taken very seriously, but it emphasizes the kind of obscurity we find in the play.

Clearly then, the first point to be faced about *Doctor Faustus* is that it is in construction a Morality play. This is the burthen of recent criticism, notably by Professor Kirschbaum[4] and Dr Greg[5] who have independently arrived at remarkably similar conclusions. Professor Kirschbaum insists that we must forget what we would like the play to be (a tragedy) and concentrate on what it is, a Morality. He insists that the prologue must be taken literally, when it announces the play as a spectacle of the clever fellow who excels in learning

> Till, swollen with cunning of a self-conceit,
> His waxen wings did mount above his reach,
> And melting, heavens conspired his overthrow.
>   (Prol. 20 –2 – Greg's conjectural reconstruction)

In other words, the fate of the presumptuous Icarus, the Christian moral of humility and denial of self in the presence of God. On that plane the play continues: Faustus is visited periodically by a Good and a Bad Angel who make obvious suggestions, he is warned finally by a pious and saintly Old Man, comes to a deservedly 'sticky end', and the appropriate comment is in the epilogue:

> Cut is the branch that might have grown full straight, . . .
> Faustus is gone: regard his hellish fall, . . .
>   (Epil. 1 and 4)

It is always tempting in dramatic criticism to appeal against over-subtlety and ingenuity, and to claim full attention only for what is made obvious. That is what Kirschbaum does, and if he is right we must accept the idea of Marlowe intending to write a simple Morality Play of a kind frequent in the sixteenth century. The curious thing about this is that it flatly contradicts older views as to the central interest of the play: tending to undervalue or completely ignore the Morality features, critics thought of Doctor Faustus as a kind of Renaissance superman condemned to tragic failure; a man who expresses superbly a longing for knowledge, beauty, wealth and power. The opening scene supports this view, with Faustus examining all the established lines of human knowledge and finding them all inadequate, too limited; the aim he sets himself is achievement of the supreme desires of Man:

> Oh, what a world of profit and delight,
> Of power, of honour, of omnipotence
> Is promised to the studious artizan!
>
> (i 52–4)

And these he pursues – begging Mephostophilis for information, recounting how he has made Blind Homer sing to him, and the chorus tells of his journey through the air to see the astronomical system in its entirety, and still at the end he pursues perfect physical beauty in Helen. All the great passages of the play are concerned with these notions, and they are the only positive ideas advanced: it is impossible to come away from seeing or reading it without having the magnificence of Faustus's visions uppermost in the mind. The final moral exhortation not to practise more than heavenly power permits is either forgotten, or leaves a stale and dusty taste behind it.

Kirschbaum and Greg both recognize this difficulty and seek to overcome it by postulating a gradual deterioration of Faustus's character throughout the play from noble-mindedness to mere depravity. And there, they suggest, the tragedy lies: in pursuing physical pleasure, Faustus neglects spiritual values, and deteriorates to such a weakness of will that he cannot assert himself against the temptations of the devil even when the penalty is near at hand.

There are three vital reasons why I do not think this a satisfactory view. First of all, this gradual deterioration of character does not seem to be in the play: it is foisting an idea of drama and behaviour on to Marlowe which is wholly unlike him, wholly foreign to the kind of play he and his contemporaries were composing. Faustus is certainly sometimes coarse and trivial – but no more so at the end than at the beginning of the play: in the first scene, he repeats his aims more vulgarly, or rather mixing the noble constantly with the trivial:

> Shall I make spirits fetch me what I please,
> Resolve me of all ambiguities,
> Perform what desperate enterprise I will?
> I'll have them fly to India for gold,
> Ransack the ocean for orient pearl,
> And search all corners of the new-found world
> For pleasant fruits and princely delicates.
> I'll have them read me strange philosophy
> And tell the secrets of all foreign kings;
>
> (i 78–86)

and so on: Faustus's pursuits are like this throughout the play; at one moment strange philosophy, at the next mere secrets of all foreign kings. Similarly there is a mixture of serious thought and cheap iconoclasm in Faustus's well-known rejection of the sciences, and it is followed (still in the first scene) by the less popular lines

> Philosophy is odious and obscure,
> Both law and physic are for petty wits,
> Divinity is basest of the three,
> Unpleasant, harsh, contemptible and vild.
>
> (i 105–8)

So Faustus oscillates throughout the play, turning from the nature of Hell to demanding a wife; from Blind Homer to delight in the farcical seven deadly sins. I can see no steady deterioration in all this: there is less serious thought perhaps at the end, but not much less: Faustus asks for Helen not philosophy, but he states

as early as scene vi that it is Pleasure he is after with Homer,
Alexander and Oenone and he repeats it in scene viii:

> Whilst I am here on earth let me be cloyed
> With all things that delight the heart of man.
>
> (viii 59—60)

That is immediately after the chorus tells of his journey to find
the secrets of astronomy, and at the end of the play it is for his
prodigious learning that his students remember Faustus the
sorcerer. The fact is that *we* make a distinction between Knowledge and Pleasure which is foreign to Marlowe: the philosophy
of *Faustus*, like that of *Tamburlaine*, is primarily hedonistic; the
man has appetites, and his pleasure is to satisfy them. He has an
appetite for knowledge, and another for sex; both are extreme,
for complete knowledge and for perfect sex; but the only qualitative distinction is between completeness and incompleteness.
If Faustus had deteriorated in character during the play he would
be content with any 'hot whore', not insist on Helen herself.

This seems to me the second vital objection to their theory,
and to get over it both Greg and Kirschbaum supposed the
apostrophe to Helen to be ironic: they remind us that Helen is
only a devil in disguise, the same spirit that Faustus produced to
beguile his students' senses; and further that in committing
adultery with the devil (as we are given to understand that he
does) Faustus commits the final sin, consummates his bond with
Lucifer, and from then on is acknowledged even by the Good
Angel to be beyond redemption. This is all true, but it does not
make the Helen episode ironic: if it were, the actor would be
asked to deliver a supremely persuasive erotic speech to convince
his audience of the value of Pleasure in the face of their fore-
knowledge that Helen is only a spirit – and yet, deliberately fail
to persuade them. An unlikely performance. To assert irony in a
passage where the words never suggest it, where the tone is of
exultant satisfaction, is to ignore the nature of the poetic statement: here, as elsewhere in the play, Marlowe has put conviction
into the voice of Hell, not of Heaven. Certainly there is irony
in this, but it is not of the kind Kirschbaum and Greg suggest,

degrading Faustus's 'weak sensuality' as a cause of his abandon-
ing lasting pleasure for the sake of temporary.

What emerges then, once the Morality framework is acknowledged, is the very odd state of affairs that all the positive statements of the play, supported by the finest verse, are against the
declared Christian moral. The pleasures Faustus wants are made
clear to the mind and the imagination. To the mind they are, as
usual with Marlowe, made disconcertingly clear: the mingling
of strange philosophy with the secrets of all foreign kings is
reminiscent of Tamburlaine's famous speech:

> Our souls, whose faculties can comprehend
> The wondrous architecture of the world . . .
> Still climbing after knowledge infinite . . .
> Until we reach the ripest fruit of all,
> That perfect bliss and sole felicity,
> The sweet fruition of an earthly crown.
>
> (II vii 21–9 – ed. Ellis-Fermor)

To Marlowe these apparently odd juxtapositions are not ironic: I
said before that he does not make qualitative distinctions; what
the human mind desires, it desires, and an odd assortment is the
inevitable result. His imagination fired at the crown or at
Machiavellian politics, for the power of individual expansion
they permit; but it fired at other less reputable occupations, such
as his employment as a spy which may connect with his curiosity
about the secrets of all foreign kings – for even in that there is a
sense of power.

These positive 'evils' which Faustus wants are made abun-
dantly clear then to the mind; there is no need to stress the
imaginative quality of the Helen speech, or of the first turn to
magic:

>   emperors and kings
> Are but obeyed in their several provinces,
> Nor can they raise the wind or rend the clouds;
> But his dominion that excells in this
> Stretcheth as far as doth the mind of man:

A sound magician is a demi-god;
Here tire my brains to get a deity!   (i 56–62)

But for the opposite, the Christian virtue and the hope of Heaven,
which Greg and Kirschbaum would have us believe Marlowe is
trying to recommend, not only is the imagination scarcely given
a chance to be fired by them, they are never made in the least
clear to the mind. From the dull and feeble bleatings of the Good
Angel at the beginning, to the conventional phrases of the Old
Man and the Epilogue, all statements of the 'good' moral remain
vague, flat, meaningless.

   The interpretation of the play as deliberately invoking Christian ideals is therefore as unsatisfactory as the older view of the
tragedy of aspiring man. Neither can be dismissed, neither is
anything like a complete view of *Doctor Faustus*. It is not possible
to believe that Marlowe intended a sound Christian play but
unconsciously emphasized the wrong moral: the nature of the
evidence I have examined would make such large demands on
Marlowe's unconscious as to amount to insanity. I therefore
conclude, that Marlowe chose deliberately to use the Morality
form, and to use it perversely, to invert or at least to satirize its
normal intention. To understand the significance of this, we
must imagine the position of a playwright in 1591 or 1592 when
Marlowe was writing *Faustus*: old Morality plays were still
performed, and some of them may not have been very old; but
much as the leading playwrights owed to the Morality tradition,
they did not write simple Morality plays such as *Faustus* purports
to be. The comedies of Lyly and Greene, the tragedies of Kyd,
and Marlowe's other plays, have moved a long way from puppet-
manipulation of abstractions, and even *Gorboduc* thirty years
earlier had called its Good and Bad Angels by the names of
political advisers. Abstractions appeared in popular plays much
later than that, but by 1590 the full apparatus of Morality was an
old and musty form of drama, as in their turn were Marlowe's
own plays by 1600. For Marlowe to write such a play at such a
time therefore suggests satire: it is the least likely way for him to
have chosen to express a volte-face from near-atheism of opinion,

and violent anti-Christian satire in *Tamburlaine* and *The Jew of Malta* to orthodox Christian belief. I believe that Marlowe's adoption of Morality form must be seen as a deliberate mis-use of popular old-fashioned material.

There are two possible forms this mis-use might have taken: firstly, to present *Faustus* as a simple Morality story, and to give it a bitter ironic twist right through. In this case, there could be no sustained elaboration of the opposite notion of morality ironically implied, nor could the death of the hero unrepentant be anything but a somewhat nasty joke: it offers no course of deliberate action to Faustus to enable us to understand the state of his mind in his last, wholly tragic speech. The predicament would be simply that of a silly old man paying the price of his stupidity – and there is in that nothing of the mental conflict, the doubt and terror that Marlowe expresses. The other possible mis-use of the Morality form is to invert it completely, to portray the search of a man for Hell not Heaven, to assert constantly the idea that everything is upside down, that so-called evil is in fact good, that the struggle of Faustus is to be anti-Christ, not Christian. In general terms like that, this conception is meaningless; it depends entirely on what is promulgated as the play develops. By two English writers, of course, such a deliberate inversion of the orthodox has been used to promulgate an unorthodox notion of morality: by Blake with profound seriousness in all his work, and by Bernard Shaw with less profundity in *Man and Superman*. There is no useful analogy to be pressed, the aims of these three writers are wholly different: Shaw could satirically suggest Heaven as a punishment for man, which Marlowe is very far from doing; Marlowe has no such complete system of spiritual forces to suggest as has Blake. Yet on a much smaller, less clearly realized plane, there is some similarity between Marlowe and Blake: they both suggest in behaviour conventionally understood to be immoral the right functioning of human instinct; they both base their judgment of good on a magnificent imaginative extension of all the innate desires and appetites of man, even cruelty.

But there the similarity ends: it is obvious at once that Marlowe is more orthodox than either Blake or Shaw, although he is popu-

larly supposed to have been an atheist. It seems to me clear that
Marlowe was not strictly an atheist at all: that is to say, he never
expressly denies the existence of God, not even in the wild
blasphemies Baines collected for his indictment. I should doubt
very much whether such a complete denial of the idea of an
almighty God was possible within the mental horizon of even an
advanced thinker of the 1590s;* I am certain that it was far from
Marlowe's mind. The 'atheism' for which he should have stood his
trial, and which he hints at throughout his plays, was not atheism
at all, but blasphemy, a repeated protest against the nature of
God implied in His treatment of Man, a protest whose bitterness
implies acceptance of the *existence* of God. It is for that reason
that Marlowe persistently invokes the idea of a jealous God, one
who could bear no brother near the throne. The dramatic tension
of the Faustus story as Marlowe presents it lies primarily in the
fact that Faustus is determined to satisfy the demands of his
nature as God has made him – to be himself a deity – and that
that is forbidden: it can only be achieved by a conscious rejection
of the God who created him in his own image, but denied him
(as much as Lucifer) fulfilment of that image.

It is interesting to note that nearly a hundred years later, Milton
justifying God's ways to Man, finds it necessary to deal with this
heresy that I have ascribed to Marlowe, allowing it full imaginative force in the mind of Satan, as he recovers from his Fall to
Hell:

> [He] Who now is Sovran can dispose and bid
>   What shall be right: fardest from him is best
>   Whom reason hath equald, force hath made supream
>   Above his equals. Farewel happy Fields
>   Where Joy for ever dwells: Hail horrours, hail
>   Infernal world, and thou profoundest Hell
>   Receive thy new Possessor: One who brings
>   A mind not to be chang'd by Place or Time.
>   The mind is its own place, and in it self

* A few years later Tourneur uses the word in a strict sense in *The
Atheist's Tragedy*; but as a fascinating speculative outrage.

> Can make a Heav'n of Hell, a Hell of Heav'n.
> What matter where, if I be still the same,
> And what I should be, all but less then hee
> Whom Thunder hath made greater? Here at least
> We shall be free; th'Almighty hath not built
> Here for his envy, will not drive us hence:
> Here we may reign secure, and in my choyce
> To reign is worth ambition though in Hell:
> Better to reign in Hell, then serve in Heav'n.
>
> > (*Paradise Lost*, 1 246–63)

This position could be read into the Prologue's somewhat ambiguous statement:

> Till, swollen with cunning of a self-conceit,
> His waxen wings did mount above his reach,
> And melting, heavens conspired his overthrow.
>
> > (Prol. 20–2)

If we press these lines for meaning, they leave us wondering what should be Faustus's reach, and why he is able to mount beyond it; and further, what sort of heavens it might be that '*conspired his overthrow*'. This is probably over-straining lines which are simply conventional, but the idea of reach is at once the theme of scene i, in Faustus's rejection of the sciences, his search for greater opportunity and his adoption of magic:

> But his dominion that excells in this
> Stretcheth as far as doth the mind of man:

and beyond that into explicit challenge of his aim:

> A sound magician is a demi-god;
> Here tire my brains to get a deity!   (i 59–62)

The angels appear, and as their remarks well illustrate the theological bias I have remarked, I shall quote them in full. The Good Angel opposes Faustus's aspiration only with negatives, the idea of a God of wrath and the ironic suggestion that he should read the scriptures whose inadequacy he has just asserted:

> O Faustus, lay that damnèd book aside
> And gaze not on it lest it tempt thy soul
> And heap God's heavy wrath upon thy head.
> Read, read the scriptures; that is blasphemy.

Whereas the Bad Angel repeats Faustus's own conception:

> Go forward Faustus, in that famous art
> Wherein all nature's treasury is contained:
> Be thou on earth as Jove is in the sky,
> Lord and commander of these elements.   (i 69–76)

Faustus therefore invites the aid of Valdes and Cornelius, well-known as magicians, whose dominion does not stretch anything like as far as doth the mind of man, for all their skill: this is an important point, we are made aware that magic does nothing in itself, that it is only an instrument through which Faustus's own peculiar potentiality for greatness may operate. In this sense, Marlowe's treatment of magic is comparable to his treatment of Senecan or Machiavellian ideas of princecraft: in each case what he knew to be 'evil' in any accepted sense, he invoked deliberately as a means for the individual to surmount the restrictions of social morality, to realize his potentiality for supreme power: Tamburlaine, Barabbas, and Faustus all have this in common, a vision of greatness denied by the Laws to which ordinary men are subjected; and they seek freedom by being a king above the Law,[6] by employing an infinity of obscure cunning, and lastly by the widest freedom of all, Magic. In each case, Marlowe's conception is aided by opportunities for stage spectacle which seems to have been as much to his taste as his audience's: in *Tamburlaine*, royal pageantry and colourful and bloody displays of sovereignty; in *The Jew of Malta* sinister trickery, poisons, and vats of boiling oil; in *Faustus*, fireworks, conjuring tricks and scenes of Heaven and Hell. He delighted not only in the philosophical implications of Faustus's act, but also in all the details of the Black Art in which he was widely read.[7]

Up to a point this mixture of the serious and the silly relates to what I have already said about Marlowe's philosophical position;

but it relates also to the popular dramatic tradition in which he was writing, and more particularly to the Morality plays whose form he was deliberately reviving. For the most astonishing thing to a modern reader of the Moralities is commonly how much gross *im*morality they include: that the vices have more than their fair share of the entertainment and constantly figure as genuinely entertaining rogues without whom the moralizing would be intolerable. For that reason they frequently unbalance the morals by seductive burlesque, leaving us in doubt whether the serious is so serious, whether the whole matter is after all an uproarious farce. This ambivalent outlook, as A. P. Rossiter insists, is a recurrent one from the Middle Ages to Shakespeare, leaving our school-tidy minds bewildered by a constant equivocation about the one thing of which the plays ought to be certain, until we are jolted into acknowledging that there is in this a disturbing but very real life-likeness.

With this tradition in mind, it is possible to understand something of the horseplay to which Faustus himself descends, and certainly those farcical scenes whose crudity causes so much discussion. In a 'good' morality, the clowns burlesque the virtues presented, but end 'in the mud' as they should, while the virtues triumph. In *Faustus* it is the 'bad' hero who is burlesqued by Wagner and the clowns, and the impact of their activities on the main theme must be observed. Wretchedly written their scenes may be, but if Marlowe did not actually write them, he planned their existence and they are in any case little more than plans — plans for a slapstick performance by antic clowns of the circus variety, for whom good words would be unnecessary, as well as probably wasted.

Scene ii immediately reveals Wagner as a mocking comic, teasing the scholars by withholding and then giving casually the sensational news that his master is dining with the magicians, which he ends with the equivocal (and naughty) remark: 'and so, the Lord bless you, preserve you, and keep you, my dear brethren' (ii 25–6). The scholars also give a different angle on Faustus's action, referring to Valdes and Cornelius as infamous throughout the world, seeing his friendship with them as damnable merely, bereft of all the splendour Faustus had given it.

Damnable it is meant to be, and in the next scene Faustus reveals his full consciousness of the fact, as he performs the rites of conjuration. Amongst the manuals of the Black Art available to Marlowe, the details of raising devils vary considerably, but the basic method remains always the same – the acts of worship of God are to be inverted, the consecration of devotion has to be turned into an elaborate rite of desecration. In some rites, there are protective measures to be taken, making the conjuring more of an experiment than a final act:[8] Faustus might mean that, when after listing the things he has done, he says:

> Then fear not, Faustus, to be resolute
> And try the uttermost magic can perform.
>
> (iii 14–15)

But it appears rather that he is afraid of making a mistake which would give the devil power over him instead of vice versa. This idea of resolution is always demanded of witches, and Valdes and Cornelius had stressed it: with Faustus it becomes a vital refrain, 'Faustus, be resolute', in all his dealings with the devil. Its constant re-iteration throughout the play and even in the last scene calls attention to a point which seems to be constantly overlooked: Faustus is always afraid not of the inevitable end of his twenty-four years, but of some immediate failure, the result of irresolution; of the threat the Bad Angel makes in scene vi: 'If thou repent, devils will tear thee in pieces.' On the purely theatrical aspect of Faustus's dealings in magic, then, it is not a simple question of getting power for twenty-four years at the cost of eternal damnation: Faustus gains his power at the cost of perpetual danger.

At that level, Faustus's activities do not necessarily extend beyond the commonplace wickedness envisaged by the students. But when Mephostophilis has been triumphantly produced (and bullied into a change of costume) the tone changes to intellectual seriousness, to a discussion of the real relationship of Faustus and his devil:

Faustus. Did not my conjuring speeches raise thee? Speak.
Mephostophilis. That was the cause, but yet *per accidens*:
> For when we hear one rack the name of God,
> Abjure the scriptures and his saviour Christ,
> We fly in hope to get his glorious soul;
> Nor will we come unless he use such means
> Whereby he is in danger to be damned.
> Therefore the shortest cut for conjuring
> Is stoutly to abjure the Trinity
> And pray devoutly to the prince of hell.

(iii 47–56)

Marlowe turns the cheap indignity of Hell at once into a conception of Mephostophilis as a voluntary agent, not a vulgar slave. And from that emerges the famous definition of Hell:

> Why this is hell, nor am I out of it.
> Thinkst thou that I, who saw the face of God
> And tasted the eternal joys of heaven,
> Am not tormented with ten thousand hells
> In being deprived of everlasting bliss?
> O Faustus, leave these frivolous demands,
> Which strike a terror to my fainting soul.

(iii 78–84)

This is the one passage of imaginative suggestion of Heaven, and it comes from the devil. Faustus contemptuously rejects it:

> What, is great Mephostophilis so passionate
> For being deprivèd of the joys of heaven?
> Learn thou of Faustus manly fortitude
> And scorn those joys thou never shalt possess.

(iii 85–8)

Again Faustus repeats the idea of resolution – 'manly fortitude' – but in a different context, of philosophical discussion not mere theatrical magic: in this latter part of the scene, Faustus's act is reconsidered in terms of its more profound significance. The direct negation of God is not here simply a magic formula, it is an act of Will on Faustus's part, asserted in pursuit of an idea of good in direct contradiction to the Christian idea. In this scene and constantly throughout the play (despite some commonplace insinuations by the Bad Angel at the end) Faustus is not subjected to any simple 'temptation' of the ordinary Morality kind. For instance, in the very dull play *The Conflict of Conscience*[9] printed in 1581 Philologus is reduced to a Faustian inability to repent, but by a wholly different process. Philologus begins by standing out for Protestant truth against a Roman (perhaps Marian) persecution: he is offered his worldly comforts and position in exchange for a recantation, and he succumbs. Once fallen, he exults in his freedom, but Remorse catches him and he argues his irredeemable damnation in the one interesting scene of the play, where verbal suggestions make it possible Marlowe may have studied it. But contrary (it would seem) to the dogmatic beliefs of the worthy minister of Norwich who wrote the play, Philologus is rescued in the end, and a Nuntius announces his repentance and peaceful death.

Faustus is not the victim of a straightforward temptation, like Philologus: he is in danger of persecution at the beginning from nothing but his own sense of frustration. It can be argued that this is only a subtle form of temptation, but for the present purpose that is a sophistication: about succumbing to temptation there is necessarily a negative suggestion, of failure of the Will; Faustus's self-damnation is wholly positive, achieved by an assertion not a failure of his Will. And it is of feebleness that he accuses Mephostophilis. Just as Marlowe has shown Mephostophilis to enjoy the dignity of free will, so Faustus is to be seen as choosing voluntarily, with knowledge of all that it means, Hell instead of Heaven. That is why I say that Marlowe has inverted the Morality structure: the course of Faustus's resolution is to damn himself; his temptation, his weakness, is in offers of repentance. Faustus's Hell is not at first a place of torture, it is Hell only in that it is absence of Heaven, it is an extreme of anti-God whose nature is deliberately opposed to the Angels' joyous submission to the service of the Omnipotent. Heaven is the subjection of self, Hell in this sense is the assertion of self. As I have already said, the foundation of Marlowe's philosophical position is that man has certain over-riding desires whose realization is

denied by any form of servitude, and the order o.
Milton's Satan observed, an order of servitude.

Marlowe is not, of course, propounding a practicable idea o.
how men should live (he does not envisage a race of Nietzschean
or even Shavian supermen), he is discussing the nature of Man
in relation to the God that made him in his own image, with an
urge to be like his maker, omnipotent. Hence the sin of Lucifer
prince of Hell although technically orthodox – Pride – is given an
odd twist by Mephostophilis' statement of it:

> Oh, by aspiring pride and insolence,
> For which God threw him from the face of heaven.
>
> (iii 70–1)

The ironic tone gives the lines a strange prominence: Lucifer
was expelled for precisely the attitude Faustus is now adopting,
but expelled (in these lines) by an irritated and petulant God. The
idea of the deity which Marlowe suggests here (and elsewhere) is
simply of a successful Lucifer or Faustus, one who has the absolute degree of magnificence, and cannot bear to have it dimmed
by a rival. That there is another idea of God (or perhaps another,
more humble, view of man) is insisted at once in the wholly
different tone of Mephostophilis's next words. But for Faustus's
attitude here, we must understand not only the hint of a jealous
God, but of a particular kind of jealousy.

A favourite Renaissance source for ideas on secular virtue was
Aristotle's *Ethics*. The conception, for instance, of Tudor king
or Italian prince was compared to Aristotle's description of the
Magnificent Man, or even of the μεγαλόψυχος, the Great-
souled Man; he who excels in all worldly 'goods', wealth, dignity,
popularity and so on, who is a great patron of the arts, and who is
superior to all the limitations of lesser men. But two important
aspects of the Great-souled Man Aristotle stresses: first, that he
must be wholly resolute in his pursuit of greatness, that the
slightest hesitation or weakness is alien to his nature: 'For the
great-souled man is justified in despising other people – his
estimates are correct.'[10] And secondly, that he will tolerate no
rival within his sphere of influence who might dim his glory:

'he will not go where other people take the first place' and 'he will be incapable of living at the will of another, since to do so is slavish'. It is not of course necessary to suppose that Marlowe derived his version of these ideas direct from Aristotle, but his years at Cambridge could hardly have been passed without reading the Greek.[11] At any rate, an understanding of Aristotle greatly illuminates what it is that Faustus is trying to achieve: the subjective aim of self-expansion is equated with the objective ideal of Aristotelian greatness, and not only are God and Lucifer treated as rival magnificos, but Faustus himself is aiming at that state. That is the philosophical reason for his fear of failure. If he weakens, he will be shown to be less-than-great-souled, he will have failed to gain his deity and will lay himself open to the punishment of God and the revenge of Lucifer, and be torn to pieces. In inverting the Morality pattern of rewards in Heaven and punishments in Hell, Marlowe (as I said before) does not simply reverse this: Heaven is not a punishment, nor is it a reward; it is a wholly different ethos, an idea of humble service which Faustus rejects as unworthy of his nature. Rewards and punishments have therefore both to be in Hell. Hell is used in a number of senses during the play, at a number of different levels, but the central ambiguity is I think between these two: the Hell Faustus seeks, which represents to him the free range of his Will to resolve to be what he thinks it is in his nature to be; and on the other hand the more familiar Hell of the Middle Ages, of unspeakable devils, tortures and indignity, which serves to represent Faustus's fear of failure.

These ideas are hinted in scene iii, and are developed in scenes v and vi; but in between there is a piece of clownage, Wagner directly burlesquing his master, raising devils, arrogating to himself the title of 'Master' and making a slave of the clown with a gibberish of pseudo-learning and Latin: the ironic suggestions in this of overweening and ridicule are developed later.

Scenes v–vii develop to the full the tragic drama, Faustus's mental conflict, his waverings and his sudden moves forward into devilry. He starts alone in his study, triumphantly asserting his damnation:

> Now, Faustus, must thou needs be damned, canst not be saved!
> What boots it then to think of God or heaven?
> Away with such vain fancies, and despair;
> Despair in God and trust in Beelzebub.   (v 1–5)

Nevertheless, as those lines ironically imply, Faustus is not so resolute – something soundeth in his ears – and he has to drive himself back by re-iteration of his basic intention as I see it:

> To God! He loves thee not:
> The god thou servest is thine own appetite,
>   (v 10–11)

from which he builds up to a typically Marlowan brutal hyperbole:

> And offer lukewarm blood of new-born babes.
>   (v 14)

The angels add nothing new, except that the suggestion of wealth fires Faustus's imagination and enables him to be resolute again and call Mephostophilis. Already in scene iii there is a suggestion of irony in Faustus's vaunting refusal to believe Mephostophilis on his own torment; here that suggestion becomes more marked. Mephostophilis promises to be his slave,

> And give thee more than thou hast wit to ask.
>   (v 47)

Faustus is suddenly suggested to be incapable of what he aims at – but Mephostophilis reassures him by offering him again what he wants:

> And then be thou as great as Lucifer.   (v 52)

The signing of the bond gives Faustus another moment of panic, but the knowledge of his remoteness from Heaven spurs him on to resolution in his dealings with Hell. With the bond signed, the deed done, Faustus becomes more blatantly confident; Mephostophilis defines the situation again:

> All places shall be hell that is not heaven.
>   (v 127)

And Faustus retorts 'I think hell's a fable', and proceeds
ebulliently to stress the idea that Hell is a mental state, and that
an after-life of physical torture is nothing but 'trifles and mere
old wives' tales'. With that he turns aside to the lively interchange about wives and whores and turns again to end the scene
by accepting the Book of Knowledge.

Greg conjectures plausibly that there should follow a comic
scene here: it would in fact make a better place for an interval in
modern performance than the usual act division, as scene v
should obviously follow at once both as a climax and an illumination of what has gone before. Scene vi demands an interval of
time, and opens with a new doubt in Faustus's mind, another
offer to repent. Mephostophilis counters it with a syllogism:

> But thinkst thou heaven is such a glorious thing?
> I tell thee, Faustus, it is not half so fair
> As thou or any man that breathes on earth.
> *Faustus*. How provst thou that?
> *Mephostophilis*. 'Twas made for man; then he's more excellent.

Which Faustus answers with another syllogism

> If heaven was made for man, 'twas made for me.
>
>   (vi 5–10)

It is hard to know exactly how to take these lines – our immediate
reaction is to dismiss Mephostophilis's statement as obviously
false logic; on the other hand it is of a kind with Faustus's own
arguments at the opening of the play, and with Marlowe's
statements elsewhere. At any rate, it leads to Faustus's determination to renounce this magic and repent, which immediately
recalls the Angels. Here it is apparent that the drama of Faustus's
soul has advanced: the deed of self-damnation is done, and his
mind twists in terror towards an easy if ignoble salvation more
tempting now that it is impossible. The Good Angel does tempt
him now: '*yet* God will pity thee', but the Bad Angel retorts at
once 'Thou art a spirit; God cannot pity thee' (vi 12–13). Greg
points the force of this line when he remarks that here and always
in the play, 'spirit' is used in a strict sense, meaning devil. Faustus

despairs and talks of suicide but recalls his Will by contemplation of Blind Homer, of Alexander's love and Oenone's death: his consolation is in voluptuous pleasure certainly, but it is not the degrading sensuality it has been called; it is Faustus's god of Appetite which turns him back to his purpose

> I am resolved Faustus shall not repent.   (vi 32)

He turns back to Astronomy, and the irony again asserts itself: in the first place, there is Marlowe's dilemma that he cannot display more knowledge than man possessed; but secondly, Faustus is cheated in his bond: Mephostophilis refuses to state who made the world. Faustus's attempt may be magnificent, to gain a deity, but the terrible fact remains that God is God: the challenge is not atheism, it is against the monstrous nature of a world where man is created to want to be at his finest precisely what he is not allowed to be; the God is the God of Milton's Satan – 'equald in intellect, but supream in force'.

Again Faustus tries to repent, and again the Angels appear, to stress now more obviously the cruder physical nature of Faustus's predicament, the 'machinery' of Heaven and Hell:

> *Bad Angel.* If thou repent, devils will tear thee in pieces.
> *Good Angel.* Repent, and they shall never raze thy skin.
>
> (vi 83–4)

Faustus, for the only time before the end, does repent, and calls on Christ to save him. It is the supreme weakening which offers Lucifer the chance to throw Faustus straight down from his attempted magnificence, it is a direct transgression of the bond. As at the end, the mention of Christ brings the prince of Hell straight to Faustus, now only to warn him. The presence of the Stygian Trinity restores his confidence and he renews his vows. But our awareness of his weakness, of his failure to be resolute is accentuated in the farce that follows, the Seven Deadly Sins presented as a grotesque parody of Faustus's god of Appetite: all his voluptuous aspirations are turned to vulgarity. Pride is mere disdain, Covetousness is gold locked up, and so on – for each sin, the worst is futility, Faustus's means to magnificence degraded to ends in themselves with a sterility set in bawdy farce. His comment on it is typically equivocal:

> Oh, how this sight doth delight my soul!   (vi 170)

That burlesque is followed by another, the clowns again, conjuring, shown as able to imagine no greater good to use their devils for, than to get wine enough to be drunk. The same point had been made in the last clowning scene (iv), where the clown falls a ready victim to Wagner's wit:

> The villain's out of service, and so hungry that I know he would give his soul to the devil for a shoulder of mutton, though it were blood-raw.
> *Clown.* Not so, neither; I had need to have it well roasted, and good sauce to it, if I pay so dear, I can tell you.
>
> (iv 8–12)

Wagner has his man: base mortals cannot will enough to use magic profitably. In this early scene the impact is in doubt: it either hints that Faustus is superior to ordinary mortals, or that he like them in a higher range, is also condemned to littleness, far from the aim he sets. By the end of scene vii, this latter insinuation must necessarily prevail. God's revenge comes before the end of the play, in the ever clearer ironic implication that He has kept man from deity by restricting his ability: has given him the imagination to desire greatness, but not the Will to achieve it. The urgency of the drama of Faustus lies in the protest against this inevitable torture for God's creature, man. If that *is* the constitution of the world, then this indeed is Hell, nor are we out of it, and Life is precisely the mixture of tragically doomed yet magnificent effort with mere mocking farce, that Marlowe makes his play.

The tragic concept of the play, then, is fully presented by the end of scene vii: scenes viii to xvii detail Faustus's achievements, his twenty-four years of power after Lucifer has left him to enjoy it. They are unquestionably disappointing scenes: in serious passages they lack either the tragic splendour or the intellectual insight of the scenes I have been discussing; when they turn to farce the critical comment is less biting, the sting is gone. Yet however feebly worked out it may be, the plan of the play continues intelligibly: the devil's agent provides Faustus with all he wants: knowledge, power, wealth – success in every direction, but always cheated of the supreme success, the consciousness of absolute greatness. It is absurd to pretend that these scenes represent a lowering of standard in Faustus's achievement, because for so long he trifles with vulgarity in Rome, or mere conjuring tricks in Germany; but they do reveal clearly the persistent weakness in Marlowe's work. A. P. Rossiter remarks that '[Kyd] is a true dramatist in his plotting; Marlowe, except in *Edward II*, is a dramatist only in his dramatic poetry – in great vistas of *mind*, rather than of the slipknot of fate or events pulling tight on human lives.'[12] This suggests the fault of these scenes: the story of Faustus's fame on earth has to be told, but its telling presents a dramatic problem which Marlowe has failed to solve. I have already said that it is impossible to show Faustus acquiring complete knowledge of the universe, for the obvious reason that Marlowe didn't possess it himself; so he simply states that Faustus did achieve it in two fine choruses and leaves the action to what can be shown, the power of human interference. The result is such a complete lack of balance, that the subject matter of the choruses is often forgotten, and Faustus accused of mere triviality in these scenes. The failure to invent a satisfactory organization for this matter apparently had its effect on Marlowe's writing; whether he actually wrote the scenes himself, or whether (as is usually argued, most recently by Sir Walter Greg) he left the major part of their composition to a collaborator, the conclusion is the same: that he was bored by them, and expended little effort or imaginative power on them. But Greg does not doubt that Marlowe planned them, and therefore their action and general significance are his responsibility.[13]

The Chorus before scene viii tells of Faustus's journey through the air, his discovery of all the secrets of astronomy; he is now turning to cosmography, and scene viii shows him at it, attending to a long lecture on the sights of Rome in which Mephostophilis

plays the part of a Renaissance Baedeker. He introduces the Feast
of St Peter and Faustus is delighted to witness it, repeating once
again the appetitive idea of his nature which I have stressed:

> Whilst I am here on earth let me be cloyed
> With all things that delight the heart of man.
>
> (viii 59–60)

But following that comes a suggestion of its weakness, as well as
a hint of all the trivial japing that is to follow:

> Thou knowst, within the compass of eight days
> We viewed the face of heaven, of earth, and hell:
> So high our dragons soared into the air
> That looking down the earth appeared to me
> No bigger than my hand in quantity:
> There did we view the kingdoms of the world,
> And what might please mine eye I there beheld:
> Then in this show let me an actor be,
> That this proud Pope may Faustus' cunning see.
>
> (viii 69–77)

Primarily, Faustus is expressing a desire to turn from contemplation to action, but he expressly states his feeling of the farcical
smallness of human existence (Mephostophilis understands him
as wishing to 'dash the pride of this solemnity'); and his 'action'
demonstrates this in practical joking at the Pope's expense. But
not at once, as our familiarity with the earlier truncated text
suggests: he first interferes seriously, but with a seriousness
belonging with the protestant polemical moralities such as Bale's,
Lindsay's or *The Conflict of Conscience*. He rescues the fallen anti-
Pope Bruno, with more than a hint that the gentleman was
Lutheran, or at least nationalist-protestant in sympathy. There
follows the farce he envisaged in the speech I quoted above, a
scene very tedious to us though not, it seems, to the Elizabethans:
familiar though the performance was, mocking the Pope seems
to have retained the thrill of permitted blasphemy, still to have
released the emotion of forbidden joys in kicking the until so
recently supreme Man, the head of the Catholic Church. But
vulgar in a sense it still is, and if Faustus is mocking his own

conception, the greatness of Man, the clowns re-appear to mock *him*, stealing a goblet from a more common vintner than the chief priest.

Scene xi returns to Germany, to present Faustus at last as renowned for knowledge and power as he wished, admired by his emperor and his fellow citizens and demonstrating his talents in a series of tricks and jokes which again end in clownage, literally in horseplay. Once indeed, Faustus comes out from this to make an explicit statement of his frustration and despair, but the lines are neither impressive nor revealing (xv 21–6).

With the opening of scene xviii (for which no chorus is needed) the wheel has gone full circle: Faustus is back at Wittenberg with his students, and as the twenty-four years draw to their end, the full drama reasserts itself. Faustus's last effort at achieving admiration, is to offer his scholars anything they please; they choose – and Marlowe offers no suggestion of unscholarly inappropriateness – they choose to see Helen of Troy. With the entry of the Old Man, despair returns and Faustus's tragic dilemma takes on an extra dimension: it is here that it becomes most vitally important not to over-simplify the drama of ideas, the vista of mind, if the meaning as well as the mood of the final tragedy is to be understood. The Old Man asserts at length a Christian criticism of Faustus's behaviour: a dichotomy of soul and body that Faustus has never admitted. Commenting on the raising of Helen, he says:

> Though thou hast now offended like a man,
> Do not persever in it like a devil.
> Yet, yet, thou hast an amiable soul
> If sin by custom grow not into nature;   (xviii 41–4)

Faustus does not comment on this argument, but consciousness of his own failure causes him in panic to turn to the Old Man's offer of mercy, of resignation to a power greater than himself. The Old Man has implied that there is still hope, that irretrievable damnation (represented by Helen, the supreme satisfaction of the appetite for beauty) has not yet been achieved. Faustus is torn

between despair equals repentance, and despair equals acknow-
ledgement of Hell triumphant:

> I do repent, and yet I do despair:
> Hell strives with grace for conquest in my breast.
>
> (xviii 71–2)

But the peculiar predicament which I have stressed and which
the Old Man, representing orthodox Christianity, ignores, is at
once brought out with the appearance of Mephostophilis: the
morality is still inverted, there are still rewards and punishments
in Faustus's Hell:

> Thou traitor Faustus, I arrest thy soul
> For disobedience to my sovereign lord:
> Revolt, or I'll in piecemeal tear thy flesh.
>
> (xviii 74–6)

And for the last time, Faustus revolts, expressly renews his bond
with Lucifer, and makes his final exertion of resolution for his
scholars' choice, Helen of Troy.

> One thing, good servant, let me crave of thee
> To glut the longing of my heart's desire;
> That I may have unto my paramour
> That heavenly Helen which I saw of late,
> Whose sweet embracings may extinguish clear
> Those thoughts that do dissuade me from my vow,
> And keep the oath I made to Lucifer.   (xviii 90–6)

Faustus's sin has been carried to the point at which he must make
a final choice between Heaven and Hell, and he makes it deliberately for Hell, as the Old Man (who watches him make love to
Helen) clearly states. But they see the act in different lights: to
the Old Man, Helen is the supreme temptation; to Faustus she is
the supreme expression of the appetitive Will. In choosing her
he commits his final negation of the idea of service to a God, to
the whole Elizabethan conception of the proper relation of
appetite to intellect, of right order. Faustus's appeal to Helen is
primarily moral, not an aesthetic escape from the moral. Nine-
tenths of his consciousness is fear and failure; reason and ex-

perience deny the validity of his appetitive Will, but at the last it is not to reason and humility he resorts, not even to that that his scholars invite him, but to Helen. Never before in the play does Marlowe make the opposition so explicit; the Old Man's theological conception of coition with the devil as the unforgivable sin, is shadowy; Faustus makes the climax of his fortunes a moral assertion beside which the theological looks as trivial as it is meant to be. And we should be prepared therefore to see his final speech not just as an emotional predicament, but as his ultimate moral tragedy.

Once again Marlowe caps Faustus's great moment with a suggestion of irony, of an impotent fly beating itself to death against a window pane: first the Old Man proves himself immune to the danger from devilish torture which has become a more and more immediate threat to Faustus, and then the Infernal Trinity take up their stations for the catastrophe. Mephostophilis sums up Faustus's position:

Fond worldling, now his heart-blood dries with grief,
His conscience kills it, and his labouring brain
Begets a world of idle fantasies
To overreach the devil, but all in vain:
His store of pleasures must be sauced with pain.

(xix 12–16)

God might have said the same thing. The exultant devils belittle Faustus's attempt to be their master; he cannot overreach them, cannot be as great as Lucifer. The re-entry of Faustus does not immediately re-assert his greatness, but rather detaches us from the struggle of Titans for a brief sense of normality, of teacher amongst his students. When asked why he didn't repent, he states again the simple idea of physical punishment:

Oft have I thought to have done so; but the devil threatened to tear me in pieces if I named God, to fetch me body and soul if I once gave ear to divinity; and now 'tis too late. (xix 71–3).

The complete absence in this prose scene of any profound suggestion, any poetic conception of the issues, of the reality of

God and devil, is well-judged: the passions are quieted, the audience lulled before the vast spectacle of eye and ear is built up.

The scholars leave, and Mephostophilis has his last degrading word, hinting that after all it was temptation to which Faustus succumbed:

> 'Twas I, that when thou wert i' the way to heaven,
> Dammed up thy passage; when thou tookst the book
> To view the scriptures, then I turned the leaves
> And led thine eye.   (xix 93–6)

Faustus remains silent, the Angels pronounce his doom, and introduce the visions of Heaven and Hell that remain with him if not with the audience till the end. Faustus, left alone, is at last fully conscious of his failure, of what he has lost as well as what he has failed to gain. But his predicament is not the simple one of a man in his last hour, knowing his fate: Faustus is not the simple Morality figure caught between Heaven and Hell; his last struggle is still between Heaven, his Hell, and his awareness of his own failure to reach either. When again he turns to Heaven in desperate appeal, he is caught back by the devils who exact the penalty for naming of his Christ:

> See see where Christ's blood streams in the firmament!
> One drop would save my soul, half a drop. Ah my Christ! –
> Rend not my heart for naming of my Christ.   (xix 146–8)

For the last time Faustus flirts with repentance: but it is something more than flirtation. The vividness of his perception of Christ's propitiatory sacrifice, and the corresponding intimacy of his address, 'Ah my Christ', bring what I have called the other ethos momentarily into full focus.[14] It seems that Faustus is finally able to envisage accepting God's forgiveness, and therefore God's right as well as his power to execute judgment. For the second time in the play, Marlowe enters an idea of Christianity that might have a meaning, not his usual satiric version. But at either level of experience it is still rejected: Faustus cannot repent because his mind is directed at independence still; or he cannot repent because when he mentions Christ the devils start to tear his heart; and as he offers to repeat his appeal for mercy, torture turns it to Lucifer instead of Christ, and the vision changes:

> Yet will I call on him: oh, spare me Lucifer! –
> Where is it now? 'Tis gone.   (xix 149–50)

In the end Faustus does despair, the devil he has constantly feared tears him to pieces, and the scholars draw back the curtain to reveal the gory mess that was 'admirèd man'. But, as with *Tamburlaine*, inevitable death does not make a tragedy. *Tamburlaine* is not tragic, *Faustus* is; and the difference lies in Faustus's tortured awareness that it should have been otherwise. Had his Will been what he felt it to be, he would have been triumphant, independent of angels and devils; he would have realized his supreme urge to self-originated power, and Heaven and Hell remained mere fables. But as Faustus fails, greatness as Man imagines it can only remain outside human power, must reside in superhuman God and Devil; and so in the end, it is extinction not mercy that Faustus craves:

> O soul, be changed to little water-drops
> And fall into the ocean, ne'er be found.   (xix 185–6)

That is not a Christian conclusion; at its tragic end as throughout its length, Marlowe's Morality is inverted; there are still two Hells, Lucifer's and Faustus's. But in the end, it would seem, Faustus has become fully conscious of Heaven as well. If so, he still cannot or will not accept it: it stands for a way of life he has rejected as unworthy of him; but it happens to be the one God insists upon. Faustus becomes aware, not only that he is wrong, but that the power of God is to have made man desiring a greatness he cannot achieve: that is the constant bitter irony that I have noted throughout the play – man's nature is in direct opposition to his fate. Faustus is the greatest of Marlowe's aspiring heroes in that his consciousness and his achievements are greater even than Tamburlaine's; he alone is of fully tragic stature, because only here does Marlowe match his imaginative conception of Man triumphant with a full awareness of Man the feeble and incompetent (in *Edward II* it is Man triumphant that is lacking). He states it both as a bitter and farcical irony, and as a magnificent protest against the creator of this dual nature, his cruel God in whose mouth the word love is the last and greatest mockery. I have already compared Marlowe with Blake in his idea of Hell: in the attitude to life adumbrated by the fate of Faustus, he is perhaps nearest to Ibsen, whose heroes' tragic sense also is opposed by an ironic and bitter awareness of futility.

There may seem, then, to be a consistency in Marlowe's attitude to the question of man's place in the universe, the question which forms the dramatic core of *Doctor Faustus*. But the attitude is not precisely that of his other plays. Tamburlaine is not obliged to submit to a world order which rejects his aspiration (or at least, not decidedly so). The Jew of Malta and the Guise are: the supporters of order have the last word and therefore, it would seem, Marlowe's approval in their triumph. In neither case, however, is that approval at all certain; he enlarges his exultant Vices beyond the point at which they can just be dismissed with easy approval, but he does not elucidate the implied contradiction. That is what, I think, he sets out to do in *Doctor Faustus*, where the ideas of individual freedom or subjection are presented in direct conflict. Faustus, as a Tamburlainish hero, still predominates; but there are already implications that Marlowe doubts his right to do so. There are indications as Greg points out that the last scene may have undergone revisions of which we have no clear idea: in the revision Greg suspects, from more formal Morality to the direct tragic speech we know, and certainly in the final removal of the Morality machinery in the 1604 text, there is a reduction of the tragic certainty of the conclusion. The more the Morality trappings are removed, the more Faustus is reduced towards a merely pathetic individual and deprived of the general implication of inevitable moral tragedy the play has suggested. As it stands, there are (as I have said) hints of a submission to a Divine Love that *is* compatible with human dignity. The implication is slight and obscure, and Faustus turns from it to his desire for dissolution. But the ironic emphasis that I have noted on man's inadequacy, and these suggestions of alterations in scene xix, with the development of a third term to Faustus's conflict, a credible ethic of Orthodox Christianity, all suggest that if in *Faustus* Marlowe achieved his clearest statement of his ideas, he was already losing confidence in them. *Edward II* does not 'answer' *Doctor Faustus*; rather it evades the issue altogether, but its final assertion of political Order has a conviction not apparent in any of Marlowe's earlier work. It echoes a principle accepted without serious question throughout the play; the interest is therefore largely focussed on Edward's individual weakness, his inability to conform to the moral order. It is remarkably well composed, but there is a sense of smallness, of contraction, from Marlowe's earlier work. The stature of *Doctor Faustus* is always greater, though its organization is cruder; and the greatness lies in the consistency of Marlowe's attention to a greater matter; to a moral, and not merely an individual, tragedy.

SOURCE: *Cambridge Journal*, v (1951–2).

NOTES

1. Here and in the final paragraph I am indebted to the criticisms of Dr C. Leech.

2. *Scrutiny*, June 1939.

3. Introduction to his parallel-text edition (1950).

4. In *Review of English Studies*, July 1943.

5. In *Modern Language Review*, Apr 1946.

6. See A. P. Rossiter, *English Drama from Early Times to the Elizabethans* (1950) pp. 157–9.

7. See Paul H. Kocher in *Modern Philology*, Aug 1940.

8. See E. M. Butler, *Ritual Magic* (1949).

9. See *A Select Collection of Old English Plays*, ed. R. Dodsley and W. C. Hazlitt, 15 vols. (1874–6) vi.

10. *Nichomachean Ethics*, iv iii.

11. See B. Tapper in *Studies in Philology*, Apr 1930.

12. *English Drama*, p. 160.

13. Since writing this essay, Nicholas Brooke has proposed a very different way of regarding the structure of *Doctor Faustus*. See his 'Marlowe the Dramatist', in *Stratford-upon-Avon Studies 9: Elizabethan Theatre*, ed. J. R. Brown and Bernard Harris (1966) pp. 86–105. J. J.

14. I owe this observation to Mr E. A. Horsman.

Harry Levin

SCIENCE WITHOUT CONSCIENCE
(1952)

KNOWLEDGE is power. The realization was Bacon's: *Nam et ipsa scientia potestas est.* But power corrupts, and Bacon – the Cambridge alumnus taking all knowledge for his province, the Lord Chancellor found guilty of corruption – demonstrated the incompatibility of the serpent and the dove. Hence the parable of Baldock in *Edward II*, the prodigal scholar corrupted by worldliness, was not uniquely applicable to Marlowe; given full scope, it could and did become an allegory for his century. Earlier in that century, Rabelais had voiced its self-conscious expansiveness in the famous letter purporting to have been written by the allegorical giant, Gargantua, to his even more gigantic son, Pantagruel. More than a father's thoughtful advice to a student, this was a medieval salute to the great instauration of humanism. Hailing the revival of the classics and the investigations into nature, it was charged with awareness of their potentialities for good – and likewise for evil. If the late invention of printing was an angelic inspiration, obviously gunpowder had been invented by diabolical suggestion. And Gargantua's eulogy is tempered with the warning that *science sans conscience* – science without conscience, or perhaps we should say 'without consciousness' – is but the ruin of the soul (II viii). There were lurking dangers, as well as enriching adventures, in this brave new world which was opening up before the European imagination. Yet we justifiably stress the excitement, the exploration, the experience, which no man has more fully personified than Leonardo da Vinci. The secret of power, for that powerful genius, was a desire for flight: *La potenza è solo un desiderio di fuga.* Along with his vision of a flying machine, his paintings and anatomical researches and projects of military engineering, his city planning and stage designing and endlessly fascinating notations, the artist-engineer momentarily considered the possibility of necromancy. That was a delusion, he duly noted; but if only it were possible, how much it could so easily obtain! Riches, conquest, ability to fly, everything, except escape from death.

Magic was originally the appurtenance of religion; and when religion cast it off, it subsisted in the outer darkness, along with appetites and curiosities which religion proscribed. Between magic and science, as we have more recently come to know it, the lines were not yet sharply drawn. Magicians, however, were rigorously distinguished on the basis of whether they practised white or black magic: whether they sought to control the elements through natural philosophy and supernatural wisdom, as Prospero does in *The Tempest*, or whether they trafficked with the devil and conjured up the dead, through witchcraft and particularly necromancy, as does Marlowe's ultimate protagonist. The legendary Faust was neither a creature of folklore, such as Pantagruel, nor a figure from history, such as Leonardo. His legend emerged from the flickering limbo between the admonitions of the Middle Ages and the aspirations of the Renaissance. More precisely, he was begotten by the Reformation out of the Teutonic north, like his fellow-unbeliever, the Wandering Jew, and quite unlike his Mediterranean contemporary, Don Juan, whose destiny ran so strangely parallel. That Faustus meant 'well-omened' in Latin was a paradox which did not pass unobserved. The disreputable name and vagabond career of an actual Georg Faust can be traced from one German university to another, sceptically pursued by accusations of charlatanism and suspicions of pederasty. It is rumoured that he enlivened the pedagogical technique of his classical lectures by the necromantic practice of bringing Homeric shades to life. Marlowe, to whom this feat had its perspicuous appeal, seems to class it with the so-called shadows of Cornelius Agrippa, and glories in having resurrected blind Homer to sing for his hero. More remotely Simon Magus, a charlatan hovering on the fringes of early Christianity, who was accompanied by a certain Helen and was killed in a desperate effort to fly, seems to have some bearing upon this story; and there was the Greek precedent of Empedocles, the philosopher who disappeared into Aetna. Doctor Faust lost his original Christian name and got another by being confounded with Johann Fust, one of the earliest printers and therefore the practitioner of an art still held by many to be ambiguous. The sinister repute of the prototype, thereby enhanced with an aura of Titanism, projected the shadowy image of a latter-day Prometheus, bearing gifts which were dangerous for mankind.

It is not clear how Faust gained his reputation as a god-defier, unless it be through his pretensions as a necromancer. He seems to have ended by mysteriously disappearing, leaving behind him a cloud of sensational rumours as to his 'damnable life, and deserued death', his 'Epicurish' habits and Atheistical blasphemies. These were gathered together a generation later, in 1587, and widely circulated by a pious printer, Johann Spies, through the solemnly edifying and crudely jocular redaction known as his *Faustbuch*. In 1592 it was published in the free English translation that Marlowe so closely depends upon for his play. The translator, who seems to have been more of a humanist than was the didactic Lutheran author of the chapbook, takes advantage of Faust's travels to expatiate upon Italian topography. Marlowe follows his guidance through the ruins of Rome, and the guide is responsible for such atmospheric details as the mention of Vergil's tomb. Moreover, he contributed an epithet which, though Marlowe makes no use of it, cannot have failed to affect his impression: at the University of Padua Faust registers as 'the vnsatiable Speculator'. The English *Faustbook* is at once a cautionary tale and a book of marvels, a jest-book and a theological tract. Its chapters, anecdotal and homiletic, are roughly grouped in three sections. The first deals, extensively and systematically, with the diabolical pact; the second, rather more discursively, with Faust's speculations and journeys, and the third, after a series of miscellaneous jests, with 'his fearfull and pitiful ende'. Here, amid much that was not germane to his purpose, was a vehicle for the highest and purest expression of Marlowe's *libido sciendi*, a speculative sublimation of Tamburlaine's or the Guise's insatiable thirst – a hero who, 'taking to him the wings of an Eagle, thought to flie ouer the whole world, and to know the secrets of heauen and earth'.

This desire for flight transcended the pomp and dalliance of those preceding plays which Marlowe all but repudiates at the outset of *The Tragicall History of Doctor Faustus*. Yet, although intellectual curiosity is now the activating force, it cannot finally be detached from the secondary motives that entrammel it, the will to power and the appetite for sensation. The interrelationship of thought and action is the major problem for Doctor Faustus, as it can become for Shakespeare's heroes. It is not just a historical coincidence that Hamlet and Faustus were both alumni of Martin Luther's university, Wittenberg; in other words, their consciences had been disciplined within the *feste Burg* of Protestantism. There, where Luther threw his inkstand at the devil, Faustus comes to terms with the adversary; yet, when Faustus laments his devil's bargain, he blames his alma mater: 'O would I had neuer seene *Wertenberge*, neuer read booke' (xix 45–6). When he appears at court and is scoffed at by a courtier, he displays his professional pride by humbling the scoffer and bidding him thereafter 'speake well of Scholers' (xii 112). The cry of the triumphant scholastic disputant, *sic probo*, must ring through a wider arena than the schools (ii 2); the intellect must prove itself by mastering life at large. Scholarship is rewarded by no greater satisfactions for Faustus than sovereignty is for Edward and Tamburlaine, or conspiracy for Barabas and the Guise. What is worse, the notorious alternative to that straight and narrow path is the primrose path to the everlasting bonfire. The formal pattern of Marlovian drama tends to be increasingly traditional. Having created the tragedy of ambition with *Tamburlaine* and put his stamp on the tragedy of revenge with *The Jew of Malta* and tried his hand at the chronicle with *Edward II*, Marlowe reverts to the morality play with *Doctor Faustus*. But within the latter, the most general of forms, he elaborates the most personal of themes – an Atheist's tragedy, an Epicurean's testament, a mirror for University Wits.

The prologue, after its apology for not presenting matters of

love and war, presents character in biographical synopsis and
plot in ethical perspective. The universal hero of this morality
will not be Everyman; he will be a particular private individual;
and Marlowe highlights his attainment, as usual, by emphasizing
the lowness of his birth. Nevertheless, the Muse intends to 'vaunt
his heauenly verse' upon this theme (Prol. 6); and, passing over
the unexpected gender of the personal pronoun, our attention is
directed by the adjective to the vertical scale of the drama. Its co-
ordinates will be nothing less than heaven and hell; while on the
horizontal plane, at opposite sides of the stage, the conflict of
conscience will be externalized by the debate between Good and
Evil Angels; and even as the heroes of the moralities traverse a
circle of symbolic mansions, so Faustus will pay his respects to
personifications of the World, the Flesh, and the Devil. As his
academic career proceeds, it is metaphorically described. Literally,
a scholar's name was registered in the Cambridge Grace-Book
when he took a degree, and the quibble on the word 'grace' serves
to bring out its non-theological overtones:

> So soone hee profites in Diuinitie,
> The fruitfull plot of Scholerisme grac't,
> That shortly he was grac't with Doctors name,
> Excelling all, whose sweete delight disputes
> In heauenly matters of *Theologie*,
> Till swolne with cunning, of a selfe conceit,
> His waxen wings did mount aboue his reach,
> And melting heauens conspirde his ouerthrow.
>   (Prol. 15–22)

The last three words, a Marlovian idiom for the counteraction of
antagonistic forces, recur in *Tamburlaine* (ed. C. F. Tucker
Brooke, l. 1455). In *Tamburlaine* the emblem of tragic pride is
Phaëthon, rashly attempting to drive the fiery chariot of the sun.
In *Doctor Faustus* it is Icarus, whose 'wings of waxe' had already
figured as an omen portending the tragedy of Dido (*Dido,
Queen of Carthage*, l. 1651). In each instance, it is a question of
flying too high, of falling from the loftiest height imaginable, of
seeking illumination and finding more heat than light. Faustus
prefers, like the Guise, to seek what flies beyond his reach; he is

accused, in the augmented version, of trying 'to ouer-reach the Diuell' (xix 15). After the prologue speaks of overreaching, the emphasis shifts from the heavenly to the hellish – and the phrase 'diuelish exercise' is borrowed straight from the *Faustbook*. With this shift, the rising verse subsides toward a dying fall, and the ethereal image of flight gives way to grosser images of appetite. These were anticipated by 'swolne with cunning' and will be continued by allusions to *hubris* in terms of overeating. 'Negromancy' is given unwonted stress by its overhanging monosyllable, and 'blisse' reminds us that magic is to Faustus what a crown was to Tamburlaine, gold to Barabas, or companionship to Edward:

> For falling to a diuelish exercise,
> And glutted now with learnings golden gifts,
> He surffets vpon cursed Negromancy.
> Nothing so sweete as magicke is to him
> Which he preferres before his chiefest blisse,
> And this the man that in his study sits.
>
> (Prol. 23–8)

The speaker of these lines may well be Wagner, the famulus, half-servant and half-disciple, since it is indicated that he reappears to speak the later choruses. It is a long way from his moral earnestness to the cynical tone of Machiavel introducing Barabas. But, as with *The Jew of Malta*, this introduction is completed by drawing aside the curtain to the inner stage – which in Elizabethan theatrical usage, was appropriately called 'the study'. The protagonist is then discovered in his literal study, the little room, the monkish cell that comprises his library and laboratory. His profession is not usury but divinity, which subsumes all the others, permitting him to 'leuell at the end of euery Art' (i 4). Thus his introductory soliloquy is no mere reckoning of accounts but an inventory of the Renaissance mind. Cornelius Agrippa, that disillusioned experimentalist, whose namesake plays an appropriate role in Marlowe's tragedy, had latterly made such a survey in his treatise *Of the Vanity and Uncertainty of Arts and Sciences*. Goethe's nineteenth-century Faust could do no better than bring up to date those *Fakultätswissenschaften*, those categories of learning which Marlowe now passes in review: *Philosophie, Juristerei, Medizin, Theologie*. Whatever the contemplative life can teach, his Doctor Faustus has learned. He has mastered the liberal arts, the learned professions, and the experimental sciences of his day. To be or not to be, *'on cai me on'* (i 12) – the existential dilemma seems to him insoluble; consequently, he is ready to take his leave of philosophy. Against Aristotle he quotes the axiom of Ramus that the end of logic is 'to dispute well' (i 8); and, since rhetoric itself is a means toward some further end, it does not gratify Faustus' *libido sciendi*. As for jurisprudence and medicine, though they help man to exist, they do not justify his existence. The 'bodies health' is scarcely a fulfilment of *libido sentiendi*; whereas *libido dominandi* requires more than a 'case of paltry legacies' (i 30). Yet the Roman statute that Faustus cites at random does not seem to be wholly irrelevant; it has to do with the ways and means whereby a father may disinherit a son.

Saying farewell to the other disciplines, he turns again for a moment to theology, picks up Saint Jerome's Bible, reads from the Vulgate, and comments upon two texts:

> *Stipendium peccati mors est*: ha, *Stipendium*, &c.
> The reward of sinne is death: thats hard.
> *Si peccasse negamus, fallimur, & nulla est in nobis veritas.*
> If we say that we haue no sinne,
> We deceiue our selues, and theres no truth in vs.
>
> (i 39–43)

This latter text, quoted from the very epistle of Saint John (1 i 8) that goes on to warn against worldly lust and vainglory, gives Faustus an ominous pause. Tentatively he balances it against the stern quotation from Saint Paul's epistle to the Romans (VI 23). All men are sinners, ergo all men are mortal, he syllogizes with a sophistical shrug: *'Che sera, sera'* (i 46). Such was Edward's sentiment, spoken in English rather than Italian, when he accepted his fate: 'That shalbe, shalbe' (line 1962). Faustus, whether in Calvinistic or Epicurean fatalism, is anxious to say 'Diuinitie,

adieu', to embrace the 'Metaphisickes of Magicians', and to
replace the Scriptures with 'Negromantike bookes' (i 47–9)
which, by the subversion of an adjective heretofore consecrated
to religious objects, now seem 'heauenly'. Faustus' references to
his magical art, like Prospero's, sustain the additional ambiguity
of referring us back to the author's literary artistry, to the 'lines'
and 'sceanes', the 'letters and characters' in which Marlowe himself set the end of scholarism. As a scholar-poet, Marlowe had
been taught that the aim of poetry was profit and delight. Is it the
scholar, the conjurer, or the artist who can make good this boast?

> O what a world of profit and delight,
> Of power, of honor, of omnipotence
> Is promised to the studious Artizan?
> All things that mooue betweene the quiet poles
> Shalbe at my commaund, Emperours and Kings
> Are but obeyd in their seuerall prouinces:
> Nor can they raise the winde, or rend the cloudes:
> But his dominion that exceedes in this,
> Stretcheth as farre as doth the minde of man.
> A sound Magician is a mighty god.
>
> (i 52–61)

The last line improves with the variant ending, more meaningful
in the context, 'Demi-god'. Marlowe's protagonists do not
simply out-Herod their fellow mortals; they act out their
invidious self-comparisons with the gods; and, from Aeneas to
Faustus, they see themselves deified in one manner or another.
Faustus' Evil Angel holds out the hope that he will be 'on earth
as *Ioue* is in the skie' (i 75). Ignoring his Good Angel and the
threat of 'Gods heauy wrath' (i 71), Faustus readily amplifies
the enticement, which far outdoes all other Marlovian seductions.
He envisages a hierarchy of spirits, answering his queries and
serving his whims:

> Ile haue them flye to *India* for gold,
> Ransacke the Ocean for orient pearle,
> And search all corners of the new found world
> For pleasant fruites and princely delicates. (i 81–4)

The panorama extends across the western hemisphere, where they are subsequently pictured as Indians, obeying their Spanish masters and conveying

> from *America* the golden fleece,
> That yearely stuffes olde *Philips* treasury.   (i 130–1)

But Marlowe's wandering fantasy comes home with an anti-climactic suggestion, which incidentally reveals the Canterbury boy who was sent to Corpus Christi on a scholarship:

> Ile haue them fill the publike schooles with silk,
> Wherewith the students shalbe brauely clad. (i 89–90)

Faustus has his own Rosencrantz and Guildenstern in the two adepts of the black art, Valdes and Cornelius. Abetted by their instructions, he repairs at midnight to a solitary grove, where he draws a magic circle and abjures the Trinity. Just as Sir Walter Ralegh's friends were alleged to have spelled the name of God backwards, so here the name of Jehovah is

> Forward and backward anagrammatiz'd.   (iii 9)

Blasphemy has its irreligious observances, and this is the dread ceremonial of the Black Mass. The play itself is almost macaronic in its frequent scholarly lapses into Latinity, and the incantation is deliberately heightened by what Faustus calls 'heauenly words' (iii 29) and the Clown will call 'Dutch fustian' (A iv 74). Though the demon makes his due appearance, first as a dragon and then in the garb of a friar, he does not appear as the devil's pleni-potentiary; he has responded to the conjuration, so he explains in scholastic terminology, because Faustus has jeopardized his soul. It is the first of Faustus' disappointments, and is immediately solaced by the delight that he takes in his personal relation with Mephostophilis. Again, even more emphatically than with Gaveston, the name itself is something to conjure with, all the more potent because it accounts for half a line of blank verse:

> Had I as many soules as there be starres,
> Ide giue them al for *Mephastophilis*.   (iii 104–5)

Marlowe's protagonists tend to isolate themselves; yet they also tend . . . to ally themselves with some deuteragonist. Edward had his evil genius in Gaveston, Barabas his demonic familiar in Ithamore; and Faustus has in Mephostophilis an alter ego who is both a demon and a Damon. The man has an extraordinary affection for the spirit, the spirit a mysterious attraction to the man. Mephostophilis should not be confused with Goethe's sardonic nay-sayer; neither is he an operatic villain nor a Satanic tempter. He proffers no tempting speeches and dangles no enticements; Faustus tempts himself, and succumbs to temptations which he alone has conjured up. What Mephostophilis really approximates, with his subtle insight and his profound sympathy, is the characterization of Porfiry, the examining magistrate in Dostoevsky's *Crime and Punishment.*

The dialogues between Faustus and Mephostophilis resemble those cat-and-mouse interrogations, in which Porfiry teaches the would-be criminal, Raskolnikov, to accuse and convict himself. Faustus is especially curious about the prince of darkness, whose name once proclaimed him the bearer of light; who was once an angel 'most dearely lou'd of God', as Mephostophilis points out, but was thrown from heaven for his 'aspiring pride', the primordial tragic fault.

> And what are you that liue with *Lucifer?*   (iii 72)

Faustus asks. And Mephostophilis answers:

> Vnhappy spirits that fell with *Lucifer,*
> Conspir'd against our God with *Lucifer,*
> And are for euer damnd with *Lucifer.*   (iii 73–5)

The reiteration reminds us that Faustus' plight, or any other human predicament, is the outcome of that Miltonic struggle, that fall of the angels, that tragedy of tragedies which brought original sin and consequent suffering into the world. It is ironic, of course, that Faustus should be asking to be admitted into the company of the damned. But misery loves company, and Mephostophilis will warrant his own role by quoting the proverb in

Latin. The special poignance of the relationship lies in his fore-
knowledge, and his foresuffering. Once the sin is committed, he
cannot but hold the sinner to his unholy covenant. Faustus, with
a blithe humanistic pantheism, 'confounds hell in *Eliɀium*' (iii
62). He has no ear for Mephostophilis' heart-cry,

> Why this is hel, nor am I out of it,   (iii 78)

nor for his painfully explicit amplification,

> Hell hath no limits, nor is circumscrib'd
> In one selfe place, for where we are is hell . . .
> All places shall be hell that is not heauen.   (v 122–7)

Orcanes, the noble infidel in the second part of *Tamburlaine*,
used a similar expression to affirm a belief in a god who is not
circumscriptible. Nothing like this Marlovian conception is
hinted among the fundamentalist tenets of the *Faustbook*,
although Marlowe might have learned from Lucretius that during
out lifetime we undergo what is fabled to happen afterward in
Acheron (iii 978–9). Faustus is quite as unconcerned with
'heauen, and heauenly things' (v 21), when his Good Angel
commends them to him; and when his Evil Angel bids him
'thinke of honor and wealth' (v 22), he has no compunction in
to choosing the pomps of Satan. On condition that he be enabled
'liue in al voluptuousnesse' for twenty-four years (iii 94), and that
Mephostophilis obey his commands and reply to his inquiries,
Faustus is willing to sign a legal deed empowering Mephostophilis and Lucifer 'to fetch or carry the said Iohn Faustus body
and soule, flesh, bloud, or goods, into their habitation where-
soeuer' (v 109–11). When his blood congeals, after he has stabbed
his arm, he ignores the portent; and when it streams again, having
been heated with coals, it warns him to escape while there is time:
'*Homo fuge*' (v 77). Instead, he affixes his bloody signature with
a blasphemous mockery of the last words of Jesus, according to
the gospel of Saint John (xix 30): '*Consummatum est*.'

Mephostophilis does nothing to lure Faustus on; he suffers for
him, he sympathizes with him, above all he understands him; and,

through this understanding, we participate in the dramatic irony. Faustus persists in regarding his fiendish attendant as a sort of oriental slave of the lamp, and Mephostophilis ironically promises more than his temporary master has wit to ask. Some day, after one fashion or another, Faustus will be 'as great as *Lucifer*' (v 52) – he will arrive at the kind of ambiguous greatness that Fielding would attribute to Jonathan Wild. In the interim he shrugs:

> Come, I thinke hell's a fable.   (v 128)

To which the suffering spirit replies with the bitterest of all his ironies:

> I, thinke so still, till experience change thy minde.
>   (v 129)

For Faustus, even more than for Edward or Barabas, the fruit of experience is disillusionment. As soon as the contract is signed and sealed, he is eager to resolve ambiguities, to satisfy the cosmic questions that teem in his brain. He is keenly aware that there are more things in heaven and earth than the trivium and the quadrivium; but his discussions with Mephostophilis scarcely proceed beyond the elementary data of natural history and the unquestioned assumptions of Ptolemaic astronomy. 'Tush,' Faustus cries impatiently, 'these are fresh mens suppositions' (vi 55–6). To the more searching inquiry, 'Who made the world?' (vi 69) his interlocutor must perforce be silent, since fiends are interdicted from naming God. When various books of occult and pseudo-scientific lore are provided, Faustus nervously thumbs through the black-letter pages, only to realize that he has exchanged his soul for little more than the quiddities of Wittenberg: 'O thou art deceiued' (v 178). In his undeception he listens to the conflicting angels again, and again the Evil Angel outargues the Good. Faustus, at all events, is beginning to respect the grim silences of Mephostophilis. Now it becomes the latter's task to divert him, but each diversion turns out to be a snare and a delusion. Faustus, being 'wanton and lasciuious, . . . can not liue without a wife' (v 142–3). This demand is frustrated, as the *Faustbook* emphasizes, because marriage is a sacrament; whereas, for Mephostophilis, it is 'a ceremoniall toy' (v 151). The best that Mephostophilis can provide is equivocally diverting: '*a diuell drest like a woman, with fier workes*'.

There are more and more of these ghoulish antics, which always seem to end by intensifying the actual harshness of the situation. Faustus, prompted by the Good Angel for the nonce, inevitably breaks down and calls upon Christ. Thereupon – most terrifying shock of all – it is Lucifer who rises with Beelzebub, presumably through the trap from below the stage, to hold Faustus to the letter of their agreement. As a pastime and a confirmation of his unregenerate state, they witness together Lucifer's pageant of the Seven Deadly Sins, the *Walpurgisnacht* interlude at the midpoint of the play, a sight as pleasing to Faustus as Paradise was to Adam before the fall (vi 108–9). Marlowe, interpolating this quaint procession of gargoyles, harked back to a more deeply rooted medieval tradition than the 'hellish pastimes' of the *Faustbook* – to the earliest subject of the moralities, as well as the homilies of Chaucer and Langland. Marlowe's treatment, curiously enough, bears a closer resemblance to theirs than it does to the Renaissance triumph of Lucifera in *The Faerie Queene*. Pride is the inevitable leader, and the others follow as the night the day, parading the principal weaknesses of the flesh, brandishing their respective perquisites, and speaking their pieces in highly seasoned prose. Faustus must indeed be a hardened sinner to contemplate their grossness without revulsion. Though he has a greeting for each of them, it seems to be Gluttony that inspires his reaction: 'O this feedes my soule' (vi 170). This has been heralded when the prologue touched upon the theme of satiety, is resumed when Faustus is 'glutted' with a foretaste of what lies ahead (i 77), and will be rounded out in the final scene where he diagnoses his illness as 'a surffett of deadly sinne that hath damnd both body and soule' (xix 37–8). Perdition is the more awful for Mephostophilis because he has 'tasted the eternal ioyes of heauen' (iii 80). As for Faustus, he has candidly dedicated himself to carnal egoism:

The god thou seruest is thine owne appetite.   (v 11)

His quest for knowledge leads him to taste the fruit of the tree that shaded Adam and Eve, to savour the distinction between good and evil. From that point he abandons his disinterested pursuit – or, rather, he abandons himself to the distractions that Mephostophilis scatters along his ever more far-flung itinerary. His further adventures are calculated less to fulfil his boundless ambition than to palliate his disappointment, to make the most of a bad bargain.

The rest is hedonism. It is conveniently preluded by Wagner, as expository chorus, describing how Faustus, like Phaëthon and other reckless adventurers,

> Did mount himselfe to scale *Olympus* top,
> Being seated in a chariot burning bright.
>
> (Cho. 1, 4–5)

A characteristic accomplishment of the legendary Faust was aeromancy, the magical power of flight. Unlike his resurrections and pyrotechnics, this does not lend itself very effectively to theatrical presentation. Wagner narrates his aerial voyages 'to prooue *Cosmography*' (Ch. 1, 20), and Faustus himself discusses geography with Mephostophilis, pausing significantly over that Venetian temple which 'threats the starres with her aspiring toppe' (viii 18), and ultimately alighting at papal Rome. There the slapstick banquet at the Vatican, where they snatch food and drink away from the Pope and the Cardinal of Lorraine, is at best a satirical comment upon the blind mouths of the clergy, and at worst a callow manifestation of Elizabethan Catholic-baiting. But the pith of the episode is the ceremony of anathema, which definitively places Faustus under the most solemn ban of the Church. The dirge of malediction, the curse with bell, book, and candle, 'forward and backward' (ix 99), is the religious counterpart of the sacrilegious rite he performed by anagrammatizing the name of God. He and Mephostophilis retort by beating the Friars and scattering firecrackers. The episode has been considerably augmented along these lines by Marlowe's presumptive collaborator, who introduces an antipope named Bruno – possibly in honour of Giordano Bruno – condemned to the stake and rescued by Faustus and Mephostophilis in the guise of cardinals. But it is a peculiarly Marlovian twist, an antireligious fascination with ceremonial, which animates Tamburlaine's burning of the Koran as well as Faustus' celebration of the Black Mass, and culminates in the ritual of excommunication. Faustus is pledged, as was Barabas, to pull down Christian churches. From the negative commitment of his Atheism he moves on to the positive exploit of his Epicureanism, when we next see him at the court of the Holy Roman Emperor. There we first behold him exercising his distinctive gift of sciomancy, and raising – in a more or less elaborated dumb show – the shades of Alexander and his paramour, evidently the fabulous Thaïs.

It must be admitted that Faustus is more impressive as an Atheist than as an Epicurean. We might have expected more for the price he is paying, after his terrible renunciation, than the jaunty hocus-pocus that produces grapes out of season for a pregnant duchess or defrauds a horse dealer and fobs him off with a leg-pulling practical joke. Such conjuring tricks may be mildly amusing, but are they worthy of the inspiration or worth the sacrifice? Certainly not; and we ought to feel some incongruity between the monologues and the gestures, between the seemingly unlimited possibilities envisioned by Faustus' speeches and their all too concretely vulgar realization in the stage business. Putting ourselves in his position, we protest with Browning's *Paracelsus*, 'Had we means/Answering to our mind!' We probably feel the incongruity more than the Elizabethans did, for a number of reasons; and first of all, because we have lost their habit of accepting the limitations of the stage as the conventions of the theatre, of taking the word for the deed and the part for the whole. Suspending disbelief, in short, we ought to be more impressed than we usually are. Still, if we remain sceptical, we may remember that so was Marlowe; he is on record asserting that the prophets and saints of the Bible were so many jugglers. His refusal to believe in miracles may well have hindered him from making sorcery altogether credible in his plays – wherein, contrary to the custom of Shakespeare and his other contemporaries, there are no ghosts; except in *Doctor Faustus*, there are naturalistic explanations for seemingly supernatural interventions. This second consideration is neutralized by a third: whatever our doubts or Marlowe's, his audiences were convinced. His talent for lurid spectacle, supported by Henslowe's most elaborate properties, and by the intermittent discharge of squibs and crackers, undoubtedly gravelled the groundlings. A supernatural atmosphere was devised and sustained with such effectiveness that a veritable body of legends grew up around the performance of the play, most of them involving a personal appearance of the devil himself, who is temporarily mistaken for one of the capering devils of the tiring house.

Large allowances should be made for the mangled and encrusted form in which *Doctor Faustus* has survived. Its very popularity seems to have subjected it to an inordinate amount of cutting and gagging and all the other indignities that dramatic texts are heir to. It was not published until 1604, more than a decade after Marlowe's death; this first quarto and later editions based on it seem to represent an unauthorized abridgment. The quarto of 1616 and others deriving from it seem to stem independently from a fuller and more authoritative manuscript, upon which editors are inclined to place increasing weight. Unfortunately, neither one – nor the combination of both – is satisfactory. The 1616 text contains about half again as much material, and preserves the play in clearer and firmer structure; yet much of that construction is filled in by an inferior hand, and several important passages are omitted. These we know from the 1604 text, which is the one most frequently reprinted; and since it is so terse a condensation, it can be very handily performed; yet it is not devoid of extraneous matter, while some of its scenes are misplaced or unduly telescoped. The recent parallel edition of Sir Walter Greg does justice, at least, to the complexity of the problem. Moreover Sir Walter confirms, with his considerable authority, the tendency to push the dating ahead to the latest period in Marlowe's career. The argument for 1592, after the publication of the *Faustbook*, seems cogent – though it carries the surprising consequence of making *Doctor Faustus* the follower rather than the forerunner of Greene's *Friar Bacon and*

Friar Bungay. Even more perplexing is the enigma of Marlowe's collaboration. Not that there seems to be much disagreement about the identity of his collaborator, Samuel Rowley. But why should Rowley's clumsy journeywork eke out the greatest masterwork the English theatre had thus far seen? It seems unlikely, from what Kyd tells us, that Marlowe could have worked in harness with Rowley. Was his *Doctor Faustus*, then, a fragment like *Hero and Leander*? If so, was it left unfinished at his death, or had he dropped it somewhere along the wayside? All too understandably, he might have found his task an uncomfortable one. Was he inhibited from finishing it by some psychological complication, or by some more instrumental reason equally inscrutable at this date?

In spite of its uneven texture, we must view the play as a whole, since its total design is not less meaningful than its purple passages, and textual disintegration will not improve its fragmentary condition. Critics have questioned the authenticity of the comic scenes, on the grounds that Marlowe lacked a sense of humour – a premise which they support by begging the question, and denying his authorship whenever they are confronted with a humorous speech. Marlowe's laughter, to be sure, is not Shakespeare's; yet, as *The Jew of Malta* must have shown us, his wit has a salt of its own. Furthermore, Elizabethan tragedy delegates a conventional function to comedy, and *Doctor Faustus* need be no exception to that rule. Thus Wagner, the clever servant, mimics his master in chopping logic with the other students. He remarks, immediately after the scene in which Faustus has bargained with Mephostophilis, that the Clown 'would giue his soule to the Diuel for a shoulder of mutton' (iv 9–10). Similarly, the hostlers, Rafe and Robin, burlesque the conjuration of Doctor Faustus; their scene, which is out of place in the 1604 text, should come after the scene in which Mephostophilis provides Faustus with conjuring books; for Robin, it appears, has just stolen one of those potent volumes; and Rafe, with its help, expects to seduce Nan Spit the kitchen maid, even as Faustus' necromancy will capture the love of Helen of Troy. Before this comedy team joined Marlowe's dramatis personae,

Rafe and Robin had parts in Lyly's *Galatea*, where they played their pranks with alchemist's equipment; but there they had little connection with the main plot, while their roles are intrinsic — if not essential — to *Doctor Faustus*. And while the comic underplot reduces the main plot of Marlowe's drama to absurdity, the overplot is luminously adumbrated — sketched, as it were, in lightning against a black sky. It is the adumbration of Faustus' downfall, glimpsed in the aboriginal tragedy of the fallen archangel. Victor Hugo's formulation for western art, the inter-mixture of grotesque and sublime, could not adduce a more pertinent example.

How grandly all is planned! (*Wie gross ist alles angelegt!*) Goethe's appreciation of *Doctor Faustus*, as recorded by Crabb Robinson, must refer primarily to its conception. In its execution, it adheres somewhat too faithfully to the undramatic sequence of the *Faustbook*. The opening scenes are necessarily explicit in underlining the conditions of the pact; but, as a result, the play is half over before the document is ratified and Faustus can start out upon his adventures. Out of the 1,485 lines in the 1604 Quarto, 791 have gone by before he leaves Wittenberg for Rome. The 1616 Quarto augments the ensuing scenes and links them loosely together with allusions to the papal-imperial struggle, which Rowley apparently gathered from Foxe's *Book of Martyrs*. But both versions move anticlimactically from the Pope and the Emperor to the Duchess of Vanholt and the trivial incident of the grapes. This, in the text of 1604, concludes a scene which commences at the Emperor's court and includes midway the buffooneries of the Horse-Courser. Faustus is well advised to pause for an instant and meditate on the restless course of time. Such drastic telescoping seems to indicate an acting version constrained by the narrow resources of a touring com-pany. It is divided into fourteen continuous scenes, whereas the text of 1616 is subdivided into twenty scenes which editors distribute among five Acts. Viewed in outline, the plot is per-fectly classical in its climactic ascent: the conjuration of Mephos-tophilis, the compact with Lucifer, the travels to Rome and else-where, the necromantic evocations, and the catastrophe. Faustus' rise is harder to triangulate than the careers of Marlowe's other heroes, because each worldly step is a spiritual lapse. Examined more technically, the play has a strong beginning and an even stronger end; but its middle section, whether we abridge it or bombast it out with Rowley's hackwork, is unquestionably weak. The structural weakness, however, corresponds to the anticlimax of the parable; it lays bare the gap between promise and fruition, between the bright hopes of the initial scene and the abysmal consequences of the last. 'As the outline of the character is grand and daring,' William Hazlitt has said, 'the execution is abrupt and fearful.'

At the request of the Emperor, Faustus has evoked no less a shade than Alexander the Great, archetype of *libido dominandi*. For the edification and pleasure of the scholars, when he returns to the university, he evokes the archetype of *libido sentiendi*. Among all the beautiful women who ever lived, they have agreed that Helen of Troy is peerless, 'the pride of natures workes', the 'onely Paragon of excellence' (xviii 33–4). Disputation is silenced when she makes her fugitive appearance in their incongruous quarters. Since the days when Marlowe studied the classics at Cambridge, Helen had been his cynosure of comparison – comparison with Zenocrate in *Tamburlaine* and even with Gaveston in *Edward II*. But metaphor is never enough for Marlowe; he must have the real thing, beauty in person; in *The Jew of Malta* policy was personified by Machiavelli himself; and the consummation of Faustus' desire – or the consolation, at any rate, for his regret – is to have Helen as his paramour. Mephostophilis produces her 'in twinckling of an eie' (xviii 98); and the glamour of the subsequent lines has obscured this interesting verbal coinage of Marlowe's, an apt phrase for a magician's assistant engaged in bringing off his employer's most spectacular trick. This, of all occasions, is the one to which language must rise; and, in so doing, it brilliantly redeems the shortcomings of previous episodes. The apostrophe to Helen stands out from its context, not because anthologists excerpt it, but because Marlowe carefully designed it to be a set piece, a purple passage, a supreme invitation to love. Its lyrical formality, its practised handling of stylistic and prosodic devices from his established repertory, set it off from the pithy prose, the sharp dialectic, the nervous colloquies and rhythmic variations of his maturing style. Characteristically, it does not offer any physical description of the heroine. It estimates, as Homer did, her impact. How should Faustus react to the sight that had stirred the elders of Troy to forget their arguments in admiration? Chapman would render their winged words in his *Iliad*:

> What man can blame
> The Greekes and Trojans to endure, for so Admir'd a Dame,
> So many miseries, and so long? In her sweet countenance shine
> Lookes like the Goddesses. (III 167–70)

That could be a marginal gloss for Marlowe's twenty lines, which constitute three fairly symmetrical strophes. The starting point for the first, the invocation, is the most rhetorical of questions. Though it is Marlowe's culminating hyperbole, it may not strike us with the fullest impact, precisely because it has struck so often before, because it has been echoed and re-echoed as one of the striking exaggerations of poetry – like the tower of ivory in the Song of Songs. The thousand ships are not exaggerated; they are specified by Ovid's matter-of-fact account of the Trojan War in the *Metamorphoses* (XII 7); but here poetic audacity intervenes to transpose a lover's emotion into a large-scale naval operation. The topless towers are recurrent symbols for illimitable aspiration, and Marlowe habitually juxtaposes them to the all-consuming element af fire. Cavalierly he poses a moral issue, and the alternative is absolute: the destruction of a city, the calamities of war, the world well lost, all for love.

> Was this the face that lancht a thousand shippes?
> And burnt the toplesse Towres of *Ilium*?
> Sweete *Helen*, make me immortall with a kisse. (xviii 99–101)

The third line is an implicit stage direction, leading on to the enactment of a metaphysical conceit; whereupon Faustus claims that Helen's lips suck forth his soul, and then reclaims it with another kiss. Underneath their amorous byplay runs the disturbing hint that she may be a succuba; this may not be the only world that is at stake for him. When Dido wooed Aeneas and spoke of becoming 'immortall with a kisse' (line 1329), it seemed to be little more than a figure of speech. For Faustus immortality means vastly more than that, in one way if not in another, although he may actually get no closer to heaven than Helen's embrace. No wonder he changes his evaluation from otherworldly to mercenary terms:

> Here wil I dwel, for heauen be in these lips,
> And all is drosse that is not *Helena*.   (xviii 104–5)

The second strophe is in the active mode of *Tamburlaine*, and the phrase 'I wil' resounds through it. Since Helen is notoriously a *casus belli*, Faustus proposes to re-enact the Trojan War through the sack of Wittenberg. He will be Paris as, in parody, Ithamore would be Jason, with Bellamira for his golden fleece. Faustus challenges the Greek heroes to a tournament, imagined as a medieval tapestry rather than a classical frieze, a colourful but two-dimensional representation of the basic conflict between pagan and Christian values. In the third strophe the knight, returning to the lady he has championed, salutes her with a gallant array of invidious comparisons and mythological superlatives. He modulates from the threat to the persuasion, the more passive mode of *Edward II*. If he cannot visualize Helen distinctly, it is because she bedazzles him. Her fairness, outshining the starlight, surpasses the goddesses – or is it the gods?

> Brighter art thou then flaming *Iupiter*,
> When he appeard to haplesse *Semele*,
> More louely then the monarke of the skie
> In wanton *Arethusaes* azurde armes.   (xviii 114–17)

It is not to these nymphs, but to Jupiter himself, that Helen is being compared. Strange as this may seem, it is not inconsistent with the prologue's allusion to a masculine muse. It throws some light back on the offer of Mephostophilis to procure the fairest of women for Faustus, be they as chaste as Penelope, as wise as the Queen of Sheba,

or as beautiful
As was bright *Lucifer* before his fall.   (v 157–8)

Helen, whatever she is, whoever she was, says nothing. Her part is purely visual, entirely mute. Faustus might almost be talking to himself, and when we notice how many of his speeches are addressed to himself, the play becomes a kind of interior monologue. Whatever satisfaction he obtains from Helen is bound to be illusory; as a necromancer he knows in advance that the shadow is not substantial, that the apparition he has materialized will vanish sooner or later. The *Faustbook* reports that she bore him a child, which disappeared – along with its mother – on the day of Faustus' death. Was it a vision or a waking dream, or does the fair exterior disguise some hideous monster like Keats's Lamia? Lucian, in his *Dialogues of the Dead*, pictures Menippus descending into the underworld, inquiring after Helen, and being shown a skeleton. Yes, Hermes assures him, this was the skull that caused the Greeks to launch a thousand ships. And the refrain is the timeless *Ubi sunt?* Where are they now – Helen, Thaïs, Dido, Zenocrate? Marlowe cannot have been insensitive to the traditional mood so poignantly expressed by his sometime collaborator, Thomas Nashe:

> Brightnesse falls from the ayre,
> Queenes have died yong and faire,
> Dust hath closde Helens eye. . . .

It is not for nothing that Faustus characterizes Helen by her face, with the connotation of skin-deep beauty as opposed to harsh truth. His rhetoric is an ornate façade, an aesthetic surface masking an ethical reality. A third dimension is given to the speech by the entrance – after the first strophe – of a third character, who is indubitably real. This is the Old Man, whom the *Faustbook* identifies as a neighbour, the exemplary figure whom Marlowe employs as a spokesman for Christianity and a counterweight for the ideal of paganism. It is he who penetrates Faustus' conscience:

> Breake heart, drop bloud, and mingle it with teares.
>   (xviii 42)

Faustus admits his sinfulness and might be moved to repent, were it not for the threatening Mephostophilis and the enticing Helen. When Faustus sweeps her off the stage, it is the Old Man who stays to pronounce the moral; and while Faustus enjoys her elusive favours, the Old Man is 'sifted' and tried by devils; but his faith triumphs over Satan's pride, and he ascends to heaven while the fiends sink back into hell. The absence of this crucial speech is a reason for continuing to distrust the 1616 Quarto.

With every scene the pace of the drama accelerates, reaching a climax with the final monologue, which syncopates an hour into fifty-nine lines. This is much too fast, and we share the suspense with Faustus, whose contract expires at midnight; and yet, in a sense, it is slow enough to fathom – as it were – the thoughts of a drowning man. It is a soliloquy in the profoundest sense, since it isolates the speaker; at the end, as at the beginning, we find him alone in his study. Tragedy is an isolating experience. To each of us, as to Proust on the death of his grandmother, it conveys the realization that we are truly alone. When the time comes, each tragic protagonist must say, with Shakespeare's Juliet:

> My dismall Sceane, I needs must act alone.
>
> (IV iii 19)

So with Faustus, whose fellow scholars rally him for becoming 'ouer solitary' (xix 33). They must leave him to his solitude, just as the friends of Everyman desert him on his way to the grave. In contradistinction to the specious grandeur of Faustus' apostrophe to Helen, his last words are an inner revelation, the excruciated agony of a lost soul. It is now too late for vaunting or pleading; it is Marlowe's occasion to develop the less characteristic mode of lamentation; and he does so with the utmost resourcefulness, timing and complicating his flexible rhythms to catch the agitations of Faustus' tortured mind. It is hard to think of another single speech, even in Shakespeare, which demands more from the actor or offers him more. Edward Alleyn, in a surplice with a cross upon it, was famed for his portrayal of the part and may well have left some marks upon these lines. They begin, with a portentous sound effect, at the stroke of eleven:

Ah Faustus,
Now hast thou but one bare hower to liue,
And then thou must be damnd perpetually.

(xix 133–5)

Time is the essence, and also the substance of the soliloquy. Its underlying contrast between eternity and transience is heavily enforced, in this distich, by a slow succession of monosyllables leading up to the rapid adverb, with the hypermetrical syllable, 'perpetually'. Words of comparable significance – 'ever', 'still', 'forever', 'everlasting' – abound throughout. Where Edward implored the sun to gallop apace and hasten events, Faustus now bids the planetary system stand still. A humanist to the last, he recalls a line from Ovid's *Elegies*:

> *O lente, lente curite noctis equi.* (xix 142)

The utterance falls ironically, but not inappropriately, from the lips of the scholar turned sensualist, the erstwhile lover of Helen of Troy. The difference is vast between his motive for wanting the dawn to be postponed and the classical lover's plea to Aurora. As Marlowe himself had rendered it:

> Now in her tender armes I sweetly bide,
> If euer, now well lies she by my side.
> The aire is cold, and sleepe is sweetest now
> And birdes send forth shrill notes from euery bough:
> Whither runst thou, that men, and women loue not?
> Hold in thy rosy horses that they moue not . . .
> But heldst thou in thine armes some *Cephalus*,
> Then wouldst thou cry, stay night and runne not thus.

(1 xiii 5–40)

Such a miracle might be accomplished at the behest of the gods, as Jupiter boasted in *Dido*; but for Faustus, all too human, the spheres go on revolving. Soon it will be his turn to be tormented; and he is not armed, as the Old Man was, with faith. Suddenly he seems to witness an epiphany. 'See see,' he exclaims, 'where Christs blood streames in the firmament' (xix 146). The line echoes and answers Tamburlaine's final challenge, when he threatened to march against the powers of heaven and 'set blacke

streamers in the firmament'. The change of colours is emblematic
of two opposing attitudes towards death: massacre for the man of
war, sacrifice for the man of peace. When Faustus excommuni-
cated himself by signing the deed, his own blood was ominously
reluctant to flow. He asked, 'Why streames it not?' (v 66) and
coals were brought to warm it – more omens. Blood, for the
Guise, was the only fluid that could extinguish the flames of
lawless ambition; but Faustus is denied the blood of Christ, the
only thing that could save him, because of his own denial. 'The
heauy wrath of God' (xix 153), as the good Angel admonished,
is now on his head; and his diction grows scriptural, echoing the
Prophets and the Apocalypse, as he vainly thinks of hiding from
the 'irefull browes' of Jehovah. The striking of the half-hour
alerts him again to temporal considerations, both relative and
absolute.

> O no end is limited to damned soules.   (xix 171)

Damnation is an unlooked-for way of transcending limits and
approaching infinity; it is immortality with a vengeance; and
Faustus would rather be a soulless beast and look forward to
oblivion. Marlowe elsewhere uses the trope of 'water drops'
when he reckons innumerable quantities. Here, with fire in the
offing, they are a welcome mirage of dissolution; now, from the
combining elements, a vapour ascends. If time oscillates between
swiftness and slowness, space is measured by the span between
heaven and hell. Although those two words are paired off
against each other in this speech and through the play, somehow
'hell' and its cognates occur fifty-eight times to forty-nine
occurrences for 'heaven' – the proportion is forty-five to twenty-
seven in the shorter edition. Faustus is accorded a glimpse of
paradise in the *Faustbook*; the 1616 Quarto directs the 'throne',
the Elizabethan god-in-the-machine, briefly to descend from the
'heavens', the roof of the stage; while hell, which is also conveniently adjacent to the localities of the play, yawns in a
discovery scene. The denouement is a foregone conclusion: 'for
vaine pleasure of 24 yeares hath Faustus lost eternall ioy and
felicitie' (xix 64–6).

As the clock strikes twelve, with thunder and lightning, the leaping demons enter to carry him off; in terror he makes his last offer to burn his books, and his very last word is the shriek, '*Mephostophilis*'. He makes his definitive exit through the monstrous jaws of the hell-mouth. That popular but obsolete property, which Marlowe resurrected from the mysteries, symbolizes pain and punishment more terribly than the sordid details of Edward's murder and more pitifully than the crude melodrama of Barabas' caldron. There is one more scene in the 1616 version, where the scholars interchange proper moral sentiments; like the sextet at the end of *Don Giovanni*, it seems unduly sententious after what has just happened; and, with some justification, it is not printed in the Quarto of 1604. The Chorus, or Wagner, draws the arras across the inner stage, and the black curtain prevails over the smoking red grotesquerie. If the classical imagery of the epilogue is at odds with its medieval purport, this reflects the tension of the play. If the branch is cut, if Apollo's laurel is burnt, let it be an object lesson for those 'forward wits' who are so enticed by 'deepnesse'. The celestial-infernal anti-thesis is conclusively asserted, and the workings of 'heauenly power' are discerned in the 'hellish fall' of Doctor Faustus. Thus the tragedy is framed by the fundamental dogmas of Christian morality. How far, then, should they be taken literally? How far do they merely furnish Marlowe with expressionistic scenery? How far was he utilizing theology as a modern playwright might utilize psychology? Faustus has maintained that hell is a fable, and Mephostophilis has declared – in an unexpected burst of humanistic fervour – that man is more excellent than heaven. Doctor Faustus' worst mistake has been to confound hell with Elysium. Between the classic shades and the quenchless flames, even in *Tamburlaine*, Marlowe had discriminated. If heaven was placed in hell, or hell in heaven, the inversion had to be reversed; and the reversal is all the more decisive in *Doctor Faustus* because it comes as a recognition, and because the movement of Marlowe's imagination – at its uppermost – turns and takes a plunge into the abyss.

Unless, with the credulous members of his audience, we regard his fireworks as sparks of hellfire, we must assume that Marlowe's Inferno is a genuine but unlocalized phenomenon. In the same spirit, Paracelsus repeatedly averred that there is a heaven in each of us, and Milton's Satan announces: 'My self am Hell' (IV 75). There is a god infused through the universe, so it was affirmed in *Tamburlaine*; and there is a hell which has no limits, Faustus is informed by Mephostophilis. Every man, according to his lights and through his own endeavours, has a chance to know both; and Milton is not being paradoxical when Satan announces in *Paradise Lost*:

> The mind is its own place, and in it self
> Can make a Heav'n of Hell, a Hell of Heav'n.
>
> (I 254–5)

The Seven Deadly Sins, the Good and Evil Angels, Mephostophilis himself, upon this level, may be regarded as materializations like Helen of Troy. 'Hell striues with grace' in a *psychomachia*, a spiritual battle within the breast of Faustus (xviii 72). Pointedly the Old Man rebukes him for excluding 'the grace of heauen' from his soul (xviii 120). It is plainly lacking, but has he excluded it? Before his blood was dry on the parchment, he was thoroughly remorseful; and his remorse, increasing over his pleasure, gradually deepens into the hopeless despair of his concluding soliloquy.

> Contrition, prayer, repentance: what of them?   (v 17)

he has wondered; he has resolved to renounce his magic, and been distracted by his Evil Angel. Later, when his Good Angel all but persuades him to repent, he tries; but his heart is so hardened that he can scarcely utter such words as 'saluation, faith, or heauen' (vi 19). Yet he does so, with no little eloquence; and, by uttering the name of God, he prays – albeit no more effectually than Claudius in *Hamlet*. As between the 'Neuer too late' of the Good Angel and the 'Too late' of the Evil Angel, the latter prevails with a Manichæan fatality (vi 81–2). Christian doctrine vouchsafes mercy to repentant sinners:

> Tush, Christ did call the thiefe vpon the Crosse. (xv 25)

Even 'the Serpent that tempted *Eue* may be sau'd (xix 41–2). Then why not Faustus? Having become a spirit in form and substance, has he ceased to be a man? Why, when the Old Man all but converts him, should Faustus accept the dagger of Mephostophilis? Why, when he calls upon Christ, is it Lucifer who emerges? George Santayana, acting as devil's advocate, and felicitously stating the case for Faustus as a martyr to the ideals of the Renaissance, would argue that he 'is damned by accident or by predestination; he is brow-beaten by the devil and forbidden to repent when he has really repented'. The pedestrian counter-argument would be based on the *Faustbook*'s account of Faustus, 'neuer falling to repentance truly' but 'in all his opinions doubtfull, without faith or hope'. Luther, followed by such English theologians as Richard Hooker, in his revolt against Catholicism had made contrition so difficult that at times it seemed virtually unattainable. What was worse for Faustus, he was no ordinary sinner; he was, like Marlowe himself, that impenitent and wilful miscreant whom Elizabethan preachers termed a scorner. Far from denying sin or its wages, death, his course of action was premised on their inevitability: *Che sera, sera*. This led him, not to fatalism, but to an extreme act of the will – namely, the commission of an unpardonable sin, a sin against the Holy Ghost. Casuistry could have found theological loopholes, had a penitent Faustus been conceivable. But that would have presupposed an orthodox Marlowe.

As a measure of his heterodoxy, it has proved suggestive to compare *Doctor Faustus* with *El Mágico Prodigioso*, the sacramental drama of Calderón, grounded upon the analogous legend of Saint Cyprian. There the magician repents, forswears his magic, is converted to Christianity and undergoes martyrdom – to be reunited in heaven with his lady, who also dies a Christian martyr. Death is a happy ending in the next world, after the uncertainties and horrors of life here below. Tragedy is intercepted by eschatology. Extremes meet, when we glance away from that simple and reassuring cosmos toward the chaos of modernity, and to the magistral exploration of it that Goethe achieved in his *Faust*. Goethe's Faust is a man of affirmations, bedeviled by a spirit of denial, whom he overreaches in the end by what – to sterner moralists – might well seem a legalistic ruse. He is free to stray so long as he strives; the forfeit need only be paid when he is satisfied with the passing moment. Though he is momentarily tempted to express such satisfaction, it is not occasioned by the present but by the prospect of a better world in the future. Hence his soul remains his own, on condition that he persist in his strivings toward the infinite, aided and comforted by eternal womanhood. Tragedy is here defeated by optimism. Enlightenment and humanitarianism absolve and regenerate Faust, just as salvation cancels out sin in that unworldly world of the Middle Ages which is still reflected by Calderón. Balancing precariously between those two worlds, Marlowe achieves his tragic equilibrium: the conviction of sin without the belief in salvation. That is sheer damnation; but damnation is man's unmitigated lot; this is hell, nor are we out of it. Such a pessimistic view is woefully incomplete; but tragedy is an intensive rather than a comprehensive inquiry, which concentrates upon the problem of evil and the nature of suffering. When Marlowe swerved from his predilection for the good things of life, he concentrated upon the evils with unflinching – not to say unbearable – intensity.

Doctor Faustus does not have the coherence of Calderón's ethos or the stature of Goethe's protagonist; yet, contrasted with the English play, the Spanish seems naïve and the German sentimental. We need not push these contrasts invidiously, given the differences in time and place, in poetic language and dramatic convention. Given the unchallengeable greatness of Goethe's achievement, it is noteworthy that certain readers have preferred Marlowe's treatment of the legend – notably Scott and Coleridge, Lamb and Hazlitt, all of them conceivably biased by their cultural leanings, and by their unfamiliarity with the second part of *Faust*. The first part, the romantic and domestic drama of Gretchen, admittedly belongs to Goethe's little world; it may have been in emulation of Marlowe that Goethe went on to investigate the macrocosm. It may well be that Faustus has less in common with Faust than with Euphorion, the hybrid offspring of Faust and Goethe's Helena, who meets a premature death by attempting to fly. It may well be, in spite of Marlowe's narrower range and less philosophical outlook, that he grasped the core of his subject more objectively and with a keener awareness of its implications; that, because his background was nearer to obscurantism than to enlightenment, he appreciated the hazards and pangs of free-thinking. A later epoch than Goethe's with less faith in progress or hope for individualism, may feel itself in closer accord with the earlier poet. It cannot dream about flying, with Leonardo, since the dream has not only come true but turned into a nightmare. It can add very little, except for amen, to the admonition of Rabelais that science is ruinous without conscience. It cannot but discern its culture-hero in the ancient myth of Icarus, in Cervantes' twice-told tale of the curious impertinent, above all in Marlowe's tragedy of the scientific libertine who gained control over nature while losing control of himself.

'The reason Milton wrote in fetters when he wrote of Angels & God, and at liberty when of Devils & Hell, is because he was a true Poet and of the Devil's party without knowing it.' Blake's problematic note to *The Marriage of Heaven and Hell*, like most paradoxes, stresses a neglected facet of a complicated truth, at the expense of what is more obvious. Marlowe, much more obviously than Milton, is committed to this kind of poetic diabolism; and, conversely, Marlowe can write with genuine yearning of paradise lost. No doubt he yearns all the more avidly with Faustus, but with Faustus he condemns himself; the Good Angel and the Old Man are at liberty, while Mephostophilis is in perpetual fetters. Yet, it is just at this point that Marlowe abandons his preoccupation with unfettered soaring, and seems to submit himself to ideas of durance, torment, and constraint. If he is imaginatively identified with any character, it is no longer Faustus; it is Mephostophilis, who suffers with Faustus like a second self yet also plays the cosmic ironist, wise in his guilty knowledge and powerful in his defeated rebellion. Through his agency Marlowe succeeds in setting the parable of intelligence and experience within a Christian framework, even while hinting that the framework is arbitrary and occasionally glancing beyond it. Such is the attitude of ambivalent supplication that Hart Crane rephrases in his poem 'For the Marriage of Faustus and Helen';

> Distinctly praise the years, whose volatile
> Blamed bleeding hands extend and thresh the height
> The imagination spans beyond despair,
> Outpacing bargain, vocable and prayer.

Such is the way in which Goethe's Faust eluded his devil's bargain, and it applies to Marlowe if not to Faustus. If hell is destruction, it follows that heaven is creation; and perhaps the highest form of creation is that engendered out of the very forces of destruction, the imagination spanning beyond despair. Perhaps we may say of Marlowe what the Florentines said of Dante: this man has been in hell. As we broadly interpret that concept, many men have been there; but few have mastered their terrors and returned to communicate that mastery.

SOURCE: *Christopher Marlowe: The Overreacher* (1954). Originally published in the United States as *The Overreacher: A Study of Christopher Marlowe* (1952).

Robert Ornstein

THE COMIC SYNTHESIS IN
DOCTOR FAUSTUS (1955)

I do not propose in this article to argue Marlowe's authorship of the prose comedy in *Doctor Faustus*, though for convenience I will follow tradition in attributing to him those scenes under discussion. Actually, the problem of authorship is irrelevant here, for my concern is with the integrity of the play as a work of dramatic art, not with the integrity of the text as a literary document. I use the traditional version of *Doctor Faustus* because it is the one known to the vast majority of readers.[1] But my discussion would, in general, apply as well to Dr Greg's conjectural reconstruction of the B-Text.[2] I intend no apology for the crude buffoonery in *Doctor Faustus*. I would suggest, however, that there is more than one level of comedy in the play – that the slapstick scenes which tickled groundling fancies unite with the seemingly fragmented main action to form a subtly ironic tragic design.

To begin with, let us admit that Sir Philip Sidney's criticism of the Elizabethan stage was well taken though somewhat academic. Marlowe's contemporaries did mingle kings and clowns 'not because the matter so carrieth', but because an Elizabethan audience expected variety and comedy. After all, high seriousness and buffoonery had long before joined hands in the Miracles and Moralities, and popular taste weighed more heavily than critical theory in the public theatres. But the custom of mingling kings and clowns could not remain a naïve literary practice as Elizabethan drama matured. Like all literary practices, it was sophisticated for better and for worse. When imagination faltered, clowns – the musicians in *Romeo and Juliet*, for instance – made purely routine appearances in tragedy. But when inspiration mounted, the Elizabethan comedians found themselves in more significant roles: as the grave-diggers in *Hamlet* or as the drunken Porter in *Macbeth* (a character rejected by Coleridge, ironically enough, as a 'disgusting' interpolation by the actors).

It was inevitable too that incongruous mixtures of kings and clowns should have developed into formalized contrasts used to enhance the beauty and substance of a main dramatic action. The highly stylized device of the antimasque merely refined the once indiscriminate jostle of coarse and courtly elements in the masque. The popular drama produced less formalized, more satiric 'antimasques' of clownish servants who aped the manners and pretensions of their betters. In Shakespeare's romantic comedies a pair of rustic sweethearts stumble through the arabesques of courtship, naturalizing by their improbable amour the artificial languors and melancholies of courtly heroes and heroines. In Ford's tragedies we find comic foils remarkably similar in one respect to the clowns in *Doctor Faustus*. Like Rafe and Robin, they are not very amusing. The best are innocuous, the majority unattractive, and the rest simply offensive. Ford, lacking a sense of humor, and at times a sense of decency, tried to use comic lewdness to set off more delicate and consuming passions.* His was the last and least successful attempt to subtilize the comic contrasts of Elizabethan drama. Marlowe's was an imperfect but brilliant innovation.

Comparing Marlowe's clowns to those in Ford's tragedies, however, merely underlines the unique function of the comic contrasts in *Doctor Faustus*. Obviously Marlowe does not enhance the main action of his tragedy by reducing it to absurdity scene by scene. He does not magnify Faustus' achievements by having clowns parody them immediately afterwards. (By analogy, no Elizabethan would try to heighten the beauty of a masque by closing it with grotesque dances. The antimasque must come first; it must prepare the audience for the familiar contrast, for the metamorphosis of antic into courtly elegance.) Yet the pattern of *Doctor Faustus* is consistently 'wrong'. In the first scene Faustus announces his intellectual supremacy and his

---

* See, for instance, *Love's Sacrifice*, in which the witty lecheries of Ferentes contrast with the nobler passions of Fernando and Bianca.

decision to gain a deity through magic. In the second scene Wagner apes his master's display of learning by chopping logic with two scholars. In the third scene Faustus agrees to sell his soul for power and voluptuousness. Immediately afterwards the Clown considers bartering his soul for a shoulder of mutton and a taste of wenching. In the following scenes Faustus makes his compact with the Devil, discusses astronomy with Mephistophilis, and is entertained by the Seven Deadly Sins. He then launches his career as a magician by snatching away the Pope's food and drink. Next Rafe and Robin burlesque Faustus' conjurations and try to steal a goblet from a Vintner.

Judging by their enthusiasm for the play, however, Marlowe's contemporaries did not find the pattern of *Doctor Faustus* 'wrong'. Perhaps because parody is its own excuse for being when its target is the heroic stance. Is there not something infinitely reassuring in the clown who apes the manner and the mannerism of the superman? And the ironic comedy in *Doctor Faustus* is more than reassuring. Its intention, I think, is both didactic and comic. Simultaneously nonsensical and profound, it clarifies our perception of moral values.

We see the world through the lenses of custom: when false values. pass current, even elemental truths appear distorted, naïve, or absurd. The ironist often deals in elemental absurdities – the absurdity of eating children to cure poverty or of mortgaging one's immortal soul for a piece of mutton (if it be well roasted). We smile at such absurdities because we have a more sensible and realistic appraisal of the world. We know that society does not and would not eat children. We know that no man, however foolish, would damn his soul to satisfy his belly – to gain infinite power, yes, but we consider such aspiration heroic. We smile, however, only until we discover beneath the surface of our sensible view of life the grim absurdity depicted by the ironist – only until sensible or grandiose appearance and absurd reality melt into one. Because the ironist (like the Shakespearean Fool) is licensed to reveal 'absurd' truths only when he amuses his audience, Marlowe entertains us with Clowns and with the ancient but eternally successful comedy of futility. It is hardly accidental that in the crucial scene when Faustus first repents Lucifer appears, impresario-like, with the Seven Deadly Sins. Faustus 'feeds' on the spectacle and jests with these harmless bogies of the superstitious mind. Entranced by Lucifer's vaudeville show he forgets salvation. Lucifer is also entertained but on a more intellectual plane. The consummate cynic, he diverts his victim with a picture gallery that suggests Faustus' own futility.

Professor Harry Levin describes Marlowe's Deadly Sins as a 'quaint procession of gargoyles' and interprets Faustus' unalloyed amusement as a sin of moral decay.[3] I would agree but also add that the Deadly Sins are supposed to be as amusing in *Doctor Faustus* as they are in much of medieval literature. The fourteenth century artist took sin seriously enough and yet caricatured it even as he caricatured Satan, arch-enemy of God, who appears in the Miracles and Moralities as a comic villain beaten off the stage to the accompaniment of divine and human laughter. The medieval playwright gave the Devil his due; he showed the human soul caught in a satanic web of pleasure and deceit. But he showed also the inevitable triumph of God's love which made the efforts of satanic evil vain and risible. In short, the medieval mind understood the ludicrousness of insatiable desire. It knew that vice (to use Santayana's definition) is 'human nature strangled by the suicide of attempting the impossible'.*

Of course Faustus is never ludicrous; he is no fustian villain ranting of his powers. But from the beginning there is casuistic self-deception in his speeches. Blind to the ever-present possibility of grace, he facilely reduces theology to the dogma of pitiless damnation. Misunderstanding his relationship with God, he completely mistakes his rapport with the Devil. He thinks that through magic he has gained control of the spirit world and

---

* In his essay on Dickens (from *Soliloquies in England and Later Soliloquies* (1922)), Santayana argues that we do not connect Dickens' caricatures with real personalities because we cannot face the honesty of his comic realism. Our failure to connect Marlowe's clowns, caricatures of the tragic hero, with Faustus is perhaps due to a comparable failure to recognize that Marlowe was also, in a sense, a comic and moral realist.

of Mephistophilis, who appears at his command and changes shape to please him. Faustus finds Mephistophilis 'pliant . . . full of obedience and humility'. Mephistophilis, a scrupulous corrupter, insists that he has only one master – Lucifer – but Faustus will not believe him. When Mephistophilis shudders at the terrors of damnation, Faustus sets himself up as an example of fortitude to the angel who openly warred against God. Later he argues with Mephistophilis about the reality of hell even though indisputable evidence of its reality stands before him.

Fleeing his own Master, Faustus contracts with the Devil for the services of Mephistophilis, who, like the cunning slave of Roman comedy, quickly gains the upper hand. Frightening and distracting Faustus from salvation, he caters to his sensuality and diverts his creative energies into court performances and practical jokes. Though at times compassionate, Mephistophilis has his joke with Faustus on the subject of lechery. Lucifer toys with his dupe on a grander scale. He assures Faustus that 'in hell is all manner of delight' and promises an excursion through it:

> . . . I will send for thee at midnight.
> In meantime take this book; peruse it thoroughly
> And thou shalt turn thyself into what shape thou wilt.
>
> (vi 174–6)

The Devil is as good as his word. He does send for Faustus at midnight. And he does help Faustus to change his shape. But the transformation is from aspiring hero to despairing libertine.

At the beginning of the play Faustus' plans, though egocentric and grandiose, are constructive. He wants pleasure, riches, and power, but he also intends to make all learning his province, better the lot of students, improve geography, and defeat tyranny. Faustus' dreams of creativity, however, are only dreams; indeed, the measure of his tragic fall is the increasing disparity between his aspirations and his achievements. He travels at first, takes in the wonders of the world, and wins fame as a magician. But on the stage itself Faustus' accomplishments grow increasingly petty; he discomforts the Pope, horns a Knight, entertains an Emperor, cheats a Horse-Courser, and delights a Duchess with grapes out of season. Here is travesty of a high order! In the latter half of the play, the mighty Faustus parodies his own highvaulting thoughts and ambitions even as Wagner and the Clown had parodied them earlier. Or more correctly, as Faustus changes shape the tragic – comic contrast begins to coalesce. Scene by scene the apposing images approach one another until at last we discover beneath the exalted appearance of the fearless rebel the figure of the fool. When Faustus steals the Pope's cup and Robin steals the Vintner's goblet the tragic and comic images nearly merge. The difference between hero and clown is one of degree, not of kind.

We need no acquaintance with Elizabethan ethical psychology to appreciate the ironic fate of a hero who in striving to be a god becomes less than a man. Only a dimwitted Clown would sell his soul for a mutton roast and a bit of lechery. Yet Faustus ends his days in 'belly cheer', carousing and swilling with the students. The scholar who pursued knowledge beyond the utmost bound of human thought finally takes Helen for his paramour to drown vexatious thought in wantonness.* Actually it does not matter whether one sells one's soul for infinite power or for belly cheer. Both transactions are ridiculous, the first even more than the second because it is far less realistic. Faustus, who dreamed of commanding the powers of heaven and earth, finds that he cannot check the movement of the stars when death threatens. In his vain rebellion there is comedy; in his fall from grace irrevocable tragedy.†

* The ecstatic poetry of Faustus' apostrophe to Helen (xviii 99–118) does not mask the corruption of his genius. Once before in despair he had summoned Homer, the 'maker', who sang of Troy. In the lines to Helen, however, he identifies himself with an effeminate Paris, whose sensuality destroyed the topless towers of Ilium. As the comparison to Jupiter and Semele suggests, Faustus does not take Helen – he abandons himself to her.

† The balance of tragic and comic elements in *Faustus* is somewhat comparable to that in *Paradise Lost*. C. S. Lewis has suggested that Satan might have been a comic figure had Milton chosen to emphasize, more than he does, the absurdity of diabolical ambition (*A Preface to Paradise Lost* (1952) pp. 92–3). Like Faustus, Satan changes his shape; the brightest of angels becomes the scarred fallen leader who, reaching

I do not mean to suggest any ambiguity or ambivalence in Marlowe's attitude towards his tragic hero. Despite persistent arguments,[4] it is difficult to believe that Marlowe secretly identified himself with Faustus and that Faustus' catastrophe is a sop to Nemesis or to conventional morality. For Marlowe gives an almost Dostoievskian sense of damnation as an earthly as well as spiritual fact; he depicts the corruption of the mind that destroys the soul. Like Mephistophilis (and like Ivan Karamazov)* Faustus makes his own personal hell of negation, a hell that 'hath no limits, nor is circumscrib'd/In one self place'. But he attempts to escape it in death by losing himself in the natural forces that were to have been his agents of creation:

> Mountains and hills, come, come and fall on me,
> And hide me from the heavy wrath of God!
> That when you vomit forth into the air,
> My limbs may issue from your smoky mouths.
> No! no!
> Then will I headlong run into the earth;
>
> .   .   .
>
> O, it strikes, it strikes! Now, body, turn to air,
> Or Lucifer will bear thee quick to hell.
>
> *Thunder and lightning*
>
> O soul, be chang'd into little water-drops,
> And fall into the ocean – ne'er be found.
>
> (xix 152–86)

---

toward heaven, transforms himself into cormorant, toad, and 'monstrous Serpent'. Satan, however, is the unwitting fool of God, the brilliant schemer whose victory turns to ashes and whose evil will produces good, the 'fortunate' fall of man. Faustus' destiny is more obscure and pathetic; he is Lucifer's fool, not God's.

* Compare the two intellectuals, Faustus and Ivan Karamazov. Both rebel against God because they cannot believe in His redeeming love; and they cannot believe because they are detached, superior beings incapable of ordinary human sympathies. Both reject intellectually what they cannot emotionally 'conceive of' and accept. Spiritually isolated, trapped by their own dialectical subtleties, they dissipate their creative gifts. They escape the restrictive bonds of morality only to discover too late that they have cut themselves off from the humanity of those who would save them.

Here is the ultimate irony; Faustus would escape the negation of hell by annihilating body and soul. The diseased creative will succumbs at last to frenzied desire for self-destruction – for nothingness. *Consummatum est!*

To say that *Doctor Faustus* can be read as the tragedy of a creative mind destroying itself in fascination with the esoteric is not to make of the play a secularized Christian allegory. Marlowe adds new dimension to the Morality framework; he does not use it as a literary, 'mythical' apparatus. Hell is a reality in *Doctor Faustus* whether experienced in an earthly nihilistic despair or in the horror of an eternal void. Marlowe's religious thought may be heterodox in some respects, but his ethics are sound. We are always aware that Faustus the aspiring Titan is also the self-deluded fool of Lucifer. The emancipated intellectual who confounds hell in Elysium spends his last hours as a lonely, terrified penitent.

Doctor Faustus, then, is not the tragical history of a glorious rebellion. For Marlowe shared with his admiring contemporary, George Chapman, the disenchanted vision of the aspiring mind – the knowledge that the Comic Spirit hovers over the Icarian flight of the self-announced superman.

SOURCE: *Journal of English Literary History*, XXII iii (1955).

NOTES

1. My text of *Faustus* will be that edited by C. F. T. Brooke and N. B. Paradise, *English Drama 1508–1642* (New York, 1933).

2. W. W. Greg, *Doctor Faustus: A Conjectural Reconstruction* (1950). Dr Greg has argued convincingly for the superiority oft he B-Text over the 'A', traditionally used as the basis for editions of *Faustus*. See *Doctor Faustus: Parallel Texts* (1950), Introduction.

3. Harry Levin, *The Overreacher: A Study of Christopher Marlowe* (Cambridge, Mass., 1952) p. 119.

4. See, for example, Paul H. Kocher, *Christopher Marlowe: A Study of his Thought, Learning, and Character* (Chapel Hill, 1946) pp. 118–119.

J. P. Brockbank

DAMNED PERPETUALLY (1962)

FAUSTUS'S great final soliloquy consummates the play in both its aspects – Morality and Heroic Tragedy – and each in its own way triumphs over the other. In fear we acquiesce in the littleness and powerlessness of man, and in pity we share his sufferings and endorse his protest.

The horrible prospect of a man being burnt alive, which Marlowe (like the Christianity he honours) does not spare us, accounts for little of the pathos and power. In the first lines we are much more moved by the magnificent futility of the human protest against the inexorable movement of time as it enacts an inexorable moral law. We are reminded that 'all things that move between the quiet poles' are at the command of the process Faustus would escape: the 'ever-moving spheres' cannot by definition 'stand still'. Faustus had explained the seasonal 'circles' to the Duchess, who marvelled at the winter grapes (xvii 27–33), and he had numbered the cycles of the spheres, but now his knowledge is of a different order. The cosmic rhythms evoked by the sense of the poetry seem to hold dominion over its movement. The first equably stressed eleven words echo the striking clock – 'Ah Faustus, Now hast thou but one bare hour to live'; the 'perpetually' that falls with finality at the end of the first sentence returns in the mocking oxymoron 'perpetual day'; and 'rise, rise again' invokes precisely the diurnal motion it seeks to arrest.

The irony of the quotation from Ovid has long been celebrated. In the *Amores* (I xiii 40) it is the plea of ecstatic love, *Clamares*, '*lente currite, noctis equi*', which Marlowe had poorly translated, 'Then wouldst thou cry, stay night and runne not thus.' But here the Latin words in their English setting sound like a last attempt to cast a spell whose vanity is betrayed by the rhythm as the horses seem to quicken pace through the line, and confessed in 'the stars move still, time runs, the clock will strike'. Were the soliloquy to end here we should feel that confinement to time is the cruellest fact of man's condition.

In the next lines, however, his ordeal is confinement to earth: 'Oh, I'll leap up to my God! Who pulls me down?' The image affirming the immensity of Christ's Testament also declares its unreachable remoteness: 'See see where Christ's blood streams in the firmament.' Marlowe may be remembering both the gulf between heaven and hell (Luke, XVI 26) and Tamburlaine, defiant in his mortal sickness:

> Come let us march against the powers of heaven,
> And set blacke streamers in the firmament,
> To signify the slaughter of the Gods.
> Ah friends, what shall I do? I cannot stand.
>
> (2 *Tamburlaine*, lines 4441–4)

Christ has accomplished the triumph over mortality that Tamburlaine's labouring brain could only imagine. The imperial pageant hyperbole of the earlier play has in the later been made to express the superhuman power of Christ; but he conquers by sacrifice not by slaughter – humility has become heroic. Even without appeal to Christian symbolism, the play has made the streaming blood emblematic of eternal life. Blood refuses to flow when Faustus cuts his arm, it 'dries with grief' as his 'conscience kills it', and it gushes forth from his eyes 'instead of tears'. As Faustus pleads that 'one drop' then 'half a drop' would save his soul, he confesses his barren littleness of life in the vastness of the moral universe.

As the vision of blood fades, Faustus meets the unappeased wrath of God and cries for the mountains and hills to fall on him (see, e.g., Luke XXIII 30, Revelation VI 16, Hosea X 8). Burial in earth becomes a privilege refused to the last paroxysms of Faustus's will. He is again re-enacting the fall of Lucifer, the figure in Isaiah who is 'brought down to hell, to the sides of the pit' and 'cast out of the grave like an abominable branch' (Isaiah XIV). When Faustus hopes for a refining ordeal of dissolution and rebirth in 'the entrails of yon labouring clouds' which might 'vomit forth' his limbs and let his soul 'ascend to heaven' his words seem haunted by Lucifer's – 'I will ascend above the heights of the clouds, I will be like the Most High'; and the same chapter could supply the stretching arm of God and the smoke of the Last Day (Isaiah, xiv). Marlowe has assimilated and re-created the Biblical imagery, however, and it is dramatically valid whether or not we suppose it allusive. Faustus, the damned hero as the play has fashioned him, has become the fittest witness of apocalyptic vision. No chorus could speak with such moving authority, for Faustus alone has enacted all the futilities of pride.

The first phase of the soliloquy discovers the futility of human pretensions to power in the face of overwhelming cataclysm, the second makes us feel the futility of knowledge and speculation. Faustus's plea for 'some end to my incessant pain' (recalling the Faust-book and the Spira story and play [*The Conflict of Conscience*]) sums up that side of the Christian tradition which, with Augustine, is 'Against those that exclude both men and devils from pain eternal' (*City of God*, xxii xxiii). Like 'Pythagoras' metempsychosis' it is wishful thinking. *The French Academy* (ii 85) could have occasioned the allusion to Pythagoras and supplied the distinction between the souls of brutes (made of 'elements') and those of men ('created of nothing'). And it would challenge Faustus's readiness to accuse the stars that reigned at his nativity by asking, 'how should the heavens, stars and planets give that to the soul which they themselves have not?' (ii 87).

Faustus moderates his struggle to escape the pain of responsibility as he curses his parents (see Luke xxiii 29) and then checks himself: 'No Faustus, curse thyself, curse Lucifer That hath deprived thee of the joys of heaven.' Again, if we read 'Lucifer' as a metaphor for Pride, the problem of responsibility recedes; but it returns when we think of the devil as a person and evil as a power outside the consciousness of man. In either case, it is fitting that the pride of knowledge should be finally purged with 'I'll burn my books!' and the fellowship of sin perpetuated with 'Ah Mephostophilis!'

In the last scene, as in Shakespeare's tragedies, normal life must

resume as best it can. Marlowe (there is no need to suppose a
collaborator) abstains from the grotesque nastiness of the Faustbook catastrophe, and strikes an apt balance between horror,
dismay and due reverence. If the noise that the scholars report
seems a concession to popular taste, we may reflect that it might
be a clue to the acting of Faustus's closing words, from 'My God,
my God! Look not so fierce on me', and remember Psalm xxii:

> My God, my God, why hast thou forsaken me? why art thou
> so far from helping me, and from the words of my roaring?

Source: *Marlowe: Dr Faustus* (1962).

J. B. Steane

THE INSTABILITY OF FAUST⌐⌐
(1964)

IF *Faustus* is a great work, it is also a flawed one. It is not merely a matter of two poor scenes and two which degenerate into nonsense, a sequence of trivial episodes and two occasions where the climax is disappointingly followed up. There is also, more seriously, a lack of sustained concentrated writing in places where one might have hoped for it, and often, by Shakespearean standards at any rate, a poverty of poetic texture. Sometimes, as one is thinking how to describe something in the play, a Shakespearean phrase comes to mind: Faustus, for instance, might be described as

> destil'd
> Almost to *Ielly* with the Act of feare.
> > (*Hamlet*, I ii)

It is a very unremarkable phrase in the richness of its context but would represent a remarkable enrichment of vocabulary in a Marlovian context. How far Marlowe is *responsible* for these shortcomings is an irrelevant query when one is concerned . . . with the text as the object or fact which exists for us.

This 'fact' has rarely been the critics' prime apparent interest in the play. Perhaps an exception is Mr James Smith, whose essay in *Scrutiny* (VIII (1939)) was limited to certain aspects of *Faustus* as a work of art. But the prime concern seems to have been with *Faustus* as a significant phenomenon rather than a work of art. Mr Levin's close study, for instance, appears to have as its prime concern an act of relating or connecting; that is, it seems for the most part to be interested in the text when it can be related to something outside itself, a whole body of European culture, adduced with breadth and knowledge, but involving the play more as a portent, a significance, than a work of art. This is true also of Miss Mahood's penetrating remarks in *Poetry and Humanism*. The effect of this kind of interest has been both to shrug off too lightly the flaws in the play (its 'significance' remains) *and* to insulate the reader from the full force of the work (as opposed to recognition of the 'phenomenon').

It is true that some of these flaws are not beyond defence. The middle section, writes Harry Levin, 'is unquestionably weak. The structural weakness, however, corresponds to the anti-climax of the parable; it lays bare the gap between promise and fruition, between the bright hopes of the initial scene and the abysmal consequences of the last.' There are other points of correspondence. I understand Mr Levin to mean that these middle scenes act, in their weakness, as a gap between the first and last sections, throwing them and the contrast between them into relief. He seems, then, to be referring to the *ultimate* fruition. But the disappointment of the immediate fruition is enforced also. The 'world of profit and delight' turns out, as dramatised, to be sadly trivial, even progressively trivial, and ever-less vital. There is a certain wonder in Faustus' European travel, as described by himself and the Chorus; also a certain zest about the doings in the Vatican. Both the wonder and the fun degenerate in the scene with the Emperor. The fun is at its lowest with the Horse-Courser, and wonder is practically extinguished in the Vanholt scene. So that this middle section does not exactly 'lay bare' the gap between the promise of the first scene and the fruition of the last, but shows the stages between them. The scenes illustrate the growing emptiness of the way of life Faustus has chosen. That is (and must have been then to the sensitive part of the audience) the moral effect; though there is some relevance in the objection that there are better ways of presenting boredom than by being boring, or triviality than by being trivial.

It is not likely that Goethe had this sort of discussion in mind when he made that famous remark, 'How greatly is it all planned.' Yet these are the points that need facing in order to say it and mean anything very much by it. This dictum, like the middle section of the play, has something to be said for it, not so much by virtue of its doubtful intentions, but because, in itself and as it stands, it has point. (The intended meaning seems not to be what the modern critic would like to make it, for the adjective *gross* suggests something more like 'on a large scale', great in the sense of large, rather than a qualitative judgment; and, although in English the emphasis of the sentence comes meaningfully on 'planned', in German the emphasis probably falls on *gross* rather than *angelegt*, which anyway suggests 'laid out' as of a park or garden, which is not really very appropriate to *Faustus*.)

The great planning, however, is plentifully in evidence. Miss Mahood justifies the term by reference to the 'philosophical structure'; and one might add the creation and development of character, the working of dramatic climax, and the linking backwards and forwards, by means open to the dramatic poet (and Marlowe is primarily that, not a philosopher), of lines and phrases which thus gain in intensity and relevance.

Other kinds of planning it clearly has not. Any complex interplay of plots and characters, for example. It has the structural bareness of the fifteenth-century *Everyman* which in several ways it resembles. The grave dignity of that play is absent (in its mirth and knockabout mixed with serious matter, *Faustus* is more like the normal Morality than *Everyman* is). Moreover, Marlowe has, characteristically, reversed much in the traditional Morality pattern. *Everyman* and *Mankind*, for instance, dramatise Holy Dying and Holy Living respectively: *Faustus* is about evil living and consequently desperate dying. Mankind and Everyman crawl up to their God; Faustus even in his last hour still aspires to leap, and it can't be done. The earlier pair, in a pilgrim's progress, climb the steep ascent of Heaven, and flights of angels sing Everyman to his rest; Faustus, the Devil's disciple, goes the primrose way and Hell calls with a roaring voice. But the admonitions of *Everyman* are those of *Faustus*:

> The story sayth: man, in the begynnynge
> Loke well and take good heed to the endynge,
> Be you never so gay.

And in both plays, a man's soul is the stage; the forces from without correspond to forces within, and Heaven and Hell play for the victory.

The people of the mediæval psychomachia have the representative characters of their names. That is, they are not distinctive characters at all, however convincingly human in their reaction to the given situation. Faustus is an individual in spite of the tendency the morality element has to categorise him among the 'forward wits'. He is inevitably one of a class or type – the young extremist, eager and buoyant, with a brilliantly energetic, inquiring mind, intoxicated by his enthusiasms, heady in his dislikes, and fundamentally superficial in both. But the character develops. After the Vatican scene, the boyish quality disappears and there is a sense of ageing. The keynote of the weak Vanholt scene is its courtesy, and in that and the two later scenes with the scholars it is a quieter and more mature Faustus who is admired. As in the beginning he was placed in a relationship of youth with age by the 'sage conference' of Valdes and Cornelius, so in the last Act he is felt to be a senior man in company with the scholars. His sheer energy has declined. 'Confound these passions with a quiet sleepe'; later the scenes with Helen have almost the quiet dignity of an Indian summer; and his sighs in the last scene with the scholars are those of a man whose vitality is weakened. But in all these things he is still, partly, representative. In other respects he is a very unusual man indeed.

He is a chaos of will and impotence. His humanism, proud and aspiring, is expressed in the lines:

> All things that mooue betweene the quiet poles
> Shalbe at my commaund, Emperours and Kings
> Are but obeyd in their seuerall prouinces:
> Nor can they raise the winde, or rend the cloudes:
> But his dominion that exceedes in this,
> Stretcheth as farre as doth the minde of man.   (i 55–60)

'The mind of man' is the nearest thing in creation to infinity; it is creation's crown. But it is checked by nature: the winds and clouds are nothing in the scale of being, yet they remain as symbols of intractable matter. Man is limited (this is the feeling) not by his own nature, but by the nature of the world that encloses him. Miss Mahood says, 'Pride in man's potentialities is swiftly reversed to despair at his limitations':

> Yet art thou still but *Faustus*, and a man.   (i 23)

She also writes of the 'extreme swings of the pendulum' in Faustus: 'contemptuous pride and incredulous despair'. What sets the pendulum in motion concerns the will; here there is a fundamental instability. Faustus sees the will as the ultimate power within man, but it is a will which at the same time he morbidly suspects to be illusory and governed by something outside itself.

He dismisses Divinity because it seems to involve a hateful determinism which denies the real freedom to 'settle', 'begin' and 'be'. Faustus is intent, as the essential means to any worth-while end, on asserting his will. His first speech is that of a man determined not to run on wheels; he is to make the existentialist choice and start living. His will may, as he implies to Mephasto-philis, be boundless and crazy. He may assert it in something like Gide's *acte gratuit*:

> Be it to make the Moone drop from her spheare,
> Or the Ocean to ouerwhelme the world.   (iii 40–1)

He might in fact will to act out Ulysses' Order speech, 'and make a soppe of all this solid Globe': 'Then euery thing includes it selfe in ... Will.'

But the rejected biblical texts also proclaimed (in their truncated form) a necessary, fated damnation. It is no accident that precisely those texts are chosen, or that Faustus should have overlooked or have deliberately and proudly set his face against that text which follows the quotation from St John: 'But if we confess our sins, he is faithful and just to forgive us our sins, and cleanse us from all unrighteousness.' That is the Christian doctrine of grace, and Faustus has no conception of it. Clearly, then, in his mind, he must be damned if there is any truth in Divinity. He has made a gesture of dismissal towards Divinity and acted on the assumption that he has done more than that. But

he has not in fact dismissed it from his mind at all. This lurking
sense of damnation *precedes* the invocation to Mephastophilis,
and the conviction of it precedes the formal deed with Lucifer:

> Now *Faustus* must thou needes be damnd
> And canst thou not be saued? . . .
> To God? he loues thee not,
> The god thou seruest is thine owne appetite.
>
> (v 1–2, 10–11)

In this speech is expressed not only the certainty of damnation
but a deep sense of sinfulness: he does not deserve God's love for
he has served his appetite ('Will into Appetite'). Again, the sinfulness is not just the result of his dealings with the devil but also
the cause of them: it was not his 'coniuring speeches' that raised
Mephastophilis, but his spiritual condition. The conviction of
worthlessness and inevitable damnation grows:

> If vnto God hee'le throwe thee downe to hell. (v 78)

The words of the Evil Angel strengthen it:

> Thou art a spirite, God cannot pitty thee.   (vi 13)

And the fearful echo of Faustus' own thought: 'Too late'.
Scepticism, hope and attempted repentance all challenge this
conviction in Faustus, but it is deeply embedded in his thought
and emerges ultimately in the last speech:

> You starres that raignd at my natiuitie,
> Whose influence hath alotted death and hel. . . .
>
> (xix 157–8)

The free-thinking Renaissance humanist only hides a tradi-
tionalism which is basically mediæval: the conservatism of
Lear's Gloucester as against the bright scepticism of the 'new
man' Edmund.

   The forces represented in this tension within the individual
are deep in European civilisation, and that explains why commentators have been so much concerned with *Faustus* as a
'significance'. Strangely, the man whose story comes to mind as
being most Faust-like in this way lived neither in the Renaissance

nor the Middle Ages, but in the 'Age of Reason'. Cowper's biography contains a terrible latter-day psychomachia: 'His bedroom was every night the battle-ground of a struggle between good and evil spirits, and . . . in the end the evil always vanquished the good, and then "Bring him out!" they would cry, "bring him out!".' Cowper was convinced of his damnation: 'On the night of 24 February he had a dream. What it precisely was no one knows; but in it amid circumstances of unspeakable horror, he heard from the lips of God himself the certain and irrevocable sentence of his damnation. . . . Within the centre of his consciousness remained unaltered the conviction that he was damned, that every day he passed brought him a day nearer to an eternity of torment; and he had fixed his eyes exclusively on such things as could still give him pleasure, had laboriously derived from them the whole elaborate scheme of occupation and habit and amusement which was his mode of life, in order to distract himself from the frightful fate that awaited him.'[1] This is from what another writer has described as 'the saddest and sweetest life in English literature'![2] Here are two of Cowper's own utterances, the first from an early poem (*Hatred and Vengeance*):

> Damned below Judas; more abhorred than he was,
> Who for a few pence sold his holy Master!
> Twice betrayed, Jesus me, the last delinquent,
> > Deems the profanest.

And the second from his diary:

Friday, Nov. 16th . . . Dreamt that in a state of the most insupportable misery, I looked through the window of a strange room, being all alone, and saw preparations being made for my execution. That it was about four days distant and that then I was destined to suffer everlasting martyrdom in the fire, my body being prepared for the purpose and my dissolution made a thing impossible. Rose overwhelmed with infinite despair, and came down into the study, execrating the day I was born with inexpressible bitterness.

This 'sweet, sad life' is, in this, not unlike what Marlowe presents us with in *Faustus*. Conscious of the Romantic heresy, one wonders whether it has anything in common with Marlowe's own.

The involvement of the author in his work is, of course, much debated. John Bakeless 'feels an autobiographical touch, feels it keenly too'. Miss Josephine Preston Peabody, quoted by Bakeless, had no doubt about it. She makes the Marlowe of her play cry: 'I am the man, the devil and the soul.' Others imply it in their judgments. Michel Poirier writes: 'That more or less conscious distortion of the Christian doctrine is rather to be ascribed to the author's nature, to his narrow logic, to his incapacity to understand the grandeur and beauty of the message of the Gospel.' That is to make Marlowe 'the man' at least, and virtually 'the devil' as well. Critics in the opposing camp include Miss Mahood, James Smith and Roy Battenhouse.

A decision here depends partly on the attitude one already has to questions of this kind, and partly on the amount of weight one allows such biographical evidence as the Baines note. With P. H. Kocher, I take the note seriously. As Faustus had used 'such meanes whereby he [was] in danger to be damnd', so (the evidence suggests) had Marlowe. It does not follow that Marlowe is making a personal recantation as some have thought, or that he had no more idea of grace than Faustus had (as Poirier implies), or that the play is essentially a sermon on the explicit 'moral' of the Epilogue. But when Miss Mahood says that 'In his tragic heroes he has embodied the spiritual adventures of his own generation, as he observed them', one has to add that as he was himself 'of his own generation' he probably, like his introspective Faustus, observed his own spiritual adventures with particular closeness. He does in fact seem to me to be 'giving of his own substance', as Professor Waldock says of Milton;[3] and this does not open him to Dr Leavis's charge which he makes – justly, I think – against Milton, of failing to depersonalise 'the relevant interests and impulses of his private life'.

For if 'his own substance' is there, and if the biographical evidence for supposing this is true, then Marlowe achieved a rare degree of detachment. The Marlowe of the Baines note and the tales is treated with little respect. The knight in the Emperor's court, for instance, is in some ways an enlightened freethinker. He will not accept Faustus on authority: 'Ifaith he lookes much like a coniurer.' That, according to the Baines note, was very much Marlowe's attitude to the reputation of Moses. The knight is contemptuous of the conjuring, and smart in the style of his commenting. In his promise to the Emperor, Faustus has allowed himself a fairly generous logical loop-hole. The knight observes it and says 'Ifaith thats iust nothing at all.' One might suppose this sceptical intelligence to be congenial to Marlowe, but in fact the knight is humiliated. This scene may not be Marlowe's own, but the same is true of Faustus himself in a scene which is certainly authentic. He too is a freethinker with advanced notions: 'Come, I thinke hell's a fable.' And later:

> Thinkst thou that Faustus is so fond, to imagine,
> That after this life there is any paine?
> Tush, these are trifles and meere olde wiues tales.

(v 134–6)

And:

> This word damnation terrifies not him,
> For he confounds hell in *Elizium*.
> His ghost be with the olde Philosophers.[4]

(iii 61–3)

These are all in spirit like the Marlowe of the Baines note, willing men 'not to be afeard of bugbeares and hobgoblins' and persuading them 'to Atheism'. This boastfully independent free-thinking always carries with it a dramatic irony in the play, and provokes the bitterly ironical comment of Mephastophilis: 'I, thinke so still, till experience change thy minde.'

Perhaps it would seem that Marlowe could not have the views attributed to him by the Baines note and at the same time hold them up to irony and humiliation in the play. But it surely is possible, understandable and moving. It would only argue in Marlowe a division and uncertainty like that he dramatises with this characteristic see-saw or wave motion in Faustus. Indeed if there is any truth in his reputation as it has come down to us, some such division is surely inevitable. However firmly a man believed with his reason that traditional religion is essentially superstition, he must also, in his soul, have felt that traditional wisdom affirming the religion could not be so utterly mistaken. The Baines note shows a nonconformist, confident in his attack and almost heroic in his boldness. But the weight of ages cannot be shaken off, and if the ages are not wrong then the freethinker must be. If he is wrong, they are right; and if they are right there is pain after this life; and for those who abjure the Scriptures, exercising their pitiful intelligence where a blind understanding is required, the ten thousand doors of hell wait ajar. The Marlowe who wrote *Faustus* need not have renounced publicly or privately the nonconformity of the Baines note, but he must have known doubts and fears of an agonising kind. Such a tension would involve a very Faust-like instability.

Instability is fundamental in the play, as a theme and a characteristic. *Faustus* is a play of violent contrasts within a rigorous structural unity. Hilarity and agony, seriousness and irresponsibility: even on the most cautious theories of authorship, Marlowe is responsible at times for all these extremes. This artistic instability matches the instability of the hero. The extremes of optimism and depression, enthusiasm and hatred, commitment to Hell and aspiration to Heaven, pride and shame: these are the swings of the pendulum in Faustus' world, and they are reflected by the sickening to-and-fro motion of the verse – an ambivalence first felt in the Prologue's 'forme of *Faustus* fortunes good or bad'. But this to-and-fro of extremes is not the only movement in the play. The other movement (and this seems to me fundamental in Marlowe's career as a writer, as it is in this play) is one of *shrinkage*. Faustus stands on his own two feet, a proud thing in creation, as he conjures in his lusty grove; but in the end, he cowers and hides, wishing his manhood to be shrunk to the stature of a brutish beast and finally to that of the lowest, least individual thing in the creation he once thought to dominate. He is bent and shrunk not merely by his contact with evil, but because in the first place he would not bend and shrink submissively to the will of the powers that shape the world. Man has to crawl between heaven and hell. In *Tamburlaine* that space seemed so ample that he could strut wonderfully and challenge the other worlds to match his splendour. In *Faustus* this world (and Faustus like a millionaire tourist has 'done it all') yields less. In the other plays it is to yield less still.

SOURCE: *Marlowe: A Critical Study* (1964).

NOTES

1. Quotations from Lord David Cecil, *The Stricken Deer* (1929).
2. George Sampson, *The Concise Cambridge History of English Literature* (1961).
3. *Paradise Lost and Its Critics* (1947).
4. J. C. Maxwell (*Notes and Queries*, CXCIV) has noted the identity of the last line with a saying attributed to the Arabic philosopher Averroes, expressing his hostility to Christianity.

D. J. Palmer

MAGIC AND POETRY IN
DOCTOR FAUSTUS (1964)

MAGIC is not only the subject of *Doctor Faustus*, it is the means by which the dramatic illusion generates power and conviction. As in *Tamburlaine*, Marlowe evidently conceives the stage as an area liberated from the limitations which nature imposes on the world around; the restraining conditions of probability here seem to be in abeyance, and Marlowe's stage affords scope to realise the gigantic fantasies of his heroes. In *Doctor Faustus* the stage assumes the properties of a magic circle, within which dramatic spectacle is transformed into enchanted vision, and poetry is endowed with the power of conjuring spirits. We do wrong to feel, as many critics have done, a kind of embarrassment, or even intellectual superiority towards the necromantic elements in the play, for it is precisely through the business of magic that Marlowe effects the heightening and tension necessary to the tragic experience. Few would claim that the play maintains its tragic intensity throughout, or that a sense of structure was one of Marlowe's strengths as a playwright. The farcical episodes which occupy the middle of the action do not have a very sophisticated appeal, and whoever actually wrote them, they remain Marlowe's responsibility as the chief architect of the play. However, the clowning with the Pope, Emperor and the rest, frivolous as it is, should not obscure from us the subtler effects which Marlowe obtains from stage-magic elsewhere in the tragedy. Theatrical trickery is certainly stuff to thrill the groundlings, but the same exploitation of Faustus' supernatural powers in terms of dramatic illusion also underlies those moments of poetic rapture and tragic grandeur that constitute Marlowe's supreme achievement. There was one controlling idea behind the dramatising of the Faust Book: that the drama, particularly the poetic drama, is itself a kind of enchantment.

The notion of drama as the art of illusion is at least as ancient as the rival view that drama imitates life; the two concepts are not really contradictory, though they have their respective origins in the literary theories of Plato and Aristotle. Shakespeare, as we should expect, lent his support to both views: Hamlet's advice to the players restates the mimetic function of drama, 'whose end, both at the first and now, was and is to hold, as 'twere, the mirror up to nature', while in *The Tempest* Prospero's speech at the conclusion of the masque pays memorable tribute to the imaginative power of illusion. But most of our critical terminology for discussing drama has come down to us through the Aristotelian tradition of mimesis, and in judging characterisation and action in all kinds of drama we almost inevitably look for probability and truth to nature. Sir Philip Sidney, surveying the popular drama of his day in *An Apologie for Poetry*, scorned it for the neglect of those unities of time and place which critical authority held to be the basis of credible dramatic action:

. . . you shal have *Asia* of the one side, and *Affrick* of the other, and so many other under-kingdoms, that the Player, when he commeth in, must ever begin with telling where he is, or els the tale wil not be conceived. Now ye shal have three Ladies walke to gather flowers, and then we must beleeve the stage to be a Garden. By and by, we heare newes of shipwracke in the same place, and then wee are to blame if we accept it not for a Rock. Upon the backe of that, comes out a hidious Monster, with fire and smoke, and then the miserable beholders are bounde to take it for a Cave. While in the meantime two Armies flye in, represented with foure swords and bucklers, and then what harde heart will not receive it for a pitched fielde? Now, of time they are much more liberall, for ordinary it is that two young Princes fall in love. After many traverces, she is got with childe, delivered of a faire boy; he is lost, groweth a man, falls in love, and is ready to get another child; and all this in two hours space. . . .

Sidney did not live to see Marlowe endow the popular stage with poetic genius, but whether his criteria would have been different if he had written during the 1590s, during the flourishing of the London theatres, is of less interest than the fact that Sidney's description here suits exactly the treatment of time and place which we find in *Doctor Faustus*. The action covers twenty-four years of Faustus' life, and ranges over most of Europe in presenting his adventures: far from trying to concentrate his plot in the manner of a Corneille or a Racine, by observing on his stage the same physical limitations which would govern it as a location in the real world, Marlowe exploits the stage as a world free from the laws of time and place. His stage is exciting precisely because it is not true to nature in the respects laid down by Sidney, and evidently in this disregard for probability he was perpetuating the habits of popular drama. No doubt Marlowe's play, like those of his predecessors, would have been better constructed if more attention had been paid to the unities, affording concentration and probability, and no doubt some tightening-up along these lines would have spared us from the low farce in the middle of the play (the episodes included in the 1616 Quarto but omitted from the 1604 Quarto suggest a play of potentially variable length: with twenty-four adventure-packed years to choose from in the source book there was no lack of material). But a neo-classical *Doctor Faustus* would be a radically different play, for the most successful effects of Marlowe's tragedy are also derived from his conception of dramatic illusion. The meaning of the play is expressed through an awareness of illusion.

The methods with which Marlowe, Shakespeare and their contemporaries went to work make it easy to understand why the unities of time and place were never properly accepted in Elizabethan drama. It was essentially a narrative art, transposing for the stage stories from non-dramatic sources, and retaining that multiplicity of incident which was so much to Elizabethan taste, as we can also see in the *Faerie Queene* and the *Arcadia*. The chronicle play, with its seemingly intractable material drawn from the flux of history, was a characteristic Elizabethan invention. In dramatising these narratives playwrights found certain means of compressing or externalising action in the stage conventions surviving from the moralities and interludes. Thus,

Marlowe uses the rather awkward device of the Good and Bad Angels to project the conflict over Faustus' soul as though he were the Everyman of the older allegorical drama, and the counsel offered by the saintly Old Man is clearly derived from the same tradition. The conventions of the soliloquy permitted Marlowe to schematise and compress a train of thought, as in the opening scene of the play, where Faustus' review and rejection of each branch of learning is presented in formal terms that summarise and represent an interior process independent of time. The physical shape of the projecting stage itself, in a theatre open to the sky, also assisted the playwright in freeing his scenes from any localised setting.

On a stage where the laws of material reality are suspended at will, Marlowe's disregard of probability is at one with Faustus' flouting of divine commandment, and Faustus' illusion of demonic power over nature is both image and source of the drama's hold upon its spectators. We are, as literally as possible, spellbound. As with Tamburlaine's astounding progress, the spectators collaborate readily in this vicarious experience of infinitely extended power, which affords a conscious exhilaration and sense of release. At its simplest level, the illusion enlists merely a kind of wish-fulfilment or indulged fantasy; the havoc which Faustus creates at the Pope's banquet, like Tamburlaine's treatment of captive kings, is an obvious appeal to our secret and anarchic fantasies, thinly veiled in good Protestant sentiment.

Few Elizabethan playwrights had any qualms about the spectacular, and in *Doctor Faustus* Marlowe seems to exult in the power of dramatic illusion: the first entrance of Mephostophilis, the pageant of the Seven Deadly Sins, the vision of Helen, each show Marlowe's love of strong visual appeal. But the pull of the magic stage is not dependent on spectacle alone, and what Marlowe cannot present in material form he conjures in lyrical, almost ecstatic poetry, so that we are caught up in Faustus' swelling aspirations of becoming a 'demi-god':

> How am I glutted with conceit of this!
> Shall I make spirits fetch me what I please,

> Resolve me of all ambiguities,
> Perform what desperate enterprise I will?
> I'll have them fly to India for gold,
> Ransack the ocean for orient pearl,
> And search all corners of the new-found world
> For pleasant fruits and princely delicates;
> I'll have them read me strange philosophy
> And tell the secrets of all foreign kings;
> I'll have them wall all Germany with brass
> And make swift Rhine circle fair Wittenberg. . . .

In later scenes there is more in this vein, which recalls Tamburlaine's vaunting speeches, where the insistent future tense opens up vistas of fantastic splendour. The characteristic Marlovian mode extends the boundaries of the drama far beyond the physical limits of the stage, and the elemental powers of the universe seem to attend at the summons of this mighty rhetoric. Well might Faustus say, 'I see there's virtue in my heavenly words.' The visions which haunt the imaginations of Marlowe's ambitious heroes are as much a part of the action as the machinery of spectacular showmanship, and expressed with that vividness and brilliance which the Elizabethans termed *enargia*. Marlowe's poetry is an important vehicle of dramatic illusion; its purpose is to make us feel as much aware of the visions described as though we were seeing them with our own eyes:

> Learned Faustus,
> To find the secrets of astronomy,
> Graven in the book of Jove's high firmament,
> Did mount him up to scale Olympus' top,
> Where, sitting in a chariot burning bright
> Drawn by the strength of yoked dragons' necks,
> He views the clouds, the planets, and the stars,
> The tropics, zones, and quarters of the sky,
> From the bright circle of the horned moon
> Even to the height of *primum mobile*;
> And, whirling round with this circumference
> Within the concave compass of the pole,
> From east to west his dragons swiftly glide
> And in eight days did bring him home again.

Here the verbal tense shifts from past to present to reinforce the illusion, and under the spell of this poetry the invisible regions are revealed before us, transcending the narrow confines of the stage: the poetry partakes of that power with which language seems to call forth the spirits of another world. Whatever else in Marlowe's play would have displeased Sir Philip Sidney, here indeed is that 'vigor of his owne invention' which Sidney attributed to the true poet, in a passage that draws more upon Platonism than upon the Aristotelian doctrine of mimesis:

Nature can never set forth the earth in so rich tapistry as divers Poets have done, neither with pleasant rivers, fruitful trees, sweet smelling flowers, nor whatsoever els may make the too much loved earth more lovely. Her world is brasen, the Poets only deliver a golden.

By creating a world more compelling in its imaginary vastness and beauty than the actors' scaffold which, stripped of the illusion, is all that actually exists, Marlowe's verse is performing the tasks which Elizabethans assumed to constitute the art of poetry. To move, to persuade, to convince, were the ends to which the poet applied his mastery over language, while the rhetoricians and figurists documented the means by which he was able to sway those whom he addressed.

Yet the transforming spell which this rhetoric exerts upon the drama never rests complete, for the tragedy will show that the magic is a cheat, and that Faustus, who would be a 'demi-god', is 'but a man condemn'd to die'. The tragedy demands simultaneously the breathtaking sense of infinite time and space, the persuasive vision of supernatural wealth and beauty, and also the awareness that these are illusions, an underlying feeling of disenchantment. This sense of the emptiness of Faustus' ambitions, however vast and splendid they are, is first apparent in his interrogation of Mephostophilis, through the revelation that the demon has come of his own accord, not under the compulsion of Faustus' conjuring. In fact the characterisation of Mephostophilis in his grave and melancholy replies to Faustus, invests him and the infernal regions whence he came with a reality and dignity

besides which the bravado of Faustus is now seen with critical
detachment as a foolish deception we can no longer share:

Faustus. Tell me, what is that Lucifer thy lord?
Mephostophilis. Arch-regent and commander of all spirits.
Faustus. Was not that Lucifer an angel once?
Mephostophilis. Yes, Faustus, and most dearly lov'd of God.
Faustus. How comes it then that he is prince of devils?
Mephostophilis. O, by aspiring pride and insolence,
    For which God threw him from the face of heaven.
Faustus. And what are you that live with Lucifer?
Mephostophilis. Unhappy spirits that fell with Lucifer,
    Conspir'd against our God with Lucifer,
    And are for ever damn'd with Lucifer.
Faustus. Where are you damn'd?
Mephostophilis.   In hell.
Faustus. How comes it then that thou art out of hell?
Mephostophilis. Why, this is hell, nor am I out of it.
    Think'st thou that I, who saw the face of God
    And tasted the eternal joys of heaven,
    Am not tormented with ten thousand hells
    In being depriv'd of everlasting bliss?
    O Faustus, leave these frivolous demands,
    Which strike a terror to my fainting soul.
Faustus. What, is great Mephostophilis so passionate
    For being deprived of the joys of heaven?
    Learn thou of Faustus manly fortitude
    And scorn those joys thou never shalt possess.

In this first part of the play, the initiative seems to pass from
Faustus to his attendant spirit: his disbelief in the pains of hell,
his hubristic blindness, strike hollow against the measured
affirmation of Mephostophilis that 'Where we are is hell,/ And
where hell is, there must we ever be', and his magic powers
dwindle to a mere means of diversion when Faustus dismisses
the subject and asks to be given a wife. Later, he calls upon
Christ, and with a terrifying stroke of irony, he is confronted
instead by Beelzebub. It seems as though the satanic powers have
assumed complete control. There is a shift in the dramatic
illusion; the fantasies of magic lose their conviction in the face of

Mephostophilis' passionate suffering, Faustus' hubris serves as a foil to heighten the awesome reality of hell, and the demon seems paradoxically more tragic and human than the man. Having at the outset enlisted our belief in a stage free from the limitations of natural probability, Marlowe now sets off those boundless visions of enchantment against the eternal tortures of the damned, an imprisonment infinitely more terrible than the circumscription of nature's law, and in the device of this new perspective which secures our acquiescence, it is an illusion of much more compelling reality. Sufficiently compelling, at least, to foster one or two strange stories about contemporary performances, such as the following:

Certaine Players at Exeter, acting upon the stage the tragicall storie of Dr. Faustus the Conjurer; as a certain nomber of Devels kept everie one his circle there, and as Faustus was busie in his magicall invocations, on a sudden they were all dasht, every one harkning other in the eare, for they were all perswaded, there was one devell too many amongst them; and so after a little pause desired the people to pardon them, they could go no further with this matter; the people also understanding the thing as it was, every man hastened to be first out of dores. The players (as I heard it) contrarye to their custome spending the night in reading and in prayer got them out of the town the next morning.

The scenes with Mephostophilis in the first half of the play are a remarkable piece of dramatic writing. The creation of dialogue does not seem to have come easily to Marlowe, who preferred wherever possible the direct impact upon the audience conveyed in set speeches, with their greater scope for the soaring rhetoric of his mighty line. Even the earliest of Shakespeare's plays have a fluency and genuine engagement between the characters in dialogue that are seldom found in Marlowe's work. The dialogue between Faustus and Mephostophilis is a catechism, a formal interrogation, in which the demon expounds theology and astronomy and explains the terms of the bond Faustus wishes to make. Yet Marlowe manages to transform this rather cramped framework into a vehicle of astonishing dramatic interest: Mephostophilis is characterised through his reluctance to dwell upon the suffering that Faustus cannot grasp as real, and through those baffling retorts which reveal his unsuspected independent volition:

> *Faustus.* Did not he charge thee to appear to me?
> *Mephostophilis.* No, I came hither of mine own accord.
> *Faustus.* Did not my conjuring speeches raise thee? Speak.
> *Mephostophilis.* That was the cause, but yet *per accidens*.

The middle scenes of the play lack tragic and poetic intensity, although Marlowe's general intentions (whoever carried them out) are clear enough. This descent to buffoonery and knock-about horseplay is an attempt to develop the popular convention which mixed clowns with kings, by integrating the 'comic relief' with the serious themes of the tragedy. The tragic hero is himself the clown in these scenes, his trifling and conjuring tricks fore-shadowed by the terrible frivolity he has already shown in his manner of quizzing Mephostophilis. This streak of reckless sportiveness, with its grimly ironic undertones, is found in Marlowe's other heroes, above all in Barrabas, and T. S. Eliot's description of the dominant mode in *The Jew of Malta* as savage farce is not altogether inappropriate to the kind of comedy occupying the middle action of *Doctor Faustus*. The frivolity has an uneasy edge to it; the illusions effected by the conjurer and his assistant disguise but at the same time manifest the illusion and self-deception in which Faustus exists. Neverthe-less, the thematic point is made at a heavy cost in terms of artistic quality, and this part of the play is not wholly redeemed by the recognition of its relationship to the overall design of the work.

The vision of Helen is remembered for the brilliance of Faustus' invocation. Yet this scene depends too upon the presentation of magic in terms of theatrical spectacle. From its context the rapturous hymn to beauty gains a richness of meaning and implication which eludes us if we read it as a detachable piece of lyric verse:

> Was this the face that launch'd a thousand ships
> And burnt the topless towers of Ilium?

> Sweet Helen, make me immortal with a kiss.
> Her lips suck forth my soul: see where it flies!
> Come, Helen, come, give me my soul again.
> Here will I dwell, for heaven is in these lips,
> And all is dross that is not Helena.
> I will be Paris, and for love of thee
> Instead of Troy, shall Wittenberg be sack'd,
> And I will combat with weak Menelaus
> And wear thy colours on my plumed crest,
> Yea, I will wound Achilles in the heel
> And then return to Helen for a kiss.
> O, thou art fairer than the evening air
> Clad in the beauty of a thousand stars,
> Brighter art thou than flaming Jupiter
> When he appear'd to hapless Semele,
> More lovely than the monarch of the sky
> In wanton Arethusa's azur'd arms,
> And none but thou shalt be my paramour.

The speech is wonderfully articulated in three sweeping movements, the second strophe beginning with that evocation of the heroic world which reaches a minor climax in returning 'to Helen for a kiss' before the final strophe takes flight to a yet more ecstatic pitch. Faustus commences, we notice, with a tribute to the power of beauty, as though he recognises in Helen's charms an enchantment akin to his own demonic powers: both are destructive. The properties of magic communicate themselves through the poetry, which in its imagery and rhythm first transforms Faustus and Wittenberg into Paris and Troy, and then metamorphoses Helen and her lover into gods. Here in the final part of the speech there is a curious reversal of rôles implied in the images: Helen's appearance before Faustus is compared to that of Jupiter to Semele, and that of Apollo to Arethusa. In each case the literal sense asserts that Helen's beauty is figured in the male god, but the inclusion of Semele and 'wanton Arethusa' assist the transposition which we naturally make, so that what we actually understand by these lines is that Faustus has himself assumed the majesty (and immortality) of the gods, while Helen really takes her place with the nymphs. It is a subtle effect, a species of enchantment that not only deifies but also suggests a sexual metamorphosis in the union with Helen.

Faustus' poetry invests Helen and himself with mythological splendour; it lifts them into another dimension of illusion, and clothes the nakedness of the stage. It is a kind of speech used on several occasions by Shakespeare, whenever the presence of a character was of itself insufficient to create the heightened awareness and romantic mood he required. So Romeo identifies the vision of Juliet at her balcony with the beauty of the stars, in a speech which simultaneously lends to Juliet an added loveliness and creates the necessary setting of night; Portia is transformed to a fabulous treasure in Bassanio's words, even before we have seen her,

> ... the four winds blow in from every coast
> Renowned suitors, and her sunny locks
> Hang on her temples like a golden fleece,
> Which makes her seat of Belmont Colchos' strand,
> And many Jasons come in quest of her ...;

and, most magical of all, the silent Hermione is at last restored to her husband, transformed to a statue, before she becomes alive indeed: a double metamorphosis. Faustus' verbal transfiguration of Helen may help to disguise the limitations of the boy actor, but as the rhapsodic verse sweeps us from Bankside and Wittenberg to the Golden Age, we become aware of an undertone of dramatic irony which runs counter to the soaring curve of his vision. His very urgency, while it impels our imaginative participation, yet betrays his desperation; there is no mistaking the anguished recollection of his bond in the cry,

> Sweet Helen, make me immortal with a kiss,

or the hint in the succeeding lines that Helen is a phantom, a demonic spirit who would indeed suck forth his soul:

> Here will I dwell, for *heaven* is in these lips,
> And all is *dross* that is not Helena.

The ironies reveal a lurking horror even to those spectators who failed to recall the *Metamorphoses* of Ovid, where Semele was reduced to ashes by her heavenly visitor, and where the embrace of Arethusa was unattainable, since she was transformed into rippling water to evade the lustful clutches of Alpheus. The dramatic excitement in the speech is generated entirely in terms of illusion: we are made to confess to both the glamour and the sham of the vision, for each have a 'reality' of their own. The tragic insight depends upon this double awareness.

Marlowe skilfully manages the foreboding which now gathers over the closing episodes of the play. Faustus' farewell to the scholars is well placed as a subdued and elegiac prose prelude to the catastrophe, that sustained soliloquy which by a staggering *tour de force* keys the emotional pitch of the tragedy to almost unendurable climax. In sheer virtuosity there was nothing in Elizabethan drama to match Faustus' last speech for several years to come. The kind of advance in the technique of the soliloquy which it represents can be measured by comparing it with the soliloquy at the opening of the play. There Faustus' rejection of legitimate studies is displayed in a schematised logical progression which summarises and crystallises the steps which led him to necromancy. The speech is evidently contrived, and within its conventions it does not require us to suppose that it represents any particular moment in Faustus' psychological history. The conception of the final soliloquy is radically different: it does move in the plane of time, as the stark simplicity of the first monosyllables announces:

> Ah, Faustus,
> Now hast thou but one bare hour to live.

The effects Marlowe is striving for here are those of spontaneity; the conception is much more inward, and dramatises the fleeting thoughts as though they were actually passing through Faustus' mind at the time. Instead of the predictable controlled development of the opening soliloquy, here are confusion and contradiction, the very process of the struggle to come to terms with the situation. Of course, the deliberate preconceived movement of the earlier speech befits our impression of the confident

Faustus which the beginning of the play requires, and the action must open on a comparatively low emotional pitch, while at the catastrophe the situation demands a frantic and desperate Faustus, and high tension. But the soliloquies are not accounted for in terms of their contexts alone: there is an essential difference in their dramatic representation of inner processes. In the final speech, Marlowe created what was virtually a new vehicle for articulating with immediacy the flux and uncertainty of a mind under pressure. It is only the exaggeration of this vital difference to say that previous soliloquies demanded an orator, while this calls for an actor. As an attempt to turn the speech of distraction into poetry, Faustus' last soliloquy is comparable with Kyd's development of Senecan rhetoric, particularly with the way Kyd deploys stage madness as an occasion for wild and whirling words.

The licence Marlowe boldly permits himself with metre here is the fundamental means of creating an impression of bursts of rapid speech punctuated by irregular pauses. Figures of repetition, like 'Fair nature's eye, rise, rise again', 'See, see, where Christ's blood...', 'Mountains and hills, come, come', and climactic constructions, such as

> The stars move still, time runs, the clock will strike,
> The devil will come, and Faustus must be damn'd,

allow the poetry to take wing, until the flight is sharply arrested often by means of a heavy caesura. A static delivery is impossible, and the strenuous vehemence carried by the disjointed verse insists upon the physical movements implied by the sense. It is impossible to give full weight to 'O, I'll leap up to my God! Who pulls me down?' with the same gesture as in

> Then will I headlong run into the earth.
> Earth, gape! O, no, it will not harbour me.

The chimes of the clock are a further cue for action, and this device illustrates how Marlowe succeeds in organically relating the speech to the stage, compared with the static and perhaps literally sedate character of the opening soliloquy. This final scene has returned to Faustus' study, where the play began; yet however localised, the swift transitions which the soliloquy makes in its verbal imagery, from the heavens and planets, to the earth with her mountains and thence to the ugly gaping of hell-mouth, seem to conjure the whole creation to witness the catastrophe. It is a magnificent recollection of the medieval stage which transforms Faustus' study into a microcosm.

This is the supreme example of Marlowe's ability to create dramatic illusion through his poetry. Faustus' flights into other magical realms, away from the here and now, have in earlier scenes been the dramatic occasions for extending the fixed 'realities' of the stage into the imaginary dimensions of poetry. The resources of the dramatist have corresponded to those of the magician. Not elation but terror now inspires Faustus' vision of all that lies beyond the physical boundaries of the stage. He conjures the elements in vain, and even if Marlowe's groundlings failed to applaud the full brilliance of giving such a strange context to a line from Ovid, 'O lente lente currite noctis equi', they would nevertheless recognise in the Latin another esoteric piece of sorcery, which it is. Faustus' magic is no longer of any help to him, but in the imagery of his lines we as spectators seem to become part of a cosmic audience attending his last hour. The theatre scarcely seems able to contain the scene, and yet, paradoxically, Faustus' utter helplessness conveys an almost claustrophobic awareness of confinement, as though the study is a cage from which he is frantically trying to escape.

One cannot say which is the more 'real', the illusion of a vast scene embracing heaven, earth and hell, or the illusion of a stage that has shrunk to cramping dimensions. But both are mutually dependent. Faustus is at bay, trapped in a corner, and yet his end is a universal drama. The dramatic effect, perfectly accommodated to the physical conditions of the Elizabethan stage, is derived principally from Marlowe's solution to the problems of space and time, the same problems which neo-classicism solved in terms of the unities. The awareness of Faustus' existence in these two simultaneous illusions of space generates tremendous dramatic tension and corresponds to a similar duality in the plane

of time, each equally illusory. Faustus is now trapped by the
clock, and by a bold theatrical device time passes with unerring
swiftness: the minutes have diminished to seconds, just as the
stage seems to have contracted, and closed in upon the doomed
man. Yet we are intensely aware too of timeless infinity, of the
imminence of perpetual damnation. The whole tragic conflict is
epitomised and crowded into this final scene, for these contrary
tensions dramatise that antithesis between human and superhuman for which Marlowe saw no certain reconciliation.

Doctor Faustus in its own time considerably extended the
range of dramatic techniques, and it is not surprising that the
play had its imitators. The treatment of necromancy in Greene's
Friar Bacon and Friar Bungay, and Shakespeare's *Henry VI*
Part 2 (where Margery Jourdain the witch is introduced), merely
exploit the unsophisticated appeal of spectacular conjuring tricks,
and owe nothing to Marlowe's play. But Shakespeare seems to
have made an unsuccessful attempt to reproduce the effects of
Faustus' last soliloquy in Richard the Third's speech on the eve
of his defeat:

> Have mercy, Jesu! Soft! I did but dream.
> O coward conscience, how thou dost afflict me!
> The lights burn blue. It is now dead midnight.
> Cold fearful drops stand on my trembling flesh.
> What do I fear? Myself? There's none else by.
> Richard loves Richard; that is, I am I.
> Is there a murderer here? No – yes, I am.
> Then fly. What, from myself? Great reason why –
> Lest I revenge. What, myself upon myself?
> Alack, I love myself. Wherefore? For any good
> That I myself have done unto myself?
> O no! Alas, I rather hate myself
> For hateful deeds committed by myself. ...

There is ample evidence that the popularity of *Doctor Faustus*
survived the turn of the century, and even Jonson's *Alchemist*
pays homage to Marlowe's play, reducing the theme to comic
terms by presenting the illusion of magic power as a series of
delusions: Sir Epicure Mammon's luxurious fantasies suggest a

parody of the rhapsodic poetry of Faustus. Ultimately, however, it was Shakespeare who learned most from Marlowe's exploitation of theatrical illusion, and he developed the dramatic ideas found in *Doctor Faustus* nowhere more effectively than in *Macbeth* and *The Tempest*. The fear and guilt that haunt Macbeth and his wife through their soliloquies and hallucinations transform the stage to a nightmare world that supplants 'reality', 'and nothing is but what is not'. As Faustus was shown the pageant of the Seven Deadly Sins, so the witches reveal the procession of phantom kings before Macbeth. In *The Tempest*, however, the powers of magic are not satanic: Prospero's virtue is a condition of his art, which he employs in the cause of merciful justice. The image of the stage itself as a magic circle becomes explicit in the closing lines of Prospero's Epilogue, and we may not be deceived if we catch an echo of that earlier magician in his words:

> Now I want
> Spirits to enforce, art to enchant;
> And my ending is despair
> Unless I be reliev'd by prayer,
> Which pierces so that it assaults
> Mercy itself, and frees all faults.
> As you from crimes would pardon'd be,
> Let your indulgence set me free.

The conceit is well-turned, for the spectators are here reminded of the necessary part they themselves bear in working the enchantment. Shakespeare bade farewell to the theatre with a play that celebrated his own art through the nobility and virtue of a magician. What better tribute could be paid to Marlowe, whose Faustus was damned, but whose genius redeemed the magic of stage illusion from the censure that it lacked both dignity and beauty?

Source: *Critical Quarterly*, VI (1964). Revised for publication in the present volume.

L. C. Knights

THE STRANGE CASE OF
DOCTOR FAUSTUS (1964)

CRITICISM . . . should beware of interpreting particular works in the light of general notions imputed, on various grounds, to their author. *Doctor Faustus* is important for what it is – a work of art in which the desire for effortless and unlimited power is subjected to the scrutiny of a powerful mind – and not merely as a document in the history of Marlowe's religious beliefs. In attempting a total estimate of the dramatist, however, it is impossible not to be puzzled by the relation between the orthodoxy so emphatically asserted in the play and the opinions attributed to Marlowe both by Kyd and Baines. And the fact that there *is* a puzzle may throw some light on the play itself.

Marlowe's persistent concern with religion was certainly not confined to exposing the gulf between the beliefs and the practices of professing Christians, and Kocher is right to insist on that fundamental aspect of Marlowe's thought. It is doubtful, however, whether he was the dedicated rationalist that Kocher makes him out to be. In the documents to which I have referred there are strictly rational arguments and objections to the fundamentalist strain in contemporary Christian thought, but there are also merely exasperated assertions of anti-Christian attitudes. And although the latter may be explained in part by the failure of his Christian contemporaries to meet him – as a Hooker could have met him – with more than dogmatic assertions, there is a residue of what seems like mere obsessive blasphemy. Referring to some of Marlowe's more outrageous statements, Kyd said, 'he would so suddenly take slight occasion to slip [them] out'. 'Almost into every company he cometh,' said Baines, 'he persuades men to atheism.' In both statements there is the suggestion of a compulsive need; and although it would be useless and impertinent to try to trace this compulsion to its sources, it may nevertheless offer a clue to the ambivalent effect of *Doctor Faustus*.

No one who studies the play with any care can subscribe to the view that Marlowe damns Faustus unwillingly, either as a concession to orthodoxy or because of a final failure of nerve. No one writes poetry of the order of Faustus's last terrible soliloquy without being wholly engaged,[1] and more than in any other of his plays Marlowe shows that he knows what he is doing. From the superbly presented disingenuousness of the opening soliloquy, in which Faustus dismisses the traditional sciences with a series of quibbles, Marlowe is making a sustained attempt to present as it really is the perverse and infantile desire for enormous power and immediate gratifications.

> O what a world of profit and delight,
> Of power, of honour and omnipotence,
> Is promis'd to the studious artizan!
> All things that move between the quiet poles
> Shall be at my command.*

However deeply Marlowe may have been versed in demonology it is unlikely that he took very seriously the business of 'Lines, circles, letters and characters'. Baudelaire says somewhere, 'Tout homme qui n'accepte pas les conditions de la vie vend son âme';[2] and a modern writer, James Baldwin, 'Everything in a life de-

---

* If this is not sufficiently placed by the immediate context, there is the implicit comment in Faustus's words to Valdes and Cornelius (complete only in the A text) which editors have strangely found obscure:

> Know that your words have won me at the last
> To practise magic and concealed arts:
> Yet not your words only, but *mine own fantasy*,
> *That will receive no object*. . . .

Marlowe also slips in a hint or two that Faustus's prowess as a scholar had contained an element of self-inflation and aggression: his 'subtle syllogisms Gravell'd the pastors of the German church', etc. (i 112); and one can almost hear the scholar's pride with which he 'was wont to make our schools ring with *sic probo*' (ii 2).

pends on how that life accepts its limits.'[3] It is in the light of such remarks that we should see the pact with the devil and the magic: they serve as dramatic representations of the desire to ignore that 'rightness of limitation', which, according to Whitehead, 'is essential for growth of reality'.[4] Marlowe – the overreacher – was only too familiar with that desire, and the turning on himself – on the self of *Tamburlaine*, Part I – is a measure of his genius.

Some such intention as I have described, the intention of coming to terms with a corrupting day-dream, determines the main structural lines and the great passages of *Doctor Faustus*. But few even of the play's warmest admirers claim that it lives in the imagination as an entirely satisfying and consistent whole. Interest flags and is fitfully revived. And although the scenes in which Faustus's power is exhibited in such imbecile ways may be defended as presenting the gross stupidity of sin, this always feels to me, in the reading, as an explanation that has been thought up. With one or two exceptions, Faustus's capers represent an escape from seriousness and full realization – not simply on Faustus's part but on Marlowe's: and what they pad out is a crucial gap in the play's imaginative structure. For where, we may ask, are the contrasting positives against which Faustus's misdirection of his energies could be measured?

With this we return once more to the unresolved conflicts, the intrusive subjectivity, in terms of which it seems necessary to explain this remarkable play, as they are necessary to explain the obvious failures. It is not merely that – unlike Macbeth – Faustus has no vision of the life-giving values against which he has offended: Marlowe doesn't grasp them either. And you have the uneasy feeling that Faustus's panic fear of hell is not only the inevitable result of a wilful, self-centred denial of life. It is as though Marlowe himself felt guilt about *any* of his assertive drives (understandably enough, since they were tied up with his regressions), and conceived of religion not in terms of a growth into freedom and reality but as binding and oppressing.

We may put this in another way. I have said that in some important respects Marlowe's creative fantasy did not meet sufficient resistance – the kind of resistance that is necessary for the production of the highest kind of energy, which is at once affirmation, growth and understanding. In *Doctor Faustus* the resistance is, as it were, externalized. The anarchic impulse (the Ganymede–Tamburlaine fantasy) collides with a prohibition. Because what is prohibited and rebuked in this play is indeed a denial of life, and because the rebuke is charged with the full force of that other self of Marlowe's which appears so fitfully in the other plays, the result is poetry of very great power indeed. But even in the last great despairing speech, where almost over-powering feeling moulds the language in a way in which it had never been moulded before, the reader's submission is, I suggest, of a different order from the submission one gives to the greatest art, where a sense of freedom is the concomitant of acceptance of reality, however painful this may be.

If this is indeed so, it does something to explain how the orthodoxy of *Doctor Faustus* and the animus against religion in the Baines document and elsewhere could be harboured simul-taneously. It also helps to explain the diametrically opposed views to be found among the critics of the play. It seems to me that those who see the final soliloquy as the logical culmination of the play's action are right; and that those who see a more or less deliberate suppression of Marlowe's sympathy for his hero, in order to bring about an orthodox dénouement, are wrong. But the latter are in fact responding to an unresolved emotional quality that lies behind the rational structure of the play.

SOURCE: 'The Strange Case of Christopher Marlowe', in *Further Explorations* (1965).

NOTES

1. A point developed by James Smith in a notable essay, 'Marlowe's *Dr Faustus*', in *Scrutiny*, VIII (1939).

2. Quoted by Enid Starkie, *Rimbaud* (1947) p. 123.

3. *Nobody Knows my Name: More Notes of a Native Son* (1964) p. 145.

4. A. N. Whitehead, *Religion in the Making* (1936) p. 146.

Cleanth Brooks

THE UNITY OF MARLOWE'S
DOCTOR FAUSTUS (1966)

IN his *Poetics*, Aristotle observed that a tragedy should have a beginning, a middle, and an end. The statement makes a point that seems obvious, and many a reader of our time must have dismissed it as one of the more tedious remarks of the Stagirite, or indeed put it down to one of the duller notes taken by the student whom some suppose to have heard Aristotle's lectures and preserved the substance of them for us. Yet the play without a middle does occur, and in at least three signal instances that I can think of in English literature, we have a play that lacks a proper middle or at least a play that *seems* to lack a middle. Milton's *Samson Agonistes* is one of them; Eliot's *Murder in the Cathedral*, another; and Marlowe's *Doctor Faustus*, the third. Milton presents us with Samson, in the hands of his enemies, blind, grinding at the mill with other slaves, yet in only a little while he has Samson pull down the temple roof upon his enemies. There is a beginning and there is an end, but in the interval between them has anything of real consequence happened? *Murder in the Cathedral* may seem an even more flagrant instance of an end jammed on to a beginning quite directly and without any intervening dramatic substance. Thomas has come back out of exile to assume his proper place in his cathedral and act as shepherd to his people. He is already aware of the consequences of his return, and that in all probability the decisive act has been taken that will quickly lead to his martyrdom and death.

Marlowe's *Doctor Faustus* may seem to show the same defect, for very early in the play the learned doctor makes his decision to sell his soul to the devil, and after that there seems little to do except to fill in the time before the mortgage falls due and the devil comes to collect the forfeited soul. If the consequence of

Faustus's bargain is inevitable, and if nothing can be done to alter it, then it doesn't much matter what one puts in as filler. Hence one can stuff in comedy and farce more or less *ad libitum*, the taste of the audience and its patience in sitting through the play being the only limiting factors.

In what I shall say here, I do not propose to do more than touch upon the vexed problem of the authorship of *Doctor Faustus* in either the A or B version. But I think that it is significant that the principal scenes that are confidently assigned to Marlowe turn out to be the scenes that open and close the play. To other hands is assigned the basic responsibility for supplying the comedy or sheer wonder-working or farce that makes up much of the play and is the very staple of scenes viii–xvii.

For their effectiveness, *Doctor Faustus*, *Samson Agonistes* and *Murder in the Cathedral*, all three, depend heavily upon their poetry. One could go further: the poetry tends to be intensely lyrical and in the play with which we are concerned arises from the depths of the character of Faustus himself; it expresses his aspirations, his dreams, his fears, his agonies, and his intense awareness of the conflicting feelings within himself. The poetry, it ought to be observed, is not a kind of superficial gilding, but an expression – and perhaps the inevitable expression – of the emotions of the central character. If there is indeed a 'middle' in this play – that is, a part of the play concerned with complication and development in which the character of Faustus becomes something quite different from the man whom we first meet – then the 'middle' of the play has to be sought in this area of personal self-examination and inner conflict, and the poetry will prove its most dramatic expression. One observes that something of this sort is true of *Samson Agonistes*. The Samson whom we meet at the beginning of the play is obviously incapable of undertaking the action that he performs so gloriously at the end. Something very important, I should argue, does happen to Samson in the course of the play, and his awareness of some 'rousing motions' after Harapha has left him is no accident – that is, the rousing motions did not simply happen to occur at the propitious moment. I should argue that the encounter between

Samson and his father, his wife, and the giant, all have had their part in transforming the quality of his response to the world about him, and that the sensitive auditor or reader will, if he attends to the poetry with which Milton has invested the play, come to see that this is true.

I think that a similar case can be made for Eliot's *Murder in the Cathedral*, though I must concede that Eliot has cut it very fine. An attentive reading or a good production of the play will make the reader aware that the Thomas who is presented early in the play is not yet ready for martyrdom. True, Thomas thinks he has prepared himself. He has foreseen the three tempters. But the Fourth Tempter is indeed, as he tells us, unexpected, and Thomas himself is clearly shaken by the encounter and does not experience *his* rousing motions until after a further conflict.

But before attempting to get deeper into the problem of whether *Doctor Faustus* has a proper middle, it will be useful to make one or two general observations about the play. *Doctor Faustus* is a play about knowledge, about the relation of one's knowledge of the world to his knowledge of himself – about knowledge of means and its relation to knowledge of ends. It is a play, thus, that reflects the interests of the Renaissance and indeed that looks forward to the issues of the modern day. There is even an anticipation in the play, I should suppose, of the problem of the 'two cultures'. Faustus is dissatisfied and even bored with the study of ethics and divinity and metaphysics. What has captured his imagination is magic, but we must not be misled by the associations that that term now carries for most of us. The knowledge that Faustus wants to attain is knowledge that can be put to use – what Bertrand Russell long ago called power knowledge – the knowledge that allows one to effect changes in the world around him. When Faustus rejects philosophy and divinity for magic, he chooses magic because, as he says, the pursuit of magic promises 'a world of profit and delight, / Of power, of honour, of omnipotence'. He sums it up in saying: 'A sound Magician is a mighty god.' But if one does manage to acquire the technical knowledge that will allow one to 'Wall all Germany with brass' or to beat a modern jet plane's time in flying in fresh grapes from the tropics, for what purpose is that technical knowledge to be used? How does this knowledge of means relate to one's knowledge of ends? Marlowe is too honest a dramatist to allow Faustus to escape such questions.

This last comment must not, however, be taken to imply that Marlowe has written a moral tract rather than a drama, or that he has been less than skilful in making Faustus's experiments with power knowledge bring him, again and again, up against knowledge of a more ultimate kind. Marlowe makes the process seem natural and inevitable. For example, as soon as Faustus has signed the contract with the devil and has, by giving himself to hell, gained his new knowledge, his first question to Mephistopheles, rather naturally, has to do with the nature of the place to which he has consigned himself. He says: 'First will I question with thee about hell, / Tell me, where is the place that men call hell?' In his reply, Mephistopheles explodes any notion of a local hell, and defines hell as a state of mind; but Faustus cannot believe his ears, and though getting his information from an impeccable source, indeed from the very horse's mouth, he refuses to accept the first fruits of his new knowledge. He had already come to the decision that stories of hell were merely 'old wives' tales' – one supposes that this decision was a factor in his resolution to sell his soul. Yet when Mephistopheles says that he is an instance to prove the contrary since he is damned, and is even now in hell, Faustus cannot take in the notion. 'How? Now in hell? / Nay and this be hell, I'll willingly be damned here. . . .'

The new knowledge that Faustus has acquired proves curiously unsatisfactory in other ways. For instance, Faustus demands a book in which the motions and characters of the planets are so truly set forth that, knowing these motions, he can raise up spirits directly and without the intervention of Mephistopheles. Mephistopheles at once produces the book, only to have Faustus say: 'When I behold the heavens, then I repent / . . . Because thou has deprived me of those joys.' Mephistopheles manages to distract Faustus from notions of repentance, but soon Faustus is once more making inquiries that touch upon the heavens, this time about astrology; and again, almost before he knows it, Faustus has been moved by his contemplation of the revolution of the spheres to a more ultimate question. 'Tell me who made the world,' he suddenly asks Mephistopheles, and this thought of the Creator once more wracks Faustus with a reminder of his damnation. Marlowe has throughout the play used the words *heaven* and *heavenly* in a tantalizingly double sense. *Heavenly* refers to the structure of the cosmos as seen from the earth, but it also has associations with the divine — the sphere from which Faustus has cut himself off.

Thus, technical questions about how nature works have a tendency to raise the larger questions of the Creator and the purposes of the creation. Faustus cannot be content — such is the education of a lifetime — or such was Marlowe's education, if you prefer — cannot be content with the mere workings of the machinery of the universe: he must push on to ask about ultimate purposes. Knowledge of means cannot be sealed off from knowledge of ends, and here Faustus's newly acquired knowledge cannot give him answers different from those he already knew before he forfeited his soul. The new knowledge can only forbid Faustus to dwell upon the answers to troubling questions that persist, the answers to which he knows all too well.

To come at matters in a different way, Faustus is the man who is all dressed up with no place to go. His plight is that he cannot find anything to do really worthy of the supernatural powers that he has come to possess. Faustus never carries out in practice his dreams of great accomplishments. He evidently doesn't want to wall all Germany with brass, or make the swift Rhine circle fair Wittenberg. Nor does he chase the Prince of Parma from Germany. Instead, he plays tricks on the Pope, or courts favour with the Emperor by staging magical shows for him. When he summons up at the Emperor's request Alexander the Great and his paramour, Faustus is careful to explain — Faustus in some sense remains to the end an honest man — that the Emperor will not be seeing 'the true substantial bodies of those two deceased princes which long since are consumed to dust'. The illusion is certainly life-like . . .; but even so, Alexander and his paramour are no more than apparitions. This magical world lacks substance.

With reference to the quality of Faustus's exploitations of his magical power, one may point out that Marlowe is scarcely answerable for some of the stuff that was worked into the middle of the play. Yet to judge only from the scenes acknowledged to be Marlowe's and from the ending that Marlowe devised for the play, it is inconceivable that Faustus should ever have carried out the grandiose plans which he mentions in scene iii — such matters as making a bridge through the moving air so that bands of men can pass over the ocean, or joining the hills that bind the African shore to those of Spain. Faustus's basic motivation — his yearning for self-aggrandisement — ensures that the power he has gained will be used for what are finally frivolous purposes.

I have been stressing the author's distinction between the different kinds of knowledge that Faustus craves, and his careful pointing up of the inner contradictions that exist among these kinds of knowledge. I think that these matters are important for the meaning of the play, but some of you may feel that in themselves they scarcely serve to establish the requisite middle for the play. To note the confusions and contradictions in Faustus's quest for knowledge may make Faustus appear a more human figure and even a more modern figure. (I am entirely aware that my own perspective may be such as to make the play more 'modern' than it is.) Yet, if Faustus is indeed doomed, the moment he signs with his own blood his contract with the devil, then there is no further significant action that he can take, and the rest of the play will be not so much dramatic as elegiac, as Faustus comes to lament the course that he has taken, or simply clinical, as we watch the writhings and inner torment of a character whose case is hopeless. Whether the case of Faustus becomes hopeless early in the play is, then, a matter of real consequence.

On a purely legalistic basis, of course, Faustus's case *is* hopeless. He has made a contract and he has to abide by it. This is the point that the devils insist on relentlessly. Yet there are plenty of indications that Faustus was not the prisoner of one fatal act. Before Faustus signs the bond, the good angel twice appears to him, first to beg him to lay his 'Damned book aside' and later to implore him to beware of the 'execrable art' of magic. But even after Faustus has signed the bond, the good angel appears. In scene vi he adjures Faustus to repent, saying: 'Repent yet, God will pity thee.' The bad angel, it is true, appears along with him to insist that 'God cannot pity thee.' But then the bad angel had appeared along with the good in all the early appearances too.

There are other indications that Faustus is not yet beyond the possibility of redemption. The devils, in spite of the contract, are evidently not at all sure of the soul of Faustus. They find it again and again necessary to argue with him, to bully him, and to threaten him. Mephistopheles evidently believes that it is very important to try to distract Faustus from his doleful thoughts. The assumption of the play is surely that the devils are anxious, and Mephistopheles in particular goes to a great deal of trouble to keep Faustus under control. There is never any assumption that the bond itself, signed with Faustus's blood, is quite sufficient to preserve him safe for hell. At least once, Lucifer himself has to be called in to ensure that Faustus will not escape. Lucifer appeals to Faustus's sense of logic by telling him that 'Christ cannot save thy soul, for he is just, / There's none but I have interest in the same.' But Lucifer employs an even more potent weapon: he terrifies Faustus, and as we shall see in scene xviii, a crucial scene that occurs late in the play, Faustus has little defence against terror.

In scene xviii, a new character appears, one simply called 'an Old Man'. He comes just in the nick of time, for Faustus, in his despair, is on the point of committing suicide, and Mephistopheles, apparently happy to make sure of Faustus's damnation, hands him a dagger. But the Old Man persuades Faustus to desist, telling him: 'I see an angel hovers o'er thy head, / And with a vial full of precious grace, / Offers to pour the same into thy soul: / Then call for mercy, and avoid despair.'

The Old Man has faith that Faustus can still be saved, and testifies to the presence of his good angel, waiting to pour out the necessary grace. But Faustus has indeed despaired. It may be significant that Faustus apparently does not see the angel now.

At this crisis when, as Faustus says, 'hell strives with grace for conquest in my breast', Mephistopheles accuses him of disobedience, and threatens to tear his flesh piecemeal. The threat is sufficient. A moment before, Faustus had addressed the Old Man as 'my sweet friend'. Now, in a sudden reversal, he calls Mephistopheles sweet – 'Sweet Mephistopheles, intreat thy lord / To pardon my unjust presumption, / And with my blood again I will confirm / My former vow I made to Lucifer.' The answer of Mephistopheles is interesting and even shocking. He tells Faustus: 'Do it then quickly, with unfeigned heart, / Lest greater danger do attend thy drift.' There is honour among thieves, among devils the appeal to loyalty and sincerity. 'Unfeigned heart' carries ironically the very accent of Christian piety.

Faustus, for his part, shows himself now, perhaps for the first time, to be truly a lost soul. For he suddenly rounds upon the Old Man and beseeches Mephistopheles to inflict on him the 'greatest torments that our hell affords'. The pronoun is significant. Faustus now thinks of hell as 'our hell', and the acceptance of it as part of himself and his desire to see the Old Man suffer mark surely a new stage in his development or deterioration. The shift-over may seem abrupt, but I find it credible in the total context, and I am reminded of what William Butler Yeats said about *his* Faustian play, *The Countess Cathleen*. The Countess, as you will remember, redeemed the souls of her people from the demons to whom they had sold their souls by selling her own. Many years after he had written the play, Yeats remarked that he had made a mistake, he felt, in his treatment of the Countess. As he put it in his *Autobiography*: 'The Countess sells her soul, but [in the play] she is not transformed. If I were to think out that scene to-day, she would, the moment her hand had signed, burst into loud laughter, mock at all she has held holy, horrify the peasants in the midst of their temptations.' Thus Yeats would have dramatized the commitment she had made. The comment is a valid one, and I think is relevant here. Yeats, in making the signing of the bond the decisive and effective act, is of course being more legalistic than is Marlowe, but he vindicates the psychology of the *volte face*. When Faustus does indeed become irrecoverably damned, he shows it in his conduct, and the change in conduct is startling. Faustus has now become a member of the devil's party in a sense in which he has not been before.

I think too that it is a sound psychology that makes Faustus demand at this point greater distractions and more powerful narcotics than he had earlier required. Shortly before, it was enough for Faustus to call up the vision of Helen. Now he needs to possess her. And if this final abandonment to sensual delight calls forth the most celebrated poetry in the play, the poetry is ominously fitting. Indeed, the poetry here, for all of its passion, is instinct with the desperation of Faustus's plight. Helen's was the face 'that launched a thousand ships and burnt the topless towers of Ilium'. If the wonderful lines insist upon the transcendent power of a beauty that could command the allegiance of thousands, they also refer to the destructive fire that she set alight, and perhaps hint at the hell-fire that now burns for Faustus. After this magnificent invocation, Faustus implores Helen to make his soul immortal with a kiss, but his soul is already immortal, with an immortality that he would gladly – as he says in the last scene – lose if he could.

It may be worth pointing out that the sharpest inner contradictions in Faustus's thinking are manifest in the passage that we have just discussed. Faustus is so much terrified by Mephistopheles's threat to tear his flesh piecemeal that he hysterically courts the favour of Mephistopheles by begging him to tear the flesh of the Old Man. Yet Mephistopheles in his reply actually deflates the terror by remarking of the Old Man that 'His faith is great, I cannot touch his soul'. He promises to try to afflict the Old Man's body, but he observes with business-like candour that this kind of affliction amounts to little – 'it is but little worth'.

Perhaps the most powerful testimony in the play against any shallow legalistic interpretation of Faustus's damnation occurs in one of the earlier speeches of Mephistopheles. If Mephistopheles later in the play sees to it, by using distractions, by appealing to Faustus's sense of justice, by invoking terror, that Faustus shall not escape, it is notable that early in the play he testifies to the folly of what Faustus is proposing to do with his life.

When Faustus asks Mephistopheles why it was that Lucifer fell, Mephistopheles replies with complete orthodoxy and with even Christian eloquence: 'Oh, by aspiring pride and insolence'. When Faustus asks him 'What are you that live with Lucifer?' Mephistopheles answers that he is one of the 'unhappy spirits that fell with Lucifer', and that with Lucifer he is damned forever. It is at this point that Faustus, obsessed with the notion that hell is a place, expresses his astonishment that Mephistopheles can be said at this very moment to be in hell. Mephistopheles's answer deserves to be quoted in full:

> Why this is hell, nor am I out of it:
> Think'st thou that I who saw the face of God,
> And tasted the eternal joys of Heaven,
> Am not tormented with ten thousand hells,
> In being deprived of everlasting bliss?
> Oh Faustus, leave these frivolous demands,
> Which strike a terror to my fainting soul.

Faustus is surprised that great Mephistopheles should be, as he puts it, 'so passionate' on this subject, and the reader of the play may himself wonder that Mephistopheles can be so eloquent on the side of the angels – of the good angels, that is. But Marlowe has not been careless nor is he absent-minded. The psychology is ultimately sound. In this connection, two points ought to be observed. Though there is good reason to believe that Marlowe expected his audience to accept his devils as actual beings with an objective reality of their own and not merely as projections of Faustus's state of mind, in this play – as in any other sound and believable use of ghosts, spirits, and other such supernatural beings – the devils do have a very real relation to the minds of the persons to whom they appear. Though not necessarily merely projections of the character's emotions, they are always in some sense mirrors of the inner states of the persons to whom they appear.

The second point to be observed is this: Faustus does learn something in the course of the play, and in learning it suffers change and becomes a different man. At the beginning of the play, he does seem somewhat naïve and jejune. He is fascinated by the new possibilities that his traffic with magic may open to him. Mephistopheles's use of the phrase 'these frivolous demands' is quite justified. But in a sense, the very jauntiness with which he talks to Mephistopheles is proof that he is not yet fully damned, has not involved himself completely with the agents of evil. As the play goes on, he will lose his frivolousness: he will learn to take more and more seriously the loss of heaven. Yet at the same time, this very experience of deeper involvement in evil will make more and more difficult any return to the joys of heaven.

At any rate, there is a tremendous honesty as the play is worked out. Faustus may appear at times frivolous, but he is honest with himself. With all of his yearning for the state of grace that he has lost, he always acknowledges the strength of his desire for illicit pleasures and powers. At one point in the play, before he signed the fatal bond, Faustus says to himself that he will turn to God again. But immediately he dismisses the notion: 'To God?' he asks incredulously, and then replies to himself: 'He loves thee not, / The God thou servest is thine own appetite.'

Most of all, however, Faustus is the prisoner of his own conceptions and indeed preconceptions. It is not so much that God has damned him as that he has damned himself. Faustus is trapped in his own legalism. The emphasis on such legalism seems to be a constant element in all treatments of the Faustian compact. It occurs in Yeats's *The Countess Cathleen*, when the devils, trusting in the letter of the law, are defeated and at the end find they have no power over the soul of the Countess. Legalism is also a feature of one of the most brilliant recent treatments of the story, that given by William Faulkner in *The Hamlet*.

Faustus's entrapment in legalism is easily illustrated. If the devils insist that a promise is a promise and a bond is a bond that has to be honoured – though it is plain that they are far from sure that the mere signing of the bond has effectively put Faustus's soul in their possession – Faustus himself is all too easily convinced that this is true. Apparently, he can believe in and understand a God of justice, but not a God of mercy. If Faustus's self-knowledge makes him say in scene: vi 'My heart's so hardened, I cannot repent', his sense of legal obligation makes him say in scene xviii: 'Hell calls for right, and with a roaring voice / Says, Faustus come, thine hour is come / And Faustus will come to do thee right.' Even at this point the Old Man thinks that Faustus can still be saved. The good angel has reiterated that he might be saved. The devils themselves would seem to fear that Faustus even at the last might escape them: but Faustus himself is convinced that he cannot be saved and his despair effectually prevents any action which would allow him a way out.

In one sense, then, this play is a study in despair. But the despair does not paralyze the imagination of Faustus. He knows constantly what is happening to him. He reports on his state of mind with relentless honesty. And at the end of the play, in tremendous poetry, he dramatizes for us what it is to feel the inexorable movement toward the abyss, not numbed, not dulled with apathy, but with every sense quickened and alert. (Kurtz, in Conrad's *Heart of Darkness*, shows these qualities. He is damned, knows that he's damned, indeed flees from redemption, but never deceives himself about what is happening, and mutters, 'The horror, the horror'.)

One may still ask, however, whether these changes that occur in Faustus's soul are sufficient to constitute a middle. Does Faustus act? Is there a sufficient conflict? Is Faustus so incapacitated for choice that he is a helpless victim and not a conscious re-agent with circumstance?

Yet, one must not be doctrinaire and pedantic in considering this concept of decisive action. As T. S. Eliot put it in *Murder in the Cathedral*, suffering is action and action is suffering. Faustus's suffering is not merely passive: he is constantly reaffirming at deeper and deeper levels his original rash tender of his soul to Lucifer. Moreover, if Faustus's action amounts in the end to suffering, the suffering is not meaningless. It leads to knowledge – knowledge of very much the same sort as that which Milton's Adam acquired in *Paradise Lost* – 'Knowledge of good bought dear by knowing ill' – and through something of the same process. Early in the play, Mephistopheles told him: 'Think so still till experience change thy mind.' Perhaps this is the best way in which to describe the 'middle' of the play: the middle consists of the experiences that do change Faustus's mind so that in the end he knows what hell is and has become accommodated to it, now truly damned.

My own view is that the play does have a sufficient middle, but this is not to say that it is not a play of a rather special sort — and that its dependence upon its poetry — though a legitimate dependence, I would insist — is very great.

There is no need to praise the poetry of the wonderful last scene, but I should like to make one or two brief observations about it. The drama depends, of course, upon Faustus's obsession with the clock and his sense of time's moving on inexorably, pushing him so swiftly to the final event. But this final scene really grows integrally out of the play. The agonized and eloquent clock-watching matches perfectly the legalism which has dominated Faustus from the beginning of the play. What Faustus in effect tries to do is to hold back the hand of the clock, not to change his relation to God. Incidentally, what Faustus does not notice is that like Mephistopheles earlier, he himself is now already in hell. The coming of the hour of twelve can hardly bring him into greater torment than that which now possesses him and which the poetry he utters so powerfully bodies forth.

Everybody has commented on Marlowe's brilliant use of the quotation from Ovid: 'O lente, lente currite noctis equi', in the *Amores* words murmured by the lover to his mistress in his wish that the night of passion might be prolonged, in this context so jarringly ironic. But the irony is not at all factitious. The scholar who now quotes the lines from Ovid in so different a context is the same man who a little earlier had begged the phantasm of Helen to make his soul immortal with a kiss. Now, in his agony, he demands of himself: 'Why wert thou not a creature wanting soul? / Or, why is this immortal that thou hast?'

Again, the great line, 'See, see where Christ's blood streams in the firmament', echoes a significant passage much earlier in the play. (I do not insist that the reader has to notice it, or that

Marlowe's audience would have necessarily been aware of the echo, but I see no reason why we should not admire it if we happen upon it ourselves or if someone calls it to our attention.) When Faustus prepares to sign the document that will consign his soul to the devil, he finds that he must sign in blood, and he pierces his arm to procure the sanguine ink. But his blood will hardly trickle from his arm, and he interprets his blood's unwillingness to flow as follows: 'What might the staying of my blood portend? / Is it unwilling I should write this bill? / Why streams it not, that I might write afresh?' His own blood, in an instinctive horror, refuses to stream for his damnation. Now, as he waits for the clock to strike twelve, he has a vision of Christ's blood *streaming* in the firmament for man's salvation. But in his despair he is certain that Christ's blood does not stream for his salvation.

In short, the magnificent passage in the final scene bodies forth the experience of Faustus in a kind of personal *dies irae*, but it is not a purple patch tacked on to the end of a rather amorphous play. Rather, the great outburst of poetry finds in the play a supporting context. It sums up the knowledge that Faustus has bought at so dear a price, and if it is the expression of a creature fascinated with, and made eloquent by, horror, it is still the speech of a man who, for all of his terror, somehow preserves his dignity. Faustus at the end is still a man, not a cringing wretch. The poetry saves him from abjectness. If he wishes to escape from himself, to be changed into little water drops, to be swallowed up in the great ocean of being, he maintains to the end – in spite of himself, in spite of his desire to blot out his personal being – his individuality of mind, the special quality of the restless spirit that aspired. This retention of his individuality is at once his glory and his damnation.

SOURCE: *To Nevill Coghill from Friends*, ed. J. Lawlor and W. H. Auden (1966).

Harold Hobson

ALL THIS AND HELEN, TOO (1966)

MICHEAL MACLIAMMOIR – an old friend of mine as well as an actor I greatly admire – is not a man that one could suspect of Nazi sympathies. But he is a witty and patriotic Irishman, and I daresay that when in a play in London a couple of years ago he was called on in the character of Hitler to speak some rousing words against English Imperialism, he took a certain sardonic pleasure in doing so. It is always agreeable to attack something violently, and then be able with perfect honesty to explain that you didn't really mean it.

Christopher Marlowe gave himself the same pleasure in *Doctor Faustus*, which Nevill Coghill directed last Monday at the Playhouse, Oxford, for the O.U.D.S., with the two most celebrated players to be found on any stage in Britain or America. In this clamantly Christian play the atheist author must have enjoyed enormously the opportunity of making the Pope and Cardinals ridiculous, secure in the knowledge that he could blame it all on his damned hero. This scene, often dismissed as an inept exploitation of second-rate conjuring, probably pleased Marlowe as much as the tremendous religious rhetoric with which the play closes. Anyway, Professor Coghill rightly seized upon the joke, and considerably heightened its outrageous effect by making the Holy Father and the Cardinal of Lorraine physical parodies of Lucifer and Beelzebub. For that, I am sure, Marlowe would have stood him a mighty drink down at that tavern in Deptford.

Professor Coghill has a slick hand with sensational entries. How he once made Ariel walk on the water is still a legend far beyond the lake of Worcester and the tower of Merton. In *A Midsummer Night's Dream* he breathtakingly brought on Peggy Ashcroft and John Gielgud dancing to the footlights hand in hand, clothed in absolute magic. Here the first entry of Lucifer and Beelzebub, played by David McIntosh and Jeremy Eccles, is similarly exciting. They are suddenly seen high up at the back of the stage, emerging luridly out of darkness, enskied perhaps, but far from sainted. Equally startling is the eruption of Andreas Teuber's imaginatively melancholy and ambiguous Mephistopheles behind the illustrious shoulder of Richard Burton.

That Mr Burton and Elizabeth Taylor should, as all the world knows, have been willing to break the rhythm of their careers in order to appear, for the benefit of the O.U.D.S., as Faustus and Helen of Troy, is one of the finest and most generous compliments ever paid to a University with wide experience of such things. Mr Burton thrillingly marks the three stages of Faustus's damnation, casually embarking on forbidden knowledge in a universal scholar's light-hearted contempt for all knowledge that is permitted; then smoothly and gaily accommodating himself to Marlowe's worldly jests; finally, in an ecstasy of poetry, at first drunk with admiration as the marvellous beauty of Miss Taylor incarnates Troy's miraculous destroyer, and then electric in agony as he sees Christ's blood streaming in the firmament outside the reach of his imploring hand. The terrified pleading with which he speaks the words –

> O, if my soul must suffer for my sin,
> Impose some end to my incessant pain

– is matched by the dazzled and dazzling skill with which he makes 'Was this the face that launch'd a thousand ships?' seem like a cry of wonder we have never heard before.

Even Professor Coghill, Miss Taylor, Mr Burton, and such excellent players as Robert Scott (Chorus), Mr Teuber, Mr McIntosh, Mr Eccles, Richard Carwardine (the Pope), Nicholas Loukes (the Cardinal), and David Jessel (a knight) cannot make *Doctor Faustus* a stage masterpiece. Some, though not all, of its magnificent poetry is undramatic. Marlowe is not Shakespeare, except in his comic scenes, when it would be better if he weren't. But much of it has a baleful splendour, and this production is a fitting reward to the abnegation of Miss Taylor and Mr Burton, as well as a moving climax to the career of Professor Coghill, who has brought so great value to the often separated worlds of learning and of the theatre.

SOURCE: *Sunday Times*, 20 February 1966.

SELECT BIBLIOGRAPHY

TEXTS

Throughout the present volume, references to scene-numbers and line-numbers in *Doctor Faustus* relate to:

Christopher Marlowe, *Doctor Faustus*, ed. John D. Jump, in the Revels Plays series (Methuen, 1962).

This 'Revels' edition owes much to Greg's great parallel-text edition:

Marlowe's 'Doctor Faustus' 1604–1616, ed. W. W. Greg (Clarendon Press, 1950).

BIOGRAPHICAL AND CRITICAL STUDIES

(As a rule, I have supplied comments only on those items that are not mentioned in the Introduction to the present volume.)

John Bakeless, *Christopher Marlowe* (Cape, 1938). A thorough-going biographical study.

James Smith, 'Marlowe's *Dr Faustus*', in *Scrutiny*, VIII (1939–1940) 36–55.

F. S. Boas, *Christopher Marlowe: A Biographical and Critical Study* (Clarendon Press, 1940). Unadventurous but scholarly.

Leo Kirschbaum, 'Marlowe's *Faustus*: A Reconsideration', in *Review of English Studies*, XIX (1943) 225–41.

Paul H. Kocher, *Christopher Marlowe: A Study of his Thought, Learning, and Character* (University of North Carolina Press, 1946).

W. W. Greg, 'The Damnation of Faustus', in *Modern Language Review*, XLI (1946) 97–107.

J. C. Maxwell, 'The Sin of Faustus', in *The Wind and the Rain*, IV (1947) 49–52.

Helen Gardner, 'Milton's "Satan" and the Theme of Damnation in Elizabethan Tragedy', in *English Studies*, N.S., I (1948) 46–66. Revised for inclusion as Appendix A in her *A Reading of 'Paradise Lost'* (Clarendon Press, 1965).

M. M. Mahood, 'Marlowe's Heroes', in *Poetry and Humanism* (Cape, 1950) pp. 54–86. She sees Marlowe's heroes as illustrating the self-destructive nature of anthropocentric humanism.

Michel Poirier, *Christopher Marlowe* (Chatto & Windus, 1951). A psychological portrait of the man, and an assessment of the aesthetic value of his writings. A useful general introduction.

Nicholas Brooke, 'The Moral Tragedy of Doctor Faustus', in *Cambridge Journal*, V (1951–2) 662–87.

Philip Henderson, *Christopher Marlowe* (Longmans, Green, 1952). A compact biographical and critical introduction by the author whose earlier study, *And Morning in his Eyes*, is mentioned in the Introduction to the present volume.

Lily B. Campbell, '*Doctor Faustus*: A Case of Conscience', in *Publications of the Modern Language Association of America*, LXVII (1952) 219–39.

F. P. Wilson, *Marlowe and the Early Shakespeare* (Clarendon Press, 1953). A slightly amplified version of the Clark Lectures of 1951. Lucid and scholarly.

Harry Levin, *Christopher Marlowe: The Overreacher* (Faber, 1954). Previously published as *The Overreacher: A Study of Christopher Marlowe* (Harvard University Press, 1952).

J. C. Maxwell, 'The Plays of Christopher Marlowe', in *The Pelican Guide to English Literature*, ed. B. Ford (Penguin, 1954–61), vol. II: *The Age of Shakespeare* (1955) pp. 162–78. Perceptive comments on the plays 'considered as a series of remarkable and varied individual dramas'.

Robert Ornstein, 'The Comic Synthesis in *Doctor Faustus*', in *Journal of English Literary History*, XXII (1955) 165–72.

J. P. Brockbank, *Marlowe: Dr Faustus* (Edward Arnold, 1962). Informative and penetrating; highly condensed.

Erich Heller, 'Faust's Damnation', in *The Listener*, 11 January 1962.

J. B. Steane, *Marlowe: A Critical Study* (Cambridge U.P., 1964). Criticism of Marlowe that 'has the poetry as its centre of interest'.

D. J. Palmer, 'Magic and Poetry in *Doctor Faustus*', in *Critical Quarterly*, VI (1964) 56–67.

L. C. Knights, 'The Strange Case of Christopher Marlowe', in *Further Explorations* (Chatto & Windus, 1965) pp. 75–98.

Cleanth Brooks, 'The Unity of Marlowe's *Dr Faustus*', in *To Nevill Coghill from Friends*, ed. J. Lawlor and W. H. Auden (Faber, 1966) pp. 109–24.

Harold Hobson, 'All This and Helen, Too', in *Sunday Times*, 20 February 1966.

NOTES ON CONTRIBUTORS

J. P. BROCKBANK is Professor of English Literature in the University of York and the author of *Marlowe: Dr Faustus* (1962).

NICHOLAS BROOKE, Professor of English Literature in the University of East Anglia, is the author of *Shakespeare: King Lear* (1963) and the editor of Chapman's *Bussy D'Ambois* (1964).

CLEANTH BROOKS, Gray Professor of Rhetoric at Yale, and Cultural Attaché at the American Embassy in London, 1964–6, is the author of *Modern Poetry and the Tradition* (1939), *The Well-Wrought Urn* (1947) and other books.

HELEN GARDNER, Merton Professor of English Literature at Oxford, is the author of *The Art of T. S. Eliot* (1949) and *The Business of Criticism* (1960), and the editor of the poems of Donne (1952, 1965).

W. W. GREG (d. 1959), the most distinguished of British bibliographers, was the author of many important contributions to the study of English Renaissance drama. His edition of *Doctor Faustus* (1950) is discussed in the Introduction to the present volume.

HAROLD HOBSON, dramatic critic of the *Sunday Times* since 1947, is the author of a number of books on the theatre.

L. C. KNIGHTS, King Edward VII Professor of English Literature at Cambridge, is the author of *Drama and Society in the Age of Jonson* (1937), *Explorations* (1946), *Some Shakespearean Themes* (1959), *An Approach to Hamlet* (1960), *Further Explorations* (1965).

HARRY LEVIN, Professor of English and Comparative Literature at Harvard, is the author of *James Joyce: a Critical Introduction* (1941), *Christopher Marlowe: the Overreacher* (1952), *The Question of Hamlet* (1959) and many other books.

J. C. MAXWELL, Professorial Fellow of Balliol College, Oxford, has edited a number of Shakespeare's works, and has been joint-editor of *Notes and Queries* since 1960.

ROBERT ORNSTEIN is Professor of English at Case Western Reserve University, Cleveland, and author of *The Moral Vision of Jacobean Tragedy* (1960).

D. J. PALMER, Lecturer in English in the University of Hull, is the author of *The Rise of English Studies* (1965) and a forthcoming book on Shakespeare.

JAMES SMITH, Professor of English in the University of Fribourg, Switzerland, contributed articles on literary and philosophical topics to *Scrutiny* during the nineteen thirties.

J. B. STEANE, Assistant Master, Merchant Taylor's School, London, is the author of *Marlowe: a Critical Study* (1964), and has edited plays by Dekker and Jonson.

INDEX

References to Faustus himself are naturally too numerous to be recorded here. References to other characters in the play are recorded only when they involve comments on the way these characters are presented or on the relationship of Faustus himself to them.

Aeschylus 27

Agrippa, Henricus Cornelius 71, 135, 139

Alleyn, Edward 30, 156

ANGELS, GOOD AND BAD 39–40, 51–5, 58–9, 60, 82, 87, 99, 102, 110, 113–14, 123, 138, 160, 191

ANHOLT See Vanholt, Duke and Duchess of

Aristotle 119–20, 133, 140, 189, 193, 208

Ashcroft, Peggy 222

Aubrey, John 12

Augustine, St 57, 92, 175

Averroes 187

Bacon, Francis 134

Baines, Richard 112, 184–6, 204, 207

Bakeless, John 184, 227

Baldwin, James 205–6, 207

Bale, John 126

Battenhouse, Roy 184

Baudelaire, Charles 205

BEELZEBUB 36, 60

BENVOLIO 184–5

Bible 64–5, 95, 140, 144, 148, 153, 158, 172, 174–6, 181

Blake, William 111, 132, 163

Boas, F. S. 14–15, 20, 82, 227

Brockbank, J. P. 17, 173–6, 229, 230

Brooke, Nicholas 16–17, 101–133, 228, 230

Brooks, Cleanth 18, 208–21, 229, 230

Broughton, James 29–30

Browning, Robert 148, 160

BRUNO 126

Bruno, Giordano 147

Bullen, A. H. 36–7

Burton, Richard 15, 222–4

Butler, E. M. 133

Byron, George Gordon, Lord 17, 26–7, 31

Calderón de la Barca, Pedro 92, 161, 162

Campbell, Lily B. 16, 228

Caramuelis, Johannes 87

Carwardine, Richard 223

Cecil, Lord David 183, 187

Cervantes Saavedra, Miguel de 163

Chambers, E. K. 12

Chapman, George 153, 172

Chaucer, Geoffrey 146
CLOWNS *See* Robin and Dick (Ralph)
Coghill, Nevill 221, 222–4, 229
Coleridge, S. T. 101, 162, 166
Collier, J. P. 30
Conrad, Joseph 219
Corneille, Pierre 190
CORNELIUS *See* Valdes and Cornelius
Cowper, William 183
Crane, Hart 164
Cunningham, Francis 14, 17

Damnable Life See Faustbook
Dante Alighieri 69–70, 164
DICK *See* Robin and Dick (Ralph)
Dickens, Charles 168
Dido, Queen of Carthage 138, 141, 154, 157, 207
Dilke, C. W. 13
Donne, John 96, 100
Dostoevsky, Fyodor 143, 171

Eccles, Jeremy 223
Edward II 102, 125, 131, 133, 134, 137, 139, 140, 142, 143, 145, 152, 154, 157, 159
Eliot, T. S. 196, 208–10, 219
Ellis, Havelock 14, 37–8
Ellis-Fermor, Una M. 14, 43–4
Empedocles 136
EMPEROR OF GERMANY 93, 151
Empson, William 15, 17, 41–2
Euripides 43
Everyman 138, 156, 179–80

Faulkner, William 218
Faust, Georg 135

Faustbook 37, 38, 41, 57, 59–60, 71, 81, 82, 93, 97–8, 102, 136–137, 139, 144, 145, 146, 149, 151, 155, 158, 161, 175, 176, 189
Fielding, Henry 145
Ford, John 166
Foxe, John 151
Fust, Johann 136

Gardner, Helen 16, 95–100, 228, 230
Gide, André 181
Gielgud, Sir John 222
Goethe, J. W. von 14, 15, 21, 25, 28, 29, 31, 32, 34, 37, 38, 41, 69, 86, 139–40, 143, 146, 151, 161–3, 164, 178–9
Greene, Robert 110, 149–50, 202
Greg, W. W. 16, 17, 19, 20, 71–88, 89–93, 99, 103–5, 106, 108–9, 110, 122, 125, 133, 149, 165, 172, 227, 230

Hallam, Henry 30–1
Hazlitt, William 13, 27–8, 152, 162
HELEN 25, 29, 34–5, 38, 51, 53, 58, 83–7, 89, 94, 99, 107–8, 128–9, 152–6, 160, 170, 196–9, 216
Heller, Erich 16, 229
Henderson, Philip 15, 228
Henslowe, Philip 11, 149
Hero and Leander 150
Hobson, Harold 18, 222–4, 229, 230
Homer 153

Hooker, Richard 161, 204
Hugo, Victor 151

Ibsen, Henrik 132

Jeffrey, Francis 13, 26–7
Jessel, David 223
Jew of Malta 30, 31, 69, 76, 102, 109, 110–11, 114, 132, 137, 139, 143, 145, 148, 150, 152, 154, 159, 196
Jonson, Ben 202–3

Keats, John 155
Kirschbaum, Leo 16, 17, 18, 19, 42–3, 89–92, 105–6, 108–9, 110, 133, 227
Knights, L. C. 18, 204–7, 229, 230
Kocher, Paul H. 16, 44–5, 133, 172, 184, 204, 227
Kyd, Thomas 110, 125, 150, 200, 204

Lamb, Charles 14, 28, 29, 162
Langland, William 146
Leavis, F. R. 184
Leonardo da Vinci 134–5, 163
Levin, Harry 17, 134–64, 168, 172, 177–8, 228, 231
Lewes, G. H. 31–2, 37
Lewis, C. S. 170
Lindsay, Sir David 126
Loukes, Nicholas 223
Lucian 155
LUCIFER 33, 36, 51, 60, 61, 83, 96, 108, 119, 123, 168, 169, 214
Lucretius 144
Luther, Martin 137, 161
Lyly, John 110, 151

McIntosh, David 223
MacLiammoir, Micheal 222
Mahood, M. M. 178, 179, 181, 184, 228
Maitland, Henry 13, 25–6
Mankind 179
Massacre at Paris 102, 132, 136–137, 138, 158
Maxwell, J. C. 16, 89–94, 187, 228, 231
Melton, John 12
MEPHOSTOPHILIS 31, 33, 34, 35, 36, 51, 66–8, 74, 77–9, 86, 92, 97–9, 102, 116–17, 118, 119, 121–3, 125, 130, 142–6, 159, 160, 163, 169, 171, 185, 193–6, 211–12, 214–15, 216–18
Milton, John 91, 100, 112–13, 119, 123, 143, 160, 163, 170–1, 184, 208–10, 219, 228
Mozart, W. A. 159

Nashe, Thomas 155
Nietzsche, F. W. 119
Norton, Thomas (*Gorboduc*) 110

OLD MAN 51, 58–9, 85–6, 87, 96, 105, 110, 127–9, 155–6, 191, 214–15
Ornstein, Robert 17–18, 20, 165–72, 229, 231
Ovid 153, 157, 173, 199, 201, 220
Ovid's Elegies 157, 173

Palmer, D. J. 12, 18, 188–203, 229, 231
Parker, A. A. 92
Peabody, J. Preston 184
Pepys, Samuel 12

Plato 189, 193
Poirier, Michel 184, 228
POPE 126, 147, 151
Pope, Alexander 101
Primaudaye, P. de la 175
Proust, Marcel 156
Prynne, William 12
Pythagoras 175

Rabelais, François 134, 163
Racine, Jean 190
Ralegh, Sir Walter 142
RALPH (RAFE) *See* Robin and
    Dick (Ralph)
Ramus, Petrus 140
ROBIN AND DICK (RALPH) 115,
    124, 127, 150-1, 166, 167,
    170
Robinson, H. Crabb 29, 151
Rossiter, A. P. 115, 125, 133
Rowley, Samuel 150, 151, 152
Russell, Bertrand 210

Sackville, Thomas (*Gorboduc*)
    110
Sampson, George 183, 187
Santayana, George 15, 39-40,
    49, 54, 59-60, 161, 168
Saturday Review 87
Schelling, Felix E. 40-1
SCHOLARS 62, 83, 84, 93, 115,
    127, 129, 152, 180
Scott, Robert 223
Scott, Sir Walter 25, 162
SEVEN DEADLY SINS 56-7, 79,
    80, 92, 123-4, 146-7, 160,
    168
Shakespeare, William 32, 100,
    101, 148, 150, 156, 166, 167,
    175-6, 177, 195, 198, 203, 223,

228; *Hamlet* 137 142, 160,
166, 177, 189; *2 Henry VI*
202; *King Lear* 182; *Macbeth*
166, 203, 206; *Merchant of
Venice* 198; *Midsummer
Night's Dream* 222-3; *Richard
III* 202; *Romeo and Juliet*
101, 156, 165, 198; *Tempest*
135, 141, 189, 203, 222; *Troilus
and Cressida* 181; *Winter's
Tale* 198
Shaw, G. B. 111, 119
Sidney, Sir Philip 18, 165, 189-
    190, 193
Simon Magus 135-6
Sinistrari, L. M. 86-7
Smith, James 15-16, 17, 18, 20,
    49-70, 89-94, 103, 133, 177,
    184, 207, 227, 231
Spenser, Edmund 146, 190
Spies, Johann 136
Steane, J. B. 17, 20, 177-87, 229,
    231
Swift, Jonathan 167
Swinburne, A. C. 38
Symonds, J. A. 14, 17, 35-6

Taine, H. A. 32
Tamburlaine 14, 30, 31, 37, 58,
    66, 77, 102, 103, 108, 109, 110-
    111, 114, 131, 132, 136-7, 138,
    139, 144, 148, 152, 154, 157-
    158, 159, 160, 174, 186-7, 188,
    191, 192, 206, 207
Tapper, B. 133
Taylor, Elizabeth 15, 222-4
Teuber, Andreas 223
Theophilus 33-4
Tourneur, Cyril 112

VALDES AND CORNELIUS 71–4, 77, 114, 115–16, 142, 180
VANHOLT, DUKE AND DUCHESS OF 93, 151

WAGNER 83, 115, 120, 124, 139, 150, 167
Wagner, Wilhelm 14, 33–5
Waldock, A. J. A. 184, 187
Ward, A. W. 32–3, 82, 86

Welles, Orson 15
Whitehead, A. N. 206, 207
Wilson, F. P. 228
Wilson, John ('Christopher North') 17
Woodes, Nathaniell (*Conflict of Conscience*) 16, 99–100, 118, 126, 175, 228

Yeats, W. B. 215, 218